THEOLOGY AND PSYCHOLOGY

Many people are now interested in the relationship between religion and science, but links between Christian belief and psychology have been relatively neglected. This book opens up the dialogue between Christian theology and modern scientific psychology, approaching the dialogue in both directions. Current scientific topics like consciousness and artificial intelligence are examined from a religious perspective. Christian themes such as God's purposes and activity in the world are then examined in the light of psychology. This accessible study on psychology and Christian belief offers students and general readers alike important insights into new areas of the 'science and religion' debate.

Fraser Watts is Starbridge Lecturer in Theology and Natural Science at the University of Cambridge, UK, and author of many books including *Christians and Bioethics* (SPCK); *Science Meets Faith* (SPCK), *Psychology for Christian Ministry* (Routledge), and *The Psychology of Religious Knowing* (CUP).

Ashgate Science and Religion Series

Science and religion have often been thought to be at loggerheads but much contemporary work in this flourishing interdisciplinary field suggests this is far from the case. The Ashgate Science and Religion Series presents exciting new work to advance interdisciplinary study, research and debate across key themes in science and religion, exploring the philosophical relations between the physical and social sciences on the one hand and religious belief on the other. Contemporary issues in philosophy and theology are debated, as will prevailing cultural assumptions arising from the 'post-modernist' distaste for many forms of reasoning. The series enables leading international authors from a range of different disciplinary perspectives to apply the insights of the various sciences, theology and philosophy and look at the relations between the different disciplines and the rational connections that can be made between them. These accessible, stimulating new contributions to key topics across science and religion will appeal particularly to individual academics and researchers, graduates, postgraduates and upper-undergraduate students.

Series Editors:

Roger Trigg, Department of Philosophy, University of Warwick, UK
J. Wentzel van Huyssteen, Chair in Science & Religion,
Princeton Theological Seminary, USA

Theology and Psychology

FRASER WATTS
Starbridge Lecturer in Theology and Natural Science
University of Cambridge

ASHGATE

© Fraser Watts 2002

All rights reserved. No part of this publication may be reproduced, stored in a retrieval system, or transmitted in any form or by any means, electronic, mechanical, photocopying, recording or otherwise without the prior permission of the publisher.

Published by
Ashgate Publishing Limited
Gower House
Croft Road
Aldershot
Hants GU11 3HR
England

Ashgate Publishing Company
131 Main Street
Burlington, VT 05401-5600 USA

Ashgate website: http://www.ashgate.com

British Library Cataloguing in Publication Data
Watts, Fraser
    Theology and psychology. - (Ashgate science and religion
    series)
    1. Psychology and religion
    I. Title
    261.5'15

Library of Congress Cataloging-in-Publication Data
Watts, Fraser.
    Theology and psychology / Fraser Watts.
        p. cm. -- (Ashgate science and religion series)
    Includes bibliographical references and indexes.
    ISBN 0 7546-1672-X -- ISBN 0-7546-1673-8 (pbk.)
    1. Christianity--Psychology. 2. Psychology and religion. I. Title. II. Series.

BR110 .W38 2001
261.5'15--dc21

2001046049

ISBN 0 7546 1672 X (Hbk)
ISBN 0 7546 1673 8 (Pbk)

Printed and bound in Great Britain by MPG Books Ltd, Bodmin, Cornwall

To Susan Howatch

Contents

Preface

In this book, I approach the interface between theology and psychology by looking at each discipline from the perspective of the other. This includes a religious perspective on several current hot topics in psychology such as evolution, neuroscience, and computer intelligence. I also consider theological topics like divine action, salvation history and eschatology, in each case using the psychological perspective in a different way. At the centre of the book is the psychology of religious experience, a rich interdisciplinary topic that raises a host of fascinating issues.

In interdisciplinary work it is all too easy to lack competence in one discipline or the other, but I am grateful to have had the unusual opportunity to work in both fields. After 25 years in psychology, including a long and rewarding period with the Medical Research Council, I had the opportunity to move to the Faculty of Divinity at the University of Cambridge. I am more grateful than I can say to Susan Howatch for her endowment in Cambridge of the Starbridge Lectureship in Theology and Natural Science, which I have the privilege of being the first holder.

I have benefited from conversation and collaboration with a great many people in writing this book. In particular, it has been enormously helpful to talk regularly with John Polkinghorne about issues in science and religion. I am also greatly indebted to my former student Thomas Dixon from whom I have learnt much more than I could reasonably have expected, and to Liz Gulliford who provided excellent help in the preparation of this manuscript. To them, and to the many other people who have helped me on my way, I am most grateful.

Fraser Watts
Cambridge
May 2002

Acknowledgements

Several of the chapters in this book are derived from material which has been published elsewhere, and is re-used here with permission. I am grateful to:

T. & T. Clark for permission to re-use in Chapters 2 and 5 material from my chapter on 'The multi-faceted nature of human personhood: psychological and theological perspectives', published in N.H. Grgersen, W.B. Drees and U. Gorman (eds) *The Human Person in Science and Theology*, 2000.

Oxford University Press for permission to re-use in Chapters 3 and 7 material from my chapter 'Towards a Theology of Consciousness', published in J. Cormwell (ed.) *Consciousness and Human Identity*, 1998.

Imprint Academic for permission to re-use in Chapter 3 my article 'Nothing but a pack of neurones', published in the *Journal of Consciousness Studies*, **1**, 275–9, 1994.

Templeton Foundation Press for permission to re-use as Chapter 4, my chapter on 'Artificial Intelligence', published in R.L. Herrmann (ed.) *God, Science and Humility*, 2000.

Vatican Observatory and the Center for Theology and Natural Science, Berkeley, for permission to re-use as the basis of Chapters 6 and 8 my chapter on 'Cognitive neuroscience and religious consciousness,' published in R.J. Russell, N. Murphy, T. Meyering and M. Arbib (eds) *Neuroscience and the Person*. Vatican City State, Vatican Observatory and Berkeley, Center for Theology and Natural Science.

Trinity Press International for permission to re-use as part of Chapter 10 my chapter on 'Subjective and Objective Hope', published in J. Polkinghorne and M. Welker (eds) *The End of the World and the Ends of God*, 2000.

Methodist Publishing House for permission to re-use as part of Chapter 10 my article 'Hell on Earth', published in Epworth Review, **22**, 80–87, 1995.

Modern Churchpeople's Union for permission to re-use as part of Chapter 11 material published in Modern Churchman, New Series XXXIII, No 2, 11–19, 1991.

All the above material has been revised in the context of the present volume.

Fraser Watts

Chapter 1

Introduction: Relating the Disciplines

This book is concerned with the dialogue between psychology and Christian theology. Theology is the rational reflection of the Christian tradition, and its dialogue with psychology focuses particularly on human nature.

It may he helpful at the outset to differentiate this enterprise from various other related concerns. First, the dialogue between theology and psychology can be differentiated from other ways in which psychology and religion can be brought into relation to one another, such as the psychology of religion, or pastoral psychology. Second, the dialogue between theology and psychology can be differentiated from other aspects of the broader dialogue between theology and the sciences. So far that dialogue has focused more on physics, cosmology and evolution than on the psychological sciences. It will be helpful to begin by placing the dialogue between theology and psychology in these two contexts.

Ways of Psychology and Religion

The psychological study of religion was an important part of psychology at its inception as an independent discipline in the latter part of the nineteenth century. However, the psychology of religion has followed a fluctuating course. It was initially a prominent aspect of the discipline, and the early qualitative work of William James (1902/1960) in *The Varieties of Religious Experience*, and the more quantitative work of Starbuck (1899) using questionnaire methods, were both well known. However, after the first quarter of the twentieth century, at least in the USA, the psychology of religion went into decline. In recent years, it has re-emerged as a vigorous, albeit specialized area of psychological research, though it has not regained its early importance in the discipline.

Psychology is often assumed to be hostile to religion. Certainly, some psychologists, such as Freud, have been hostile to religion, though in fact the majority of psychologists who have chosen to study religion have been sympathetic to it. Even Freud's central insight about religion, that concepts of God often arise from the individual's experience and psychic needs, can be seen as potentially constructive. There are clear indications, for example in the clinical research of Rizzuto (1979), that people's personal backgrounds can shape their thinking about God. However, this does not mean that there is no God, nor that there is no possibility of moving towards a more authentic concept of God. In fact, as Tillich (1952) pointed out, Freudian ideas about religion can be taken as providing a warning about how easily ideas about God can become trapped in limited human conceptions. Freud's contribution points to the need to move beyond such limited conceptions. The message here is very similar to that of 'negative' theology, which has stressed the importance of 'unlearning' human concepts of God, which are necessarily inadequate.

The psychology of religion has generally sought to take as neutral a view of religion as possible. Unfortunately, much empirical research has lacked either a strong theoretical motivation or direct practical application. Indeed, it is surprising how little the psychology of religion has been applied to the work of the churches, though at almost every point it would enable them to organize their work more effectively. Psychological research can provide data about which sort of people are religious, where religious experience arises, where conversion takes place, who attends Church, how children learn about religion, what causes stress in ministers, and so on. Far from being hostile to religion, such factual data is potentially of great value in planning the ministry and mission of the Church. With colleagues at Cambridge, I have recently tried to set out a wide-ranging psychological perspective on the work of the Church, drawing on empirical research in the psychology of religion (Watts *et al.*, 2001).

Another quite different point of intersection between psychology and religion has been the pastoral application of psychology. That stemmed from the new methods of psychological therapy developed by Freud and the broad range of approaches to counselling and psychological therapy derived from his pioneering work. One of the first to see the potential application of these developments in psychology to the pastoral work of the Church was Freud's friend, Oskar Pfister, a Lutheran pastor (Meissner, 1984). Between the wars, there was a very vigorous development of Christian pastoral psychology in the UK, in which the Methodist minister Leslie Weatherhead was a key figure. At this time, there was a greater degree of estrangement between psychology and the churches in the USA. Pastoral psychology developed later there, though when it did so it became more influential and widely employed. In the UK, Frank Lake's (1966) *Clinical Theology*, an integration of psychiatry, psychotherapy and theology, was another landmark development in the post-war period.

There have been fluctuating attitudes to pastoral psychology in the churches, and recent years have seen growing concern at the extent to which the churches have abandoned their own classic tradition of pastoral care in favour of approaches derived from therapeutic psychology (Pattison, 1993). Christian pastoral care is usually more informally structured than most secular counselling. It also has clearer moral values and allows the counselling process to be guided by them more explicitly. Extremes are often to be found in Christian attitudes to pastoral psychology, ranging from suspicion or even hostility to an uncritical enthusiasm that seems to assume that psychotherapy is itself the Christian gospel. It is sensible to maintain a middle course, acknowledging the value of the contribution of counselling psychology, while also maintaining the distinctive features of the Christian approach.

It is easy to see why Christians might be suspicious of secular pastoral care. For example, it is sometimes suggested that psychology excuses people's wrongdoing, though that is to confuse the explanations of behaviour offered by psychology with excuses for wrongdoing. It is also sometimes suggested that psychology results in people becoming self-preoccupied rather than God-centred, but the two are not necessarily incompatible. The journey inwards can lead to a deep experience of

God, who is present everywhere. At the other extreme, Christians have sometimes embraced secular approaches to counselling too uncritically. Christian pastoral care has distinctive features, such as the emphasis on authority or forgiveness. However, like any pastoral approach, a specifically Christian one needs to be used with care if it is not to become coercive.

It is not the purpose of this book to pursue either the psychology of religion or pastoral psychology (though the psychology of religious experience will be considered). These other points of intersection between psychology and religion have been considered briefly, only to help to indicate the rather different way of relating psychology and religion with which this book is concerned, namely the dialogue between theology and psychology. By 'theology' I mean the tradition of teaching and scholarly reflection found within the Christian religion. This book will not be primarily concerned with the practical life and work of the Christian community, neither will it attempt to consider the theologies of non-Christian faith communities.

This third way of relating psychology and religion has tended to be the poor relation, and to attract less interest than either the psychology of religion or pastoral psychology. However, such neglect is regrettable, and I am gratified by encouraging signs that it is beginning to be remedied. One reason for the weak state of the dialogue between theology and psychology is presumably that psychology is one of the most secular of the sciences, in that it has one of the lowest percentages of believing Christians of all academic disciplines. However, this is not how things began. Many of the founding fathers of psychology in the USA, such as G.T. Ladd, G.S. Hall, and J. McCosh, were committed Christians (Dixon, 1999). They have bequeathed us a substantial body of what might be called 'Christian psychology'.

Theology and Science

The dialogue between theology and psychology can also be seen as part of the more general dialogue between theology and science, which has also followed a somewhat fluctuating course. It has sometimes been suggested that there is necessarily conflict between them (Watts, 1998a, Chapter 1). However, the conflict idea only came to the fore in the last quarter of the nineteenth century, in the aftermath of the Darwinian controversies. Before the middle of the nineteenth century, most scientists were committed Christians even if some, such as Newton, were heterodox in their beliefs. The pioneers of the scientific revolution in the seventeenth century believed that, in studying nature, they were studying one of the 'books' of God, scripture being the other. It is also debatable whether the 'falling out' between science and religion in the late nineteenth century is best seen in terms of conflict, or simply separation. Since the late nineteenth century, there have always been some prominent scientists who have been openly hostile to religion. However, the majority of contemporary scientists are probably not hostile, but simply unconcerned with religion, one way or the other.

Recent decades have seen a marked revival of interest in the dialogue between theology and science, in which Ian Barbour, Arthur Peacocke and John Polkinghorne have been particularly prominent figures. It is notable that all come from a scientific background, even though their main contributions to work on the interface between theology and science were made after they had ceased to be personally active in scientific research. They have approached the dialogue with theology as scientific generalists, rather than being particularly concerned with their own areas of scientific research. There has been less interest in the dialogue between theology and science among theologians, though Charles Raven, Tom Torrance and Wolfhart Pannenberg are among the exceptions.

In fact, the sciences are very different from one another, and it is potentially misleading to talk generally about the dialogue between theology and 'science'. There are really a number of different dialogues with different sciences. The dialogue of theology with physics and cosmology has become increasingly constructive in recent decades. There has been a growing recognition that theology and cosmology are concerned with rather similar metaphysical questions, albeit from different perspectives. For example, there is an interesting parallel between the views of Stephen Hawking and St Augustine about the origin of time. Hawking has suggested that the universe did not begin at any fixed point in time because time only became defined as the universe came into being. Similarly, Augustine suggested that God created time along with the rest of creation, and that time did not exist before it. Also, the growing sense of the openness of the natural world associated with quantum indeterminacy, and even more significantly with 'chaos' theory, has made it easier to see how God can act in the world *with* the grain of the laws of nature, rather than against them. In general, the physical sciences have become open to a sense of mystery about creation.

The dialogue with the biological and human sciences is proceeding very differently. The argument about evolution continues to be heated in some quarters, though much more in the USA than the UK. Religious suspicion about evolution continues despite the fact that the main planks of a possible reconciliation between them have been clear from the outset; first, that the early chapters of Genesis are making theological points about the dependence of creation on God, and are not trying to be a scientific textbook, and second that evolution can be seen as God's way of 'doing' creation, and a fulfilment of his purposes. Recent years have also seen a growing open-mindedness about the processes by which evolution has come about.

Nevertheless, reductionism is much more prominent in the biological and human sciences than the physical sciences. This trend towards demystification that has been part of the thrust of science since the early days of the seventeenth century seems eventually to have come home to roost in the scientific study of human beings. Perhaps the ultimate challenge for science is to understand human beings themselves, and there are several 'nothing but' impulses running riot in the human sciences. The reductionist impulse in the human sciences runs so strong that it has to be a major focus of any consideration of the dialogue between theology and psychology, and several chapters in this book will have it as their main focus. The three most prominent are:

(a) that human beings are nothing but survival machines for their genes,
(b) that we are nothing but a 'bundle of neurones' (as Francis Crick put it), and
(c) that the human mind is nothing but a computer program.

Religious Suspicions of Psychology

The dialogue between psychology and theology has been handicapped by a lack of sympathetic interest on both sides. The majority of psychologists, with the notable exception of a handful of Christian psychologists, have had no knowledge of theology, nor interest in such a dialogue. Christians, on the other hand, have often been suspicious of psychology, and it is worth considering why this should have been so. One factor is the reductionist tendency in some psychology that has just been considered. Another, already referred to, is that psychology has sometimes taken a critical view of religion, and it may have been assumed that psychology had no alternative but to do that. In fact, psychology can, and has, taken a variety of views of religion, ranging from the critical, through the relatively neutral, to the sympathetic. However, the religious suspicion of psychology has many aspects, which deserve exploration.

There have been clashes of values between psychology and theology (Myers and Jeeves, 1987), though these have focused particularly on counselling psychology, rather than on the whole of the discipline. Some, such as Bergin (1980), have been sharply critical of the values which they see as implicit in counselling psychology, and have contrasted these with Christian assumptions and values. Guilt is one topic on which there has been sharp disagreement, with some people in the Christian tradition emphasizing its value in leading to repentance, but with counselling psychology seeing it as a personal problem. This apparent conflict falls away once a clear distinction is made between realistic and neurotic guilt. It is realistic guilt that Christians value, but neurotic guilt that concerns psychologists. There has been a similar debate about self esteem, with psychologists generally valuing it as a force for good adjustment, but some Christians being wary of it as promoting too much self-centredness, or disguising the need for God (McGrath and McGrath, 1992). Once again, this can be resolved by distinguishing between helpful and unhelpful aspects of self-esteem.

In the debate about the relationship between Christianity and personal growth psychology, some have seen humanistic psychologists, such as Carl Rogers (1961), as talking about many of the same things as religion, albeit in a secular language. Specifically, warmth, empathy and genuineness, Rogers's list of the hallmarks of a good counsellor, can be seen as a secular equivalent of the Christian idea of love. Others have insisted that Christian love can only be characterized adequately in more specifically theological terms. More generally, this raises the question of whether the apparent differences between humanistic psychology and the Christian religion are substantive or semantic, a matter about which there is no agreement.

Another basis of the widespread suspicion of psychology among religious people is that psychology seems to have placed too much emphasis on the individual. There has been growing emphasis on the social dimension of the Gospel, whereas psychology, in contrast has seemed narrowly individualistic. In addition, the prevailing intellectual climate of the humanities has been to emphasize the importance of general culture, and oppose what it has seen as 'individualism'. There are two responses to this objection to psychology. One is to point out the danger of trying to replace an extreme individualism with an extreme collectivism. There is surely mutual influence between the society and the individual, an issue to which we will return in Chapter 7 in connection with religious experience. The second response is to point out that psychology also has its social dimension, and it has been making its presence felt increasingly, through social constructionism, study of the effect of the social environment on personality, systems therapy, and so on. Psychology includes social psychology; it is not exclusively individualistic.

Another related unease about psychology is that it represents an approach to religion that is too 'subjective'. Theologians, in contrast, especially those of conservative outlook who have been most suspicious of psychology, have wanted to emphasize the objectivity of the Christian faith. One response to that objection is to point out that this sharp disjunction between the subjective and the objective is itself too stark. Human knowing generally occurs at the interface of the objective and the subjective, a theme that I develop in Chapter 11. It is fair to point out that the psychological study of cognition makes psychologists more aware than most people of how the objective and the subjective intersect. Though psychology is concerned with how people interpret their experience, its methodology is designed to approach that in as objective a way as possible.

Finally, some would argue that psychology has grown up within an explicitly secular culture that leaves no place for religious belief. On this view, psychology is so contaminated by that secular culture that it can be of no value whatsoever for those who wish to reestablish an explicitly Christian intellectual worldview. Such a position would parallel the case that Milbank (1990) has argued against social theory. I accept that the culture from which psychology has emerged is predominately secular, though not entirely so. It has already been noted that a number of the key founding fathers of modern psychology were committed Christians who were explicitly developing a Christian psychology. Also, it would be grossly dismissive of the achievements of contemporary psychological research for Christians to throw its discoveries overboard and start again, or to revert to the psychology that existed before the modern scientific approach. No doubt, some lines of approach in psychology need to be re-examined from a Christian perspective and to be placed in a different context. But there is much of enduring value in the psychological research of the twentieth century that no Christian should simply dismiss.

However, it is worth emphasizing that the predominantly secular approach to psychology that has dominated the twentieth century is not the only possible one, and should not be accorded an absolute supremacy. It has become increasingly apparent, as philosophy of science has proceeded through the latter part of the twentieth century, that there is no neutral scientific rationality, no 'view from nowhere'. The secular standpoint that has dominated the various different strands of twentieth-century psychology is only one viewpoint among many: it has its own prejudices and unexamined assumptions. A different set of psychological assumptions would be perfectly possible. One advantage of developing a more explicitly Christian approach to psychology, alongside the current predominately secular one, would be that everyone would become clearer about their starting point and presuppositions. If different psychologists are adopting different background assumptions, there will be less danger of any particular approach, secular or Christian, being accepted uncritically.

The Nature of Dialogue

So, if these sources of suspicion can be overcome, what kind of relationship should there be between theology and psychology? There has been much discussion of this, and it has often been framed in terms of the relationship of authority between the two (Carter and Narramore, 1979; Fleck and Carter, 1981; Jones, 1994; Johnson and Jones, 2000). For example, it has been suggested that, in relating psychology and religion, the main authority should be accorded to scripture, and that psychology should have a subsidiary role. The issue is similar to the more general one of the relationship between theology and science, on which there has also been much discussion (for example, Barbour 1998, Chapter 4). Regrettably, there seems to have been virtually no cross fertilization between the two separate literatures, on how theology should relate to psychology specifically and to science generally.

One key issue is whether either discipline should be in the ascendancy, or whether there should be a dialogue between two free standing and relatively autonomous disciplines. In the context of the relationship between theology and science, Polkinghorne (1996) has characterized this in terms of the alternatives of 'consonance' or 'assimilation'. I share his rejection of the assimilation of one discipline into the other, and would prefer to see co-ordination between two separate disciplines.

Assimilation can be attempted in either of two possible directions. Sometimes, it is felt that psychology, or science, should be the dominant partner, and that theology should be adjusted so that it is more readily consistent with it. There are two steps in this programme of assimilation, and both are controversial. One is the judgment that psychology and theology are not really compatible as they stand, and that some programme of adjustment is needed if they are to be reconciled. There can be divergent views about that, both for science generally, and for psychology specifically. As far as science is concerned, Polkinghorne sees little incompatibility himself, whereas he suggests that others such as Ian Barbour appear to see much more need for revision if theology is to be compatible with science.

If the judgment is that the two disciplines are currently incompatible, and that revision is needed to bring them into harmony, the question is which one should be adjusted. In practice, it often tends to be theology that is revised, though there is sometimes talk about theology, or scripture, having authority, and psychology, or science, being brought under its hegemony. It is implicit, for example, in Milbank's critique of secular social theory that it should be refashioned under the tutelage of theology. The parallel argument could be advanced for secular psychology. In practice, the programme of completely replacing existing secular disciplines with revised ones under the hegemony of theology seems rather unrealistic. Even if it were desirable, it is hard to see how it could be carried through.

On the first question of the compatibility of theology and psychology, my judgment is that there is no radical incompatibility between the two. However, it obviously depends to some extent where you are looking in the two disciplines. As I will indicate in a later section, both disciplines are very heterogeneous, and parallel debates can sometimes be found in them. Though my judgment is that there is no gross incompatibility between the disciplines, there is scope for constructive mutual influence between them. I would also wish to see both disciplines open to refinement as a result of the dialogue, though I recognize that the lack of interest among psychologists in the dialogue with theology would make refinements to psychology harder to carry through.

Within theology, there has always been a balance between maintaining the integrity of the tradition, and developing it in changing circumstances (see Chapter 11). Psychology can potentially contribute to that process of development, without threatening or distorting the tradition. Equally, in psychology, as with other scientific disciplines, I would hope to see a gradual emancipation, and a willingness to recognize a broader range of human processes as scientifically intelligible. I judge that is likely to happen anyway as a result of internal pressures within the discipline of psychology, but the process could perhaps be facilitated if psychology had a constructive dialogue with theology.

How far should such a dialogue go? Sometimes people speak of moving beyond dialogue towards 'integration'. If that means a state in which both disciplines lose their distinct identities in some kind of merger, it seems neither possible nor desirable. However, what is meant by integration may just be a substantial degree of mutual influence. That is something that I would welcome, though it cannot be rushed. It is only through a sustained period of fruitful dialogue between two distinct and separate disciplines such as theology and psychology that significant mutual influence can arise.

The position I am taking here is similar up to a point to that of Hunsinger (1995). Certainly, I agree with her that the two disciplines should remain distinct, but should be related to one another. As she points out, that is somewhat parallel to the Chalcedonian formulation of the relation of the persons of the Trinity to one another, distinct but related. However, Hunsinger also wants to see a hierarchical relationship between the two disciplines, and that is more controversial.

Theology is, of course, always a broad discipline. Because it relates whatever it is concerned with to God, it has the broadest possible frame of reference. A discipline like psychology is, in comparison, much more circumscribed. In that sense, there might be said to be a hierarchical relationship between the two disciplines. It is rather like relating a close-up picture to a panoramic view. However, this obvious difference in the breadth and scope of the two disciplines could easily lead to the idea that psychology is a subordinate discipline. That would be unjustifiable. If there is to be constructive dialogue between the disciplines, the relationship should not be seen as one of superiority and subordination.

Complementary Perspectives

Theology and psychology can be seen, in some ways, as offering complementary perspectives on reality, even though psychology is concerned with only a fragment of the broader reality that is the scope of theology. There is a helpful analogy to be drawn in this regard between the relationship of theology and psychology to one another, and the relationship of discourses about mind and brain (Watts, 1998b has a fuller discussion of this). By 'mind', I mean thoughts and feelings as they are experienced; whereas by 'brain' I mean the physical grey matter inside the head to which they are related. It has become increasingly clear from various lines of empirical research that there is a close correlation between the two, though the causal nature of that relationship is still open to discussion. The close relationship is evident from looking at the mental effects of head injury, and from the more recent scanning techniques that can monitor brain activity while people are engaged in various mental tasks.

Research on sleep provides a good illustration of the way in which mind and brain discourses provide complementary accounts of the same basic process. Going to sleep can be described in terms of the physical processes of the brain, usually as how the electrical rhythms become slower and more pronounced. Equally, going to sleep can be described in terms of phenomenological changes. Thought processes become more fragmentary and less deliberate, orientation is lost, and bizarre images may flit unwilled through the mind. Both descriptions are valid in their different domains, and they are complementary rather alternative. It would make no sense to ask whether sleep represented a change in brain state *or* a change in mental processes. Manifestly, it is both, and it can be described validly, but incompletely, in either discourse.

Both sets of changes tend to follow an orderly sequence, though the correlation between them appears to be only approximate. One cannot infer exactly, from knowing where someone's brain changes have got to in the trajectory towards sleep, exactly what phenomenological changes will be taking place. Both discourses describe essential aspects of the total process of going to sleep, so, neither the material nor the phenomenological accounts could be eliminated.

This bears on the claim, made by eliminative materialists, that mind language is redundant and just a convenient shorthand way of describing what could be more exactly described in terms of brain language. This claim assumes a one to one mapping of brain states on to mind states. As far as going to sleep is concerned, it looks unlikely, empirically, that there is such a one-to-one mapping. Of course, some would try to argue that if we had better and fuller descriptions of brain states, phenomenological descriptions would become redundant. However, in any case, the concept of a 'brain state' is an odd one, in that we do not know how to produce a full description of a 'brain state', especially not one that is independent of the mind state with which it is associated.

The relationship between descriptions of brain and mind provides a useful model for how scientific and theological accounts can be set side by side, complementing each other, rather than being seen as alternatives. Scientific explanations of any phenomenon can be offered, and such accounts might even become complete in their own terms, though that is not often achieved. Nevertheless, a theological account can, in principle, always be offered alongside the scientific account, complementing it and cohering with it in the way that mind accounts complement and cohere with brain accounts. Having an adequate scientific account does not make a theological account redundant, any more than having an adequate neurological account of going to sleep makes a phenomenological account redundant.

Note here that atheism corresponds directly to eliminative materialism. Both seek to simplify the situation of having two complementary discourses by eliminating one of them. It is not just that one discourse is accorded primacy over the other. Rather, one discourse is held to be adequate, and the other discourse to be redundant. Both atheism and eliminative materialism are based on the assumption that the preferred discourse renders the other discourse redundant. However, one difference between atheism and eliminative materialism is that materialism is more programmatic. Materialists admit that we do no yet know how to manage without mind discourse, even though they expect that to be possible eventually. Atheists would be more likely to claim that it is already perfectly possible to speak a completely natural, non-theological discourse.

It is sometimes assumed that talk of complementary discourses implies that the two discourses are independent. This suggestion is more often made in connection with theological and natural discourses than with mind and brain discourses. However, I believe that the independence of complementary discourses only follows if both languages are taken in a non-realist way. Like many other people, I would want to espouse some kind of critical realism, at least about reference (or entities), if not about truth claims (or theories). If even minimal realism is upheld, it is incorrect to suggest that complementary discourses are separate and unconnected (Watts, 1998b).

Further, if you espouse some kind of realism, it is appropriate to bring complementary accounts into relation with one another. Complementary explanatory accounts should not be divorced so completely that integration between them is impossible. To return to the example of going to sleep, different levels of description of going to sleep are not independent. Knowing what is happening at one level enables you to predict with reasonable (but probably not complete) accuracy what is happening at the other level. A complete understanding of sleep requires exploration of how the complementary mind and brain accounts can be coordinated.

The Diversity of the Disciplines

In considering the relationship between two disciplines such as theology and psychology, it is important to remember how diverse both are. Psychology, like every scientific discipline, has a hierarchical structure. At the bottom level, there are detailed research findings. I know of nothing demonstrated by psychological research that is incompatible with Christian theology. You could probably say the same for every science. However, research findings are always made in the broader context of theories, which themselves arise out of general research paradigms, and at the highest level are embedded in scientific world views. The further up that hierarchy you go, the more possibility there is of encountering incompatibility with theology. That is partly because theology and detailed research findings are so different in character that there is hardly any scope for them to agree or disagree with one another. In contrast, scientific paradigms and worldviews are entering the same kind of metaphysical territory as theology, and so can potentially conflict with it.

Also, psychology involves a variety of very different approaches. In fact, in some ways, it would be more appropriate to speak of psycholog*ies* than of psychology. Biological psychology, which is a natural science and quite close to disciplines such as physiology, takes a very different approach from social psychology, which is close to sociology. At one end of the spectrum of psychology, there are the introspectionist methods that were important at the inception of psychology as a discrete discipline, and that have begun to come back into vogue in the form of 'account analysis' (Good and Watts, 1996). At the other end of the spectrum, there are the behaviourist methods that came to prominence after the First World War as a reaction against introspectionism, and have been championed by B.F. Skinner. Even within specific areas of psychology, such as the study of intelligence, a variety of different controlling metaphors have been used (Sternberg, 1990). At present, it seems that the emphasis on 'cognition', the dominant approach in psychology, may offer the best hope so far of reaching an integrative paradigm that holds the biological and the social together.

There is also rich variety within the tradition of Christian theology. On many issues there is no single theological position, but a variety of views. It is perhaps when it comes to philosophical issues that the Christian tradition is most diverse, and it is of course the more philosophical end of theology that intersects most with scientific disciplines such as psychology. Let us take two brief examples to make the point. First, there has often been an emphasis on human free will in Christian theology, especially for example, in approaching the problem of evil. However, there are other traditions, especially conservative Calvinistic theology with its doctrine of predestination, that has such a strong sense of determination by God that it brings human freedom into question.

Another issue is the nature of the human soul. As we will see in Chapter 5, there were divergent views about soul in Greek philosophy, and they have continued to be reflected through Christian theology. One tradition, coming from Plato through Descartes, has emphasized the separateness of the soul from the body. The other, coming from Aristotle through Aquinas, has emphasized the embodied soul. How you coordinate theology and psychology depends on the part of the Christian tradition with which you are mainly concerned.

Parallel Debates

In fact, both theology and psychology are so diverse that it is often helpful to get beyond the question of theology versus psychology, but rather to see where and how similar debates have been played out in both disciplines. As an example, let us take one of the classic debates in Christian theology, that between Augustine and Pelagius. Very crudely, they differed in how positive or negative a view of human nature they took. Augustine, with a strong doctrine of Original Sin, took a bleak view of human nature unaided by the grace of God. Pelagius took a more positive view of human beings as made in the image of God, and able to live according to his will. One of the intriguing things about the doctrine of Original Sin is that it has entered Western consciousness so deeply that it crops up in a variety of secular guises. There are fictional treatments of the theme, of which William Golding's *Lord of the Flies* is one of the most celebrated. The theme of Original Sin, or an equivalent to it, has also arisen in psychological thought, both in sociobiology and in psychoanalysis.

The parallel between the Biblical myth of the Fall and Dawkins's (1976) modern myth of the *Selfish Gene* illustrates the close but concealed relationship there can be between theological and scientific worldviews. Goodwin (1994) in his *How the Leopard Changed His Spots* makes some interesting remarks about how the sociobiological myth of the selfish gene is basically the Christian myth of Original Sin in naturalized form. The old idea that we are born sinful resurfaces in the claim that our hereditary material is basically selfish; then the idea that our sinful nature condemns us to a life of conflict and toil resurfaces as the idea that our selfish genes lead to competitive interaction and to the constant attempt to reach competitive advantage over rivals in the fitness stakes. Finally because, as Dawkins says, we are born selfish, we will have to learn to be altruistic. That corresponds to the religious idea that there can be salvation from our selfish nature, though he seems to have no adequate notion of where that salvation might come from. It is where the analogy conspicuously breaks down. Looked at this way, you can see that, though Dawkins tries to retain something corresponding to salvation in his Darwinian myth, he does not have the resources to do this convincingly; he has no good account of how altruism is to be learned, or why it should be.

An equivalent idea of Original Sin can also be found in Freud, as various people have pointed out, including, McClelland (1964), Gellner (1985) and Webster (1995). Part of Freud's originality was to establish a concept of universal psychopathology. In his view, no one is completely free of the scars of human development, and the universality of psychopathology is one of the features that makes it parallel to the doctrine of Original Sin. The mechanism by which universal problems arise may be different (though the doctrine of Original Sin is rather vague about that), but they agree about the problems being universal. The other point of similarity is the moralistic element. In Freud's view, the universal psychological problems of humanity also prevent them from doing anything genuinely altruistic; we are locked into patterns of behaviour that meet psychological needs. The difference between the doctrine of Original Sin and psychoanalysis is the latter offers a less adequate escape route. Freud places his confidence in the process of analysis, whereas sociobiology has no escape route at all. However, what can be expected from psychoanalysis is much more limited than the redeeming grace of God held out in Christian doctrine.

More generally, you can often find parallel debates about human personality being discussed in psychology and theology, as Peter Morea (1997) has pointed out. The range of theological views he considers include those of Augustine, Kierkegaard, Thomas Merton, Pascal Teresa of Avila and Karl Rahner, while the psychologists include Freud, Jung, Rogers, Maslow, Kelly and many other personality theorists. For example, he sees links between Thomas Merton and Maslow's theory of self-actualistion, and other links between George Kelly's concept of 'man as scientist' and Rahner's 'transcendental' Christianity. There is thus a diversity of views about personality, both within modern psychology and within the Christian tradition. This means that there is a complex set of parallels to be drawn and similar debates often occur in both disciplines.

The Scope of the Current Dialogue

Just as the dialogue between theology and the natural sciences has been pursued mainly by religiously-minded scientists, for the dialogue with psychology we are mainly indebted to religiously-minded psychologists. Malcolm Jeeves, a distinguished neuropsychologist, has made an important contribution to the dialogue in a series of books that spans a quarter of a century (Jeeves 1976, 1984, 1994, 1997). He has also collaborated with the well-known social psychologist, David Myers (Myers and Jeeves, 1987). Another important contributor to the dialogue between theology and psychology is the pastoral theologian and psychologist, Don Browning, whose important books again span many years (Browning, 1966, 1980, 1987). There has also recently been a growing interest in the human person in the dialogue between theology and science (Russell *et al.*, 1999; Gregersen *et al.*, 2000).

The current dialogue between theology and psychology focuses around at least four key areas. One specialist area of the dialogue that will not be considered here concerns theological and psychological perspectives on Christian pastoral care. Pattison (1993) and Hunsinger (1995) offer different assessments of that dialogue. Then there are three further dialogues that focus on

(a)   general issues about human nature,
(b)   the nature of human religiousness, and
(c)   the concerns of systematic theology.

The first of these dialogues arises from the investigation of human functioning in mainstream scientific psychology. That includes evolutionary psychology, brain processes, learning and development, cognition, and consciousness. At its most general, this dialogue is concerned with models of human nature and influences on human functioning, and their religious significance. When the dialogue is conducted in this way, psychology sets the agenda and provides the basic material about which the dialogue is conducted. Theology takes up the role of commentator. The aim is to offer theological reflection on the approaches to the human person implicit in contemporary psychologies.

The next four chapters of this book are contributions to that kind of dialogue. Chapter 2 is concerned with the evolutionary approach to human nature that is currently so much in the ascendancy. Chapter 3 focuses on a specific aspect of psychological functioning, human consciousness, that is currently the focus of a vigorous multi-disciplinary debate (especially from the perspective of neuroscience), and seeks to offer a theological contribution. Chapter 4 offers a theological appraisal of one of the most controversial areas of contemporary science, the computer simulation of intelligence, an enterprise that carries heavy ideological presuppositions about the nature of human functioning. Then, in Chapter 5, moving beyond reductionism, I consider how a broad-based approach to the human person might proceed, in both theology and psychology, and recommend the concept of the 'self' as a particularly fruitful one for the dialogue between theology and psychology.

The second area of dialogue moves from general issues about human nature to more specific issues about human religiousness. That dialogue draws on the psychology of religion, though general psychology is still relevant in the background. Though there has been a growing amount of research activity in the psychology of religion, there has so far been surprisingly little dialogue between theology and the psychology of religion. It is curious that the interface between the two should have been so neglected. Part of the problem is that the implicit assumption of much psychology of religion is that it is offering an approach to human religiousness that is an alternative to, and replaces, the theological one. I suggest that, though the psychology of religion can be taken in that way, it doesn't have to be. For example, social psychological explanations of speaking 'in tongues' do not exclude the role of the Holy Spirit; they can be taken as indicating how the activity of the Spirit is mediated. One important contributor to the dialogue between theology and psychology who grasps this point well is the Jesuit psychoanalyst, William Meissner, especially in his *Life and Faith* (1987). His exposition of the relationship between the theology and psychology of grace is exemplary in allowing each discipline its proper space.

The chapters in this book on religious experience are a contribution to the dialogue between theology and psychology about human religiousness. Chapter 6 examines approaches to religious experience from the perspective of cognitive neuroscience, and takes up the question of whether explanations from that perspective are exhaustive, or whether they are compatible with a theological perspective. In particular, I argue for the value of a hierarchical model of cognition, an approach that is likely to be fruitful theologically and psychologically. Next, in Chapter 7, I look at approaches to religious experience that have seen it as reflecting processes of social influence, and resist the assumption that there is nothing more to religious experience than the influence of people's religious culture.

The third way of conducting the dialogue between theology and psychology allows theology to set the agenda, and invites psychology to contribute to it. There will be some who will argue that the dialogue always ought to be conducted in that way, that theology always ought to be the starting point. I see no reason to accept that requirement. It is perfectly possible to respect the distinctive place of theology in the dialogue with psychology, whichever discipline is the starting point for a particular phase of the conversation. When Christian doctrine is considered, there are various topics to which a psychological perspective is relevant, and I consider three.

In Chapter 8, I seek to harvest the implications work on religious experience for an understanding of divine action, arguing that there are good theological reasons for supposing that much divine action will be mediated through revelation to human beings. In Chapter 9, I pursue the century-old attempt to coordinate salvation history with evolution, focusing especially on the evolution of consciousness, the aspect of evolution that, I argue, it is most fruitful to consider in this endeavour. Then, in Chapter 10, I turn to the nature of eschatological hope, and in particular consider how the area of the sciences that is brought into dialogue with eschatology affects how theological discourse itself is understood. There are various ways of reading theology, and I suggest that a dialogue with the natural sciences tends to result in it being taken rather propositionally, while the dialogue with psychology tends to result in more of an emphasis on the expressive or attitudinal aspects of theology. Keeping both dialogues running alongside one another may be the best way of not distorting the nature of theology one way or the other.

In the final chapter I turn to what might be called 'metatheology', and develop a psychological perspective on the process of doing theology. I focus on the tendency of theology to operate in terms of dichotomies; there are important issues that arise here that can be elucidated from the perspective of the psychology of thinking. I caution against dichotomous thinking in theology, whether that arises in the context of epistemology, doctrine, or religious authority.

The topics considered in this book do not exhaust the contribution of psychology to theology. I have indicated elsewhere (Watts *et al.*, 2001, Chapter 15) some of the other topics it may be fruitful to consider, including psychological contributions to the doctrine of the atonement, to Biblical interpretation, and to the history of Christian life and thought. However, I hope that topics considered here indicate the scope of the constructive work that can be done on the interface of the two disciplines. If this book sets the tone for the dialogue between theology and psychology, and others are encouraged to extend it, the book will have done its job.

Chapter 2

Evolution

The next three chapters will consider the three main reductionist approaches to human nature. In each case, it will be important to distinguish the perniciously strong reductionist approaches that are sometimes put forward from the more circumspect versions that are preferable, both scientifically and theologically. We will begin here with the evolutionary approach to human nature, and examine its relationship to the Christian view. After considering neuropsychology and artificial intelligence in the next two chapters, Chapter 5 will examine more general issues in Christian and psychological approaches to human nature.

The evolutionary approach to the human person is currently being pressed very vigorously, and this has come in two waves. First, from the mid-1970s, there was an approach to social behaviour from the perspective of evolutionary biology, known as 'sociobiology', in which the two seminal works were E.O. Wilson's (1975) massive *Sociobiology*, and Richard Dawkins's (1976/1989) more popular *The Selfish Gene*. Then, in the 1990s, there has been 'evolutionary psychology', a movement within the human sciences themselves to apply a radically evolutionary perspective. So much heat has been generated by these movements that it is necessary to pause to evaluate them in general terms before going on to specifically religious issues.

Sociobiology

It is important to distinguish how successful sociobiology has been in studying animal and human social behaviour. It has made useful scientific headway with animal social behaviour. In contrast the real problems arise when it is applied to human behaviour. Though its enthusiastic proponents write confidently about human applications, what they claim is usually pure speculation, with hardly any firm scientific evidence to support it. The scientific criticisms to be made of this highly speculative application of sociobiology to human social behaviour are devastating (Kitcher, 1985). For example, there are too many discontinuities between animal and human 'altruism' to be able to transfer explanations from one to the other. I want both to acknowledge the merits of animal sociobiology, and to be strongly critical of human sociobiology.

Further, given the speculative nature of human sociobiology, it is not surprising that, when it comes to human culture, sociobiologists disagree radically among themselves. Unfortunately, this does not often give rise to healthy debate. Rather, with little discussion or explanation, one sociolobiologist just takes up a radically different position from another. Given that there is no proper contact between theory and data in human sociobiology, there is usually no scientific way of settling differences between the approaches of different sociobiologists. For example, E.O. Wilson took a strong line about the genetic control of culture, albeit on a 'long leash'. Dawkins, in contrast, seems to have given up this idea, presumably because he thought it was untenable. Instead he dreamt up the notion of cultural units that were analogous to genes in being 'replicators', and which he called 'memes', an idea that may subsequently have been taken more seriously than he intended. Though the idea of memes has attracted its adherents (Blackmore, 1999), it has given rise to little research, and seems to most people to be a too simplistic idea of how social transmission takes place to represent any scientific advance. Disagreements between sociobiologists are well analysed by John Bowker (1995) in *Is God a Virus?*

Though popular sociobiology has been successful in gaining attention and causing a stir, the quality of the scientific writing has often been inexact and potentially misleading. A classic case is Dawkins's application of the term 'selfish' to genes, though it is clear that genes are not the kind of thing to which such moral terms apply. The application enables him to make the illegitimate move from saying that we have selfish genes to saying that we ourselves are selfish. Mary Midgley (1985) has done a good job of pointing out these philosophical flaws. Dawkins also has a tendency to write as if genes somehow controlled people totally, though when he is writing more carefully, as in *The Extended Phenotype* (1982), it is clear that he knows better. However, his misleadingly exaggerated claims for the powers of genes seem not just to be eye-catching popularization, but to be designed to suit his polemical purposes.

Evolutionary Psychology

Though there has been a good deal of public debate about sociobiology, the fact remains that it has not been taken very seriously either by psychologists or social scientists, and has had minimal impact on how those disciplines are conducted. In contrast, its offspring, evolutionary psychology, is an attempted revolution from within those disciplines and represents a determined campaign to change the human sciences. The tone has been fierce and polemical, with the aim of establishing evolutionary biology as being able to provide a complete explanation of all aspects of human functioning. The seminal text was The *Adapted Mind* (Barkow *et al.*, 1992), though the best-known expositions are those of Wright (1994) and Pinker (1994, 1997). A strange feature of evolutionary psychology is that there is only a modest amount of technical scientific work underpinning the popularizations; the popularizations seem to have run ahead of the research.

At the heart of evolutionary psychology there is, first, a quest to understand how human traits and attributes might have arisen through natural selection. That contributes a valuable perspective, but it suffers from the methodological difficulty of obtaining evidence that bears on whether a particular evolutionary story is empirically correct. It is also never clear how far a particular human attribute is explicable in terms of natural selection, or whether other factors are relevant. It is always a fruitful question when considering any human capacity to ask 'what is it for?'; that is the start of an enquiry, not the basis for a dogmatic assertion that human capacities are entirely explicable in terms of their adaptive advantage.

Second, there is a concern with how far key human capacities are innate. The strongest example is that of language. Many people have now been persuaded that there is an inherited capacity for language that underpins the acquisition of particular languages in particular cultures by individual people (Pinker, 1994; Plotkin, 1997). This concern leads on to the much more speculative suggestion that other areas of human functioning might be similarly underpinned by inherited capacities in the form of 'modules' of the mind. In evolutionary psychology, it ought to be a matter of empirical enquiry how far the mind is organized in inherited modules. Unfortunately these sometimes become matters of dogma rather than scientific enquiry. The key difference between moderate and strong forms of evolutionary psychology is that the moderate form assumes that there are sometimes inherited mental modules, and looks for evidence to tell us how far a particular human capacity is underpinned by them. The strong form simply assumes, without evidence, that every human capacity is underpinned by such modules.

Finally, evolutionary psychology is often allied with a strong form of genetic determinism. It is easy simply to assume that we have genes for everything, crime for example. In fact, most high-level human capacities are influenced by many different genes, not just one. Moreover, those genes only exert influence, steering things in one direction or another, but not determining the outcome. The mechanism of the influence of genes is usually complex and interactive, not simple and direct. Interest in the power of genes has been given extra force by the current project of mapping the human genome (Ridley, 1999), and by the development of techniques for genetic engineering. (For a Christian perspective, Watts, 2000). Evolutionary psychology, at least as it has been portrayed in the media, has often formed an alliance with a naive form of genetic determinism that has enhanced either excitement or fear.

The strong version of evolutionary psychology thus claims that all key human attributes are the result of genetically controlled, innate capacities that arise through natural selection, and are instantiated as mental modules. The moderate form asks what the evolutionary advantage of human capacities might be, and looks at how inherited potential interacts with other factors in giving rise to human capacities, but it sees the evolutionary perspective as the start of the enquiry, not the basis for a dogmatic pre-empirical ideology.

Given the rather extreme way in which most evolutionary psychologists have presented their position, it is not surprising that there has been a strong counter-response (for example, Rose and Rose, 2000). Unfortunately, there is a real danger of the contribution of the evolutionary perspective to the human sciences getting lost in the resulting battle. However, there are pointers towards a better way of considering things. One of the best books on evolutionary psychology that I know is Henry Plotkin's *Evolution in Mind* (1997). Plotkin is a strong and persuasive advocate of the value of an evolutionary perspective in psychology, but he can always see both sides of a question, he keeps the research evidence at centre stage, his scientific judgment is dependable, and he does not over-state his conclusions. If all evolutionary psychology were conducted with such scientific sophistication, it could be given a whole-hearted welcome.

Many of the initial advocates of evolutionary psychology seem to have failed to learn the lessons of scientific history, and to be claiming that they can deliver more than is credible. It is unlikely that it will be possible to produce a complete explanation of why humans have the characteristics they do in terms of the survival advantage of those characteristics. My hope is that evolutionary psychology will calm down, become less pretentious, and deliver the important contribution to understanding human nature that it has the potential to make.

What Kind of Darwinism?

There have long been very different interpretations of evolutionary theory, and Barlow (1994) has provided a helpful compendium of contrasting approaches. Recently there have been especially heated debates between the narrow, strict approach that has been called 'ultra-Darwinism', represented by Dennett (1995) and a broader, pluralistic approach represented by Stephen Jay Gould (1996). The broad Darwinians, while convinced that evolution is the mechanism by which species have evolved, recognize that there are puzzles about evolution that are not yet explained, and are willing to consider other processes apart form natural selection as contributing to the evolutionary process.

Gould's three main points are:

(a) that evolution proceeds in a step-wise way with 'punctuated equilibria',
(b) that many evolutionary developments seem to have originated as neutral, non-adaptive developments, even if they eventually came to have adaptive value, and
(c) that evolution has been affected by contingencies such as climate changes and the arrival of meteorites.

In each case, it seems to me that Gould has the plausible scientific case. Gould is a Darwinian, as he himself would emphasize, but not a fundamentalist one.

There is now a substantial body of what might be called radical, post-reductionist biology that, as John Polkinghorne (2000, Chapter 4) points out, opens the way to a reconciliation of evolution with design. One important strand has been the postulation of self-organizing processes in life forms, that supplement what can be explained through mutation and natural selection. Such self-organizing tendencies have been postulated in different ways by both Brian Goodwin (1994) and Stuart Kauffman (1995), and they mark an important development in biology. Others have gone further. Michael Behe (1996) has drawn attention to a number of remarkably integrated systems, such as the intracellular transport of proteins, of the blood-clotting system, that are not easily explicable in evolutionary terms. Behe asserts that they are 'irreducible'; I would prefer to see them as challenges that we will need an expanded evolutionary biology to handle. Another intriguing development in radical biology is Rupert Sheldrake's (1988) theory of 'morphic fields' which can operate across time and space, guiding development and conveying information.

Such developments in biology make narrow, fundamentalist Darwinism look increasingly blinkered and dated. Many of these newer trends in biology are, of course, still speculative, and cannot yet be embraced with confidence. Part of the problem is that evolutionary biology has always had a shortage of data to work with, and is not able to make much use of experimentation. However, there seems absolutely no basis for the fierce dismissal found, for example, in Dennett's (1995) *Darwin's Dangerous Idea* of broader ideas about evolution. We need a period of open-minded enquiry about exactly how evolution is most likely to have occurred.

The key point is that though natural selection may explain much, it cannot explain everything. Varela *et al.* (1991) in their excellent book, *The Embodied Mind*, seek to release us from the tyranny of the extreme Darwinism that seeks to explain all characteristics of species in terms of their advantage in the battle for survival. Like other recent evolutionary thinkers they emphasize the role of the self-organizing capacities of creatures. Also, what survives is not necessarily what is *best* for survival; rather a wide range of characteristics may be selected provided they do not work *against* survival. The insight here is rather like Karl Popper's insight that we do not prove good scientific theories, it is just that our best theories survive disproof. In a similar way, the characteristics that are retained through evolution are not necessarily those that have been specifically selected, but the much more diverse range of characteristics that have not been eliminated by natural selection. There is a powerful warning here against expecting too much from evolutionary psychology.

The standard form of biological thinking about how our distinctive human capacities have emerged is that they result from the increasing complexity of the central nervous system, and the information processing capacities that arise from it. It is worth pausing, however, to note the social constructionist critique that can be offered of that kind of story. We tend perhaps to make over sharp distinctions, between genes and environment in the evolutionary process, and between the organism and the environment. Though these distinctions are helpful first approximations, they can be misleading if we hold to them too rigidly. Oyama, in her *Ontogeny of Information* (1985), has criticized the distinction between genes and environment as an artificial and misleading one. Goodwin (1994) has made similar points.

It is a widely accepted idea that human characteristics such as intelligence are part 'nature', part 'nurture'. The point that now needs to be made is that one cannot separate genes from the environment sufficiently to be able to speak of what genes do, as opposed to what the environment does. It is only a slight exaggeration to say that neither genes nor environment, on their own, have any effect whatsoever. It is the interaction between genes and environment that determines almost everything. Moreover, these interactive effects can take many forms, and can operate along many different developmental pathways; there is no invariant form of interaction between them.

It is interesting to note the attitudes of different evolutionary psychologists to this truism. Pinker (1997, p. 33) is rude about interactionism viewing it as simplistic and uninformative. Plotkin (1997), in contrast, sees the task of specifying interactionism more precisely as at the heart of evolutionary psychology. As he notes (Chapter 4), there are now some sophisticated ways of reconciling the idea of innate mental modules with processes of learning and development, particularly for the example of language, which is at the forefront of evolutionary psychology.

Just as we need to avoid an over-rigid separation of genes from environment, so Varela *et al.* (1991) also argue that we need to be careful about an over-strong separation between organism and environment. The environment that is important from most points of view is the *perceived* environment. Of course, there are constraints on this perceived environment; we cannot simply fantasize any environment we like. However, it is the environment as we perceive it that we adapt to; perceiving features of the environment opens up possibilities for adaptation that would not be present if we were oblivious of them.

This view of things underlines the point that the adaptation of human beings to their environment is radically different from that of any other species. Human beings live in what Varela *et al.* call an 'enacted' environment (i.e. one they create and construct) to a greater degree than any other creatures. Many of the ways in which we enact our world are socially shared and culturally transmitted. There are individual elements of course, but the collective determination is very strong. These considerations should give pause to a biological imperialism that wishes to explain the social and psychological features of human beings in terms of evolution; against that has to be set the fact that, for human beings, the environment within which evolution takes place is to a large degree socially constructed and enacted.

The current broadening of evolutionary theory in some quarters is welcome to theologians, because it moves away from the reductionist claim that everything can be explained in terms of genes and natural selection. However, it would be wise to watch how the scientific discussion unfolds before rushing in to build a natural theology around a broadened understanding of evolution, though it is worth noting that it is already possible at least to attempt a detailed integration of evolutionary theory and natural theology (for example, Corey, 1994). A more cautious exploration of the possibilities of integrating divine action with evolutionary theory can be found in Russell *et al.* (1998).

Culture

How far can the evolutionary perspective explain culture? One extreme position, which I would join evolutionary psychologists in rejecting, is that human culture is a matter for the social sciences alone. Some people might want to establish a demarcation within psychology, with evolutionary psychology studying some of the basic aspects of human nature, and social psychology studying the cultural aspects. On the contrary, I would want to see them as converging perspectives. I believe that the evolutionary perspective has a valuable contribution to make to understanding all aspects of human social life. On the other hand, the group processes that social psychologists study are significant for evolution. The evolutionary and social approaches to psychology are intertwined and complementary; neither is definitive nor exhaustive.

It is also necessary to have a subtle view of the relationship between natural and cultural evolution. With the development of human culture, it is clear that evolution has moved into a new phase. Cultural evolution is not identical to natural evolution, and I do not know anyone who is trying to deny that there is a distinction to be made. Though there are dissimilarities between natural and cultural evolution, they are not so sharp that the evolutionary perspective has no relevance whatever to culture. Like Pinker and others, I reject the view that Darwinism explains evolution up to a certain point in human development, and then its relevance stops.

The New Testament scholar, Gerd Theissen (1984), has offered a helpful analysis of the similarities and differences between biological and cultural evolution. He suggests that cultural variations are an equivalent of genetic mutations, that there are selection pressures in both biological and cultural evolution (though culture softens the harsh selection pressures of biological evolution,) and that cultural transmission is an equivalent of genetic propagation. Within this framework, he develops a view of Christ as a spiritual mutation, a protest against crude selection pressures, and an adaptation to ultimate reality (see Chapter 9).

The most sophisticated evolutionary approach to culture, as far as I am aware, comes from the collaborative work of Charles Lumsden and E.O. Wilson (Lumsden and Wilson, 1981, 1983). Their joint position is considerably better grounded in research, and more plausible than either Wilson's earlier ideas about the genetic control of culture, or Dawkins's rather simplistic idea of memes as self-replicating cultural units (Bowker, 1995, has an excellent comparison of these different positions). The key concept in Lumsden and Wilson's position is that of 'epigenetic rules', perceptual regularities that are grounded in neural processes, and which have important influences on how the world is perceived, and through which culturally transmitted patterns of meaning are acquired by the individual. Rather than attempting to relate genes to culture directly, mind and brain are brought into the picture in a mediating role, and that helps considerably. It permits the development of a sophisticated theory of 'co-evolution', involving both genes and culture, in which each influences the other (see Wilson, 1998, Chapter 7).

Lumsden and Wilson have a list of twelve epigenetic rules, each of which is reasonably well researched. There may be others, but their list is enough to establish that this is a well-grounded approach. However, it is important to note that epigenetic rules only predispose to certain interpretations of culture; there is no suggestion that they determine it. Also, some aspects of how we perceive the world will be more influenced by inherited epigenetic rules than others. For example, it seems highly likely that there is an inherited predisposition for humans to be frightened of spiders, but there are many other complex emotions such as guilt that are more culturally variable and less likely to be the result of inherited predispositions. In the religious domain there may well be aspects of ritual that make sense in terms of 'epigenetic rules'. Perhaps aspects of the Jewish purity code set out in Leviticus can be seen as having direct evolutionary advantages, and religion could have had evolutionary value in giving authority to that purity code. Lumsden and Wilson have offered a helpful account of how certain limited aspects of cultural life relate to inheritance and evolution, but there seems no serious prospect of it being developed into a complete evolutionary theory of culture.

Evolutionary Ethics

The aspect of culture that has been most vigorously debated from an evolutionary perspective is ethics. The arguments about evolutionary ethics have become increasingly sharp and sophisticated, and there is growing clarity about the disputed issues (Ruse, 1995, especially Chapter 9). How far can evolution 'explain' ethics? That breaks down into two rather different questions: how far evolution can give an account of the development of ethics, and how far evolution can justify ethics.

As far as the development of ethics is concerned it is perfectly possible, of course, to identify patterns of behaviour in sub-human species that are a precursor of the moral behaviour of human beings. Sociobiology has identified various kinds of animal behaviour that can loosely be called altruistic, and these can be regarded as part of the seed out of which human morality has evolved. So far, so good. One key question is how close these are to human morality; there are both similarities and differences between animal and human 'altruism', as Rottschaeffer has pointed out (1998). There is not much dispute about evolution being able to explain certain aspects of altruism; the question is whether it can give an adequate account of the evolutionary emergence of all aspects of human altruism.

It is important to remember that morality is a multi-faceted phenomenon, as has long been recognized comprising such components as moral insight, moral ideology, resistance to temptation, reactions to transgression, altruistic behaviour, and so on (see Wright, 1971). The links between these various facets of morality are not always very close, and an adequate theory of the origin of ethics would have to give a convincing account of all of them. That is something that evolutionary ethics has hardly even attempted so far. Rottschaeffer and Martinsen (1990) make a point of this kind when they suggest that evolution can explain basic moral sentiments but not full-blown moral dispositions, with an appropriate sense of moral obligation. Clarifying which aspects of morality are explicable in evolutionary terms, and which are not, is bound to expose the significant but limited value of the evolutionary approach.

It is also worth noting that evolutionists cannot agree about the relationship of evolution to morality, as Rottschaeffer (1998) pointed out. Though E.O. Wilson believes that evolution provides the basis of morality, other evolutionists have taken a different approach. Richard Alexander (1987) sees evolution as morally neutral, while George C. Williams (1989) considers that the dictates of survival are in conflict with morality. It is yet another reflection of the weak scientific status of much evolutionary thinking that there is no adequate methodology for resolving such disputes. If one accepts Williams's position, which has a good deal of plausibility, it is clear that there is no prospect of reducing ethics to evolution. Another important point of debate is whether the evolutionary emergence of human morality can be explained in terms of the direct effects of natural selection, or whether, as Franscisco Ayala argues (1987), it is a non-adaptive development that arises from more basic components that have themselves arisen through natural selection.

Even if evolution is able to explain the origin of morality, it may not be able to justify it. It is a feature of morality as we know it, that it is an approach to the regulation of conduct that claims some kind of authority. One radical response to this complaint, of course, is to say that it is a mistake to imagine that there could be any absolute justification for an ethical system (Ruse, 1995). This view admits that evolution cannot explain moral authority. However, that is not regarded as a fair criticism, because the idea of moral authority is itself seen as a mistake.

If evolutionary ethics takes this turn, it becomes clear that it is not offering an explanation of morality as we know it, but redefining morality. Some evolutionists would welcome such redefinition, and suggest that ethics could be improved by recognizing its evolutionary basis. Such a move exposes the ambiguity about whether the evolutionary approach is seeking to explain morality as we know it, or to redesign morality in its own image. My own view is that morality has multiple foundations. Emmet (1979) has set out a view of this kind, arguing that there are always strands dealing with authority, with consequences, and with character and virtue. It is because of this inherently multifaceted nature of morality that it defies reduction to any one of its foundations.

Religion

Discussion about the relation of religion to evolution has been less vigorous than that about morality, though the debate runs along somewhat parallel lines. There can be little doubt that the capacity for religion is rooted in capacities that have developed in the course of evolution. How could it be otherwise? However, religion, like morality, is a complex, multifaceted phenomenon, including beliefs, private prayer, public rituals, life-style and so on, and an evolutionary approach will have to take that into account. The complexity of religious life makes it incredible that there should be a single religion module in the brain. Though it is becoming clear that there is a degree of genetic predisposition to religion (Eaves *et al.*, 1999), it is impossible for something as complex as religion to be determined by a single gene, or that genes should completely determine religiousness. It will be a long and difficult scientific task to unravel how the variety of different genes involved can steer people towards religion or against it.

Though natural selection is no doubt relevant to religious capacities, it again seems likely that the influence is indirect. It is easy to assume that there are only two alternatives: one that religion has arisen because of the pressures of natural selection and is explicable in those terms; the other that natural selection has had no effect on religion whatsoever. As Hinde (1999) suggests, it seems most likely that religion draws on a number of basic capacities that have evolved through natural selection, rather than itself being the result of natural selection. That is comparable to Ayala's suggestion about how natural selection has contributed to morality.

Religion is an integrative phenomenon that brings together capacities for ritual, morality, relationships, reflective self-consciousness, and much more. Indeed, there is hardly anything distinctively human that does not find a place in religion. Moreover, each of the components of religion is itself complex, draws on a variety of more basic capacities, and no doubt has a complex evolutionary history. Equally, religion seems likely to draw on many different areas of the brain, each of which is involved in other things. All this makes it unlikely that simplistic questions such as 'what is the adaptive advantage of religion?' will yield any useful answers.

Most recent evolutionary theories of religious thinking assume that a religious view of the world makes use of elements that evolved in other cognitive domains, but integrates them in the service of a new approach. Thus, Sperber (1996) assumes that religious cognition springs from everyday cognition, even though it diverges from it in ways that give it its power and appeal. Similarly, Boyer (1994) assumes that assumptions from naive physics, biology and psychology have been brought together in a religious view of the world. Mithen (1996) also assumes that religious ideas arise from bringing together discrete cognitive domains of personal and impersonal intelligence. Though the details of this kind of approach remain speculative, it seems that the broad background assumption will prove durable, that religion evolved through integrating cognitive components that initially developed separately.

Some aspects of religion will probably be illuminated by an evolutionary approach more than others. However, there will be limits to the evolutionary approach to religion, and it may well turn out that the most interesting, distinctive and impressive aspects of religion are those least explicable in terms of evolutionary advantage. Certainly, there is no justification at the present time for concluding that religion is nothing but the product of natural selection.

Comparing Humans and Other Creatures

It is hard, in both theology and science to keep a balanced view of the relationship of human beings to other creatures, and to avoid exaggerating either the similarities or the differences. From a scientific point of view, I would want to emphasize the rooted-ness of human nature in the process of evolution, while also resisting the tendency to say that we are nothing but the products of evolution. From a theological point of view, I would also want to emphasize both the continuity of human beings with the natural world, but also our transcendence from it and our development into spiritual creatures. Often this balance has not been kept, either in science or in theology. There has been a tendency for Christian thinkers to want to exaggerate the differences between human beings and other creatures, and for secular thinkers to want to exaggerate the similarities.

In science, the trend in biological anthropology has been to emphasize the continuity of human beings with the rest of the animal kingdom, though I sense that the pendulum is beginning to swing back. Language has been one key area of debate, and some have tried to argue that chimpanzees, for example, have language. It now seems that they have only such limited rudiments that it is wholly misleading to say that they have language (Pinker, 1994; Plotkin, 1997). It also seems that reflective self-consciousness is something that is distinctive to human beings (Davies and Humphreys, 1993). Religion and art are also probably distinctively human.

However, it is necessary to be cautious in how these claims are stated. I am not trying to say that any human characteristics are so unique that they have no parallel in the other species. That would be biologically implausible. For example, our distinctive kind of self-consciousness must have its roots in the more limited kind of consciousness found in animals. However, it would be flying in the face of both commonsense and scientific evidence to say that human beings do not manifest capacities that are developed to a degree that is really new and distinctive.

In theology, the emphasis has tended to be on the differences between human beings and other creatures, on our unique *imago Dei* status, rather than on continuity with the natural world. However, it is not clear why this need be so. Genesis assumes that humanity is rooted in the natural world, and Ecclesiastes 3 takes a strong view of the similarities between humanity and the 'beasts'. There is no justification here for trying to divorce human beings from the rest of creation. Nevertheless, the ways in which human beings differ from other species are clearly of theological importance, because they bring us into a new moral domain and open up the possibility of a conscious relationship to God. I would want to talk about how, in human beings, the natural and spiritual worlds meet; we are both natural and spiritual creatures, and in this sense stand at the pivot of creation.

One twentieth-century theologian who gets the balance right is Karl Rahner (1978). He sees the 'transcendent' or spiritual aspects of being human as arising from their natural creatureliness. Further, he sees this as reflecting the purpose of God, including his purpose to reveal himself in human form. He is to be admired for his attempt to hold together the natural and spiritual aspects of being human in a coherent way. For theology to fail to give a proper account of either the natural or the spiritual aspects of being human obscures our pivotal place in God's creative purposes.

If there is a problem in Rahner's account, it lies in his rather different uses of the concept of 'spirit', and in an apparent slide between low and high notions of spiritual or transcendent. At the lowest level, the concept of the 'spiritual' can be used as a way of referring to the capacities that differentiate us from other animals, capacities that enable us to relate to other people and, critically from a Christian point of view, enable us to relate to God. Various lists have been produced of such characteristics. Brown (1998) suggests five, language, theory of mind, episodic memory, conscious top-down agency, and future orientation.

Calling such capacities 'spiritual' may seem to imply that they are wholly good, that they put us on the side of the angels, but I do not assume that. Neither Rahner nor I are talking about humans being the pinnacle of creation, or of our being somehow perfect. There are very contrasting approaches to the relationship between evolution and morality, and extreme views are often found. Some assume that our animal inheritance is all good, and that evil is a specifically human development. Others assume that our animal inheritance is all bad, and that goodness is a specially human virtue (for example, Campbell, 1975). Both positions fail to see the morally ambivalent nature, both of the animal kingdom and of what is distinctly human.

What we inherit from our animal ancestors seems partly good and partly bad. Though the animal world is in some ways 'red in tooth and claw', there are also species such as dolphins that seem impressively peace-loving and altruistic. Equally, our distinctive human self-consciousness is morally ambivalent. Our higher capacities are, in fact, highly ambivalent in their moral and spiritual implications. For example, the self-consciousness that enables us to meditate and pray also enables us to worry and give ourselves insomnia. (Other animals do not have insomnia or commit suicide; they are unique human achievements.) Our greater moral awareness is also ambivalent. We have a unique capacity to do good to others. Only moral creatures can properly be said to be altruistic. But if altruism is a unique human achievement, so is sin. Animals may do harm to one another, but you need moral awareness to do it in the deliberate way that counts as sin. Surely, as Bowker suggests (1995, p. 108), we should decline to take sides on the simplistic question of whether evil is 'born or bred'. Clearly it is both, though the scientifically interesting question is how exactly the two interact.

Donald Campbell (1975) is inclined to equate inherited tendencies to selfish behaviour with Original Sin, and to assume that it needs to be countered by more altruistic tendencies transmitted through socio-cultural evolution. However, it seems mistaken to load all the responsibility for Original Sin onto genetics; that seems a curiously over-naturalized approach to theology. It is also rather strange to assume that the tendency for moral evil is transmitted exclusively through our genes; 'inherited' sin here becomes an unsatisfactory scientific substitute for 'Original' Sin. It is hard to see that there could be any satisfactory theological answer to the question of when or how moral evil entered the human gene pool. Philip Hefner (1993) touches on these issues in the chapter on Original Sin in *The Human Factor*. His approach is more subtle than that of Campbell, and he suggests that the human sense of sinfulness arises from the *sense* of discrepancy between the conflicting demands of genes and culture. However, that perhaps retreats too far into merely existential questions about the sense of sinfulness.

Just as I am not assuming that human beings are necessarily good, so I am not claming that they are necessarily unique in being spiritual creatures. Some Darwinians consider that evolutionary theory leads to the conclusion that there are likely to be similar creatures elsewhere in the universe (Ruse, 2001, Chapter 8). I am not necessarily convinced by that argument, but I don't think there is as much at stake here theologically as some people assume. Humans seem to be unique amongst creatures on earth, but I make no assumptions about whether or not, elsewhere in the universe, there might be creatures like ourselves that are both natural and spiritual. If there were, I assume that God would reveal himself to them in whatever way was appropriate.

Evolution and the Purposes of God

Next, there are issues about the compatibility of evolution with the Christian doctrine of creation. Since Darwin's time, there have been those such as Charles Kingsley, who have suggested that it is a 'loftier thought' that God created primal forms capable of development than that he should have created every species already fully developed. In this view, evolution reflects God's purpose and is God's way of doing creation. Moreover, if we assume that it was God's particular purpose that there should be creatures such as ourselves capable of receiving his revelation and relating to him, we are led to the assumption that it was God's purpose that creatures such as ourselves should develop through evolution.

Others have rejected any such assumptions. Jacques Monod (1972) claimed that evolution was pure, blind chance, and as such inconsistent with the assumption of a purposeful creator. Dawkins (1986) has a slightly softer view, seeing evolution as reflecting 'tamed' chance, but he still rejects the idea that nature is the product of a purposeful creator. Suggesting that the development of spiritual creatures like ourselves represents the purpose of God may be seen to be assuming a teleological view of evolution of a kind that would be disowned by many evolutionary biologists.

The extent to which evolution reflects chance may have been exaggerated. It is usually assumed that mutations are completely random, though that is difficult to determine. There are indeed some indications, admittedly highly debatable, that if animals are put in a very different environment, there is an increase in the rate of mutations that are helpful in coping with that environment. That is a matter that calls for more investigation. However, even if we assume, as most people would, that mutations are random, natural selection is certainly not random. Mutations may be random but, as Arthur Peacocke (1993) points out, they can still provide the range of possibilities out of which the evolutionary process arises.

Seeing the evolutionary process as fulfilling God's creative purposes seems to involve some kind of assumption of evolutionary progress, and evolutionary progress is a highly controversial notion. Though it is fiercely attacked by some evolutionists, it is ardently espoused by others. Representative views on both sides can be found in Barlow (1994, Section one) and Hull and Ruse (1998, Section nine). The balance of argument is probably swinging towards those who are prepared to admit some kind of directionality in evolution (Wright, 2001), though no one is suggesting that evolution was bound to take exactly the course it did. There is an excellent discussion of evolutionary progress in relation to Christian theology in Ruse (2001).

One key point made by those who resist the assumption that there is evolutionary progress is that, much of the time, natural selection favours only what helps one particular species to survive in one particular environment. However, it would be an exaggeration to say that natural selection only ever favours such highly specific adaptations. It seems that natural selection can sometimes favour developments that would facilitate adaptation in a wide variety of environments, and can justifiably be regarded as an evolutionary advance.

There is also concern that the concept of progress is an over-anthropomorphic one, and too easily slips in the assumption that human beings are the evolutionary pinnacle. Who is to say that the adaptation of one species to its own environment represents any greater evolutionary 'progress' than that of another? That is a reasonable point, but it would be carrying it too far to deny that there has been some kind of direction in evolution. That remains true even if you leave humans out of the picture. If the fossil record were reversed, it would suggest a rather different direction in evolution from that which has actually occurred.

That having been said, it is not easy to know quite how best to formulate the direction in which evolution has been tending. Julian Huxley suggested that there has been an increase in the independence of organisms over their environment, and their ability to control it. Ayala (1988) sees it rather in terms of an enhanced ability to perceive the environment and thus to respond to it effectively. I tend to share this view that the capacity to process information efficiently and effectively is the key development, and that everything else flows from that. Control of the environment is certainly one spin off, but so is the ability to form relationships and, of central importance from a Christian perspective, to receive God's self-revelation and to respond to it.

As is so often the case, it is necessary to distinguish between strong and weak versions of the idea of evolutionary progress. The strong version would claim that there has been consistent, linear progress in evolution. That has clearly not occurred, and I know of no one who seriously maintains it. However, objections to the strong version should not be allowed to justify rejecting even moderate ideas of evolutionary progress.

I do *not* assume that evolution has proceeded along a fixed track that would in principle have been predictable had there been anyone around to make the predictions. However, I *do* assume that there are such advantages in our kind of highly developed capacity for information processing that it was likely that creatures with such capacities would develop in the end. Certainly, the advantages of information processing in natural selection are such that evolution was bound to favour creatures that were good at it. Such creatures need not have been exactly like ourselves, nor need they have evolved by exactly the route as we did. I do not assume that it was God's intention that evolution should proceed in exactly the way it did. However, I do assume that it was God's intention and purpose that, through evolution, creatures should emerge that were capable of relating to him.

Every evolutionary biologist knows that the same capacities may underpin a variety of different functions. Capacities that develop because of one particular implication in the battle for survival may turn out fortuitously to underpin a much broader range of functions. We have already noted that point in connection with the evolution of both morality and religion. It seems that both are likely to trade on developments that were initially selected for other, more basic, survival reasons. Our special capacity for information processing was presumably selected initially because it helped our ancestors to survive, but having come into existence it also subserves our capacity to form a relationship with God and to grow towards his likeness.

There is no theological problem with the idea that God has given the evolutionary process a fairly free reign, knowing that it would lead, sooner or later, to creatures capable of relating to him. It is a basic Christian assumption that God has given human beings free will, which means allowing them to do evil as well as good. God's approach to creation seems to involve a degree of *kenosis*, or 'self-emptying', parallel to what is seen in his incarnation in human form (Haught, 2000). It is thus entirely compatible with general theological assumptions to suppose that he should have allowed evolution to find its own course to his intended goal, rather than pre-determining every development.

One particular aspect of the relation between evolution and God's purposes is how human evolution relates to the fallenness of humanity, and to God's redemptive purpose revealed in Christ. However, that is too big an issue to be broached at the end of this chapter, and I will return to it in Chapter 9.

Conclusion

There are two polarities to be avoided in evolutionary explanations of human nature. One is that the evolutionary account explains everything about human beings, with the result that there is no room for any other approach whatsoever, including a religious one. The other, apparently espoused by some Christians, is that the evolutionary approach to human nature is objectionable or irrelevant. I hope it is clear that neither approach is being adopted here. The evolutionary approach to human nature is interesting and helpful, but it doesn't explain everything, and it isn't the only story to be told.

Moreover, there need be no incompatibly between evolutionary theory and Christianity, provided that neither is espoused in a naive and simplistic form. They can be seen as complementary perspectives on human nature. I would thus endorse Ruse's (2001) conclusions on this matter:

Can a Darwinian be a Christian? Absolutely! Is it always easy for a Darwinian to be a Christian? No, but whoever said that the worthwhile things in life are easy. Is the Darwinian obligated to be a Christian? No, but try to be understanding of those who are. Is the Christian obligated to be a Darwinian? No, but realise how much you are going to forswear if you do not make the effort ... (p. 217).

Chapter 3

Consciousness, Brain and God

Consciousness is a topic whose time has come. It is one of the most distinctive things about human beings, and is currently the focus of an extraordinary amount of multi-disciplinary interest. The human sciences currently see it as one of their greatest challenges. In his influential book, *Consciousness Explained*, Dennett (1991) offers an interesting reason for why consciousness is so much under discussion just now. It is that human consciousness 'is just about the last surviving mystery'. Other mysteries such as the origin of the universe, the nature of life, the appearance of design found in nature, have all been tackled, Dennett says, at least to the point 'where we know how to think about them'.

Consciousness, in contrast, remains a mystery that we do not know how to tackle. Dispelling mysteries has always been a central part of the scientific project. Indeed, apart from the practical benefits that come from the application of science, this is really what science is for. Midgley (1992) has reminded us how early modern science was committed to the view that nature was not mysterious. Now, in the late twentieth century, this programme of demystification has moved on to human beings, and it is the last challenge to see whether consciousness can be rendered non-mysterious.

There is an air of excitement about the current assault on the problem of consciousness. Flanagan concludes his book on the subject by saying that 'understanding consciousness with the conscious mind is a wonderful, giddy idea...' (Flanagan, 1992, p. 222). In part, this is an understandable expression of enthusiasm for the progress that is being made with a difficult but intriguing scientific problem, but there may be more to it than that. Is there an aspiration to some kind of God-like-ness in wanting to use our own minds to understand mind itself? Is there some kind of slightly scary thrill in entertaining the idea that we are really 'nothing but' something perfectly natural and understandable, that there is no mystery about us? It is hard to place with any exactness the sense of excitement people have about the consciousness problem. However, in reading the vast current literature on consciousness, it is an interesting task to attend to the heady, emotional undertones.

The chapter falls into four main sections. The first will consider what is meant by consciousness, distinguishing the various things that are meant by the term and looking at changing assumptions about the relationship between mind and brain. The next section will examine the critique of religion mounted by Francis Crick on the basis of the scientific study of consciousness. The third section will be concerned with the theological insight that God can be understood in some sense as a mind, rather like a human mind, or as a centre of consciousness. Then a final section will focus on immortality, which raises the possibility of a survival of some kind of disembodied consciousness. Questions about religious consciousness will be considered in Chapter 6.

Approaches to Consciousness

There are important theological reasons for being interested in consciousness. For example, the conscious awareness of the presence of God plays an important role in religious life, and we often think about God as a centre of consciousness that is in some ways like ours. This chapter will set out the broad lines of a theological approach to mind and consciousness. In doing so, it is, of course, important to engage with the emerging scientific and philosophical understanding of consciousness, reflecting on it in the light of theological concerns, and extending and recasting it from a theological perspective.

At the outset, it will be good to try to clarify what we mean by 'consciousness'. Like many terms that have become the focus of fierce debate, it has a range of different meanings, and there is a danger of arguments arising from using the same word to talk about different things. No approach to distinguishing different meanings of consciousness would be universally accepted. However, I will follow a helpful classification of meanings of consciousness set out by Copeland (1993).

First, there is a baseline meaning in which an organism is said to be conscious if it has sensory experience of the world and can perform mental operations. It is an important property of human beings that we are conscious in this minimal sense, but it does not raise any particularly controversial issues.

Next, more interestingly, there is reflective consciousness, or knowing that we know something. It is normally a hallmark of human beings that they have this reflective self-consciousness, but recently there have been some intriguing scientific demonstrations of the impairment of this capacity in the phenomenon of 'blindsight' (see below). The experience of seeing is more than just the ability to process visual information, it is not apparently a mere epiphenomenon with no function, but is crucial to the functional performance.

Third, there is consciousness in the sense of having the subjective feel of something. We know what it is like to be us, to have our experience of colour and pain and so on. We do not know for sure what it is like to have other people's experiences, though we assume their experiences are something like ours. We certainly do not know, as Thomas Nagel (1974) has famously argued, what it would be like to be a bat. Philosophers often talk about these 'feely properties' of experience as qualia. This 'feely' meaning of consciousness is the most controversial. Indeed, there are some such as Dennett (1991) who think that this aspect of consciousness is something of a mirage, and that the problems associated with explaining qualia scientifically are pseudo-problems.

Nevertheless, there are good reasons for accepting the experiential aspect of consciousness, however it is formulated, as important. For example, it seems especially important in emotion. Indeed, without it, we would be reluctant to say that someone had an emotion. Take anger for example. A person might look red in the face and be argumentative after something frustrating had happened; but if they did not *feel* angry, it would not count as a classic example of anger. Much of psychotherapy is concerned with expanding the range of potentially threatening things that people experience in a 'feely' way.

Perhaps the most compelling evidence that consciousness is more than the ability to process information comes from the study of patients with neurological conditions such as blindsight (e.g. Flanagan, 1992, Chapter 6; Weiskrantz, 1997). Sometimes, after brain damage or a brain operation, people have a particular part of their visual field in which they have no awareness of seeing anything. What is remarkable is that, even without any conscious experience of seeing, they can guess the location of a point of light with such accuracy that they clearly are registering it at some level. The experience of seeing is completely dissociable from the processing of visual information.

Though there is currently enormous scientific interest in consciousness, this conceals a serious disagreement about how important it actually is. For a long time, behaviourist psychology ignored all mental activity completely. However, even when behaviourism gave way to cognitive psychology, there remained a wariness about consciousness. Sometimes this took a strategic form, along the lines of 'we are not ready yet for big questions like consciousness, let's work on some more basic questions about mental life for now, and see where we get to'. However, other people took a more dogmatic stand that consciousness was simply not important; they said that it was relatively incidental that human beings were conscious, and that consciousness served no essential function, it was a mere 'epiphenomenon'. This provided a convenient theoretical defence for approaches to the study of human cognition that left consciousness to one side.

This is one of the few points in philosophical debates about consciousness at which scientific evidence becomes relevant. The indications are that it actually does make a difference whether we become conscious of something. There are many ways of making this argument (Baars, 1988). In the therapeutic field, accessing a previously repressed memory is often decisive in leading to personal change. It is also clear, in various forms of cognitive therapy that carefully controlled exercises involving thinking about or imagining the subject of particular preoccupations can bring about significant, measurable change. Becoming conscious of something in our environment probably allows us to adapt our behaviour more rapidly and effectively than if we were not aware of it. Those who think that consciousness makes no difference also have to respond to the argument that it is unlikely that consciousness would have evolved at all if it had no function.

These different kinds of 'conscious-shyness' are still around, though I believe that the tide is going out on them. Certainly, there is a growing body of experimental research that takes consciousness seriously (Davies and Humphries, 1993; Marcel and Bisiach, 1988). There are many strands to the current scientific interest in consciousness. In psychoanalysis, the exploration of the borderline between the conscious and the unconscious has been a key focus of theoretical and practical interest. Within cognitive psychology, now it has extricated itself from behaviourism, there is considerable interest in the paradoxes of consciousness, such as how it is possible to be conscious of something by one criterion but not by another. Brain scientists have become intensely interested in how consciousness arises within the physical structure of the brain. Within evolutionary thinking, attention is being given to how and why consciousness evolved.

Powerful as these considerations are, they are not decisive. It is still possible to accept that there is a distinct functional value in states of consciousness, but to resist the conclusion that it is the consciousness itself that gives them that value. Perhaps states of consciousness correspond to a particular kind of brain state, and it is the brain state rather than its correlate in conscious experience that has functional value for us. I do not see how this argument can be finally refuted. However, it is manifestly a highly speculative position that currently has no direct scientific support.

Despite the reality and functional importance of human consciousness, I see no reason to dissent from the prevailing assumption that our capacity for consciousness is grounded in the physical brain. I assume that the brain is involved in all human mental activity, including conscious mental processes. To put it the other way round, it is hard to see how people could think without a brain. When we think, there are presumably brain processes going on that play a critical role in underpinning our thinking.

For some people, this leads onto the formal position that for every mental event or process there must be a corresponding brain state. As an idea, it is not unreasonable; but it is worth noting that it is something of an act of faith. We do not really know how to describe mind states exactly; we can only do so in a very partial and inexact way. Even less do we know how to describe brain states. Some people talk glibly about what the relationship is between mind states and brain states, but the truth is that we do not really know how to investigate scientifically the idea that there is a one to one mapping between them (Harré, 1970).

The next question, even if we assume a correspondence between mind states and brain states, is whether it adds anything to talk about *both* mind and brain. It can be suggested that it is really redundant to talk about both, because whatever we describe in one language can in principle be said in the other. However, there are serious problems with that suggestion. First, this is to assume a much more exact correspondence between mind states and brain states than so far has any scientific warrant. Second, even if such a correspondence could be assumed, the language of mind (about thoughts, intuitions, decisions and so on) is simply talking about different kinds of things from what brain language talks about (activity in the neurons of the brain). Such considerations lead many people to say, rightly in my view, that mind language could never be dropped in favour of brain language without our losing a real way of talking about the distinctive processes of the mind.

Leaving aside these philosophical debates, a good deal of scientific progress has been made in investigating the relationship between mind and brain. Certainly, there have been considerable advances in studying how the brain supports cognitive processes. Jeeves (1993) has referred to it as a 'tightening' of the mind brain link. We now understand the highly specific linkages there can be between particular sites in the brain and particular cognitive functions. Jeeves refers, for example, to the evidence that specific neurological damage can impair our normally remarkable ability to recognize faces. There even seem to be different sites where recognition of faces from the front and from the side are localized. There are also reported cases of the ability to recognize other objects being specifically impaired in the absence of any other difficulties, such as the farmer who lost the ability to tell one cow from another but was unimpaired in all other recognition. However, in terms of the distinctions between different meanings of the term 'consciousness' made at the beginning of this section, it is clear such linkages only involve the relationship of the brain to the minimal meaning of consciousness. It does not yet establish such a tight mind–brain link for the higher aspects of consciousness, such as knowing that you know, and getting the subjective 'feel' of your experience.

There is currently a lot of interest in what sort of neurological structures would be needed to support consciousness, and various models have been proposed. Three of the better known are Gerald Edelman's (1992) theory of neural Darwinism, Francis Crick's (1994) theory of synchronized electrical rhythms, and Roger Penrose's (1989) theory of non-computable brain processes (Crick, 1997, offers a philosophically sophisticated discussion of these theories). I think it would be fair to say that all theories of the neurological basis of consciousness are currently highly speculative. There is not even agreement about what kind of theory we need in terms of the extent of localization. Should we look for 'consciousness neurons' and try and localize phenomenal consciousness quite specifically in the brain? Alternatively, should we see consciousness as emerging from the complex interactions in the structures and networks of the brain, as Dennett amongst others would do? To me the latter seems much more likely.

There are a number of popular assumptions in this area that are highly questionable, once they are critically examined. One is that there is a centre of consciousness, a kind of 'homunculus' monitoring experience, into which all brain processes lead if they are to result in consciousness. In contrast, I would share what is probably the majority scientific view that consciousness arises in a distributed way within the higher nervous system. It is also probably a mistake to think about consciousness as being the *end point* of information processing in the nervous system, and perhaps unhelpful too to look for any single gateway between information processing and conscious experience.

The current philosophical literature is characterized by an attempt to find a path between dualism and what Crick himself calls 'crude materialism'. Few people now see merit in talking about mind or soul as independent of the brain, but equally it is hard to see how they can be completely reduced to brain. In looking for a middle path, some philosophers have taken to talking about how the mind is grounded in the brain, or "supervenient" on it' (Charles and Lennon, 1992), but nevertheless not reducible to it. The assumption is that both brain and mind are 'real', that there are close links between them of an asymmetrical kind, but that the higher level is not reducible to the lower. This is a helpful direction in which to be looking. However, there is not yet a sufficiently clear consensus about exactly what 'supervenience' means. The debate about supervenience is, of course, of considerable theological interest, and it may provide a path between, on the one hand, a strong form of dualism that seems to many people to be scientifically untenable and, on the other, a strong reductionism that denies the reality or significance of higher mental powers.

Nancey Murphy (1998) is in the forefront of those who reject both reductionism and dualism in favour of some kind of non-reductive physicalism. Despite the current popularity of this position, some philosophers are arguing that it is internally incoherent to be a physicalist without also being a reductionist (Kim, 1979). Their argument is that non-reductive physicalism cannot give a coherent account of mental causation without being dragged down either into reductionism or dualism. Though non-reductive physicalism is an attractive position, I think the jury is out on whether it is coherent and tenable. Until the matter is resolved, it would be unwise to judge it as the salvation of a Christian theology of the person. (I discuss general issues about reductionism in Chapter 5).

Non-reductive physicalism is not the only path between strong reductionism and strong dualism, and it may not turn out to be the best one.

My own instinct is to espouse a 'dual aspect monism' in which mind and brain are seen as two real and important faces of the same unitary reality. Such a position retains the distinction between mind and brain, but assumes that mind and brain are so inextricably intertwined in human beings that they are not dissociable. It also resists any attempt to eliminate or play down either one of them. Much more work needs to be done before we can see what exactly is the best path between strong dualism and crude materialism. Suffice it for now to say that such a path is what we should seek, and that it seems likely to be available.

Though I assume that consciousness is grounded in the brain, there are growing reasons for thinking that we currently have too restricted a view of the extent to which mental powers are physically localized. There is growing evidence that the range of operation of consciousness goes beyond the confines of the physical body. Rupert Sheldrake (1995) set out a research programme that would establish that conclusion, and evidence in support of it has been accumulating. For example, there is good evidence that at least some dogs sense when their owners are setting off home (Sheldrake, 1999). Also, evidence is accumulating that people sense when they are being looked at (Sheldrake, 2000).

The theoretical challenge that we now face is to know how best to formulate and explain these phenomena. I do not assume that these extended powers are independent of spatial location. Indeed, the ability to sense that one is being looked at seems to be quite restricted in the range over which it operates. Also, I suggest that these phenomena do not necessarily mean that the mind is independent of the physical brain. I would also still assume that mental powers are grounded in the physical brain, even if their range is more extended than has often been supposed.

Francis Crick on Consciousness

Francis Crick (1994), in *The Astonishing Hypothesis: The Scientific Search for the Soul*, uses the scientific de-mystification of consciousness as the springboard for an attack on religious thinking. His argument trades on the assumption that consciousness and soul are virtually synonymous, and that if science can explain one it can explain the other. He further assumes that if science can explain the soul, that is a defeat for religion. There are many flaws and misunderstandings here, and they are sufficiently common that they are worth dissecting.

Crick's book begins with the question of how visual processing in the brain leads to the experience of consciously 'seeing' something. It is a good scientific question, and I agree with Crick that it is a timely one. The first part of his book summarizes the psychology of perception, and the second part presents comparable background about the physical brain. Crick does all this rather well, but there is nothing novel or remarkable in it. Then in part three comes the central question of what neuronal processes lead to conscious awareness. Here Crick is raising questions at the frontiers of current scientific understanding, and he takes us through what pointers he can find in recent scientific work. As he admits, he comes to no clear conclusions, though he makes a useful contribution to current scientific discussion.

However, it is Crick's philosophy rather than his science that has attracted most attention, as I suspect he intended. Unfortunately, the philosophy is less competent than the science, and is beset with imprecise and overly broad-brush positions. Let us begin with the 'astonishing hypothesis' itself. At the beginning of the book he puts it like this:

> The astonishing hypothesis is that 'You', your joys and your sorrows, your memories and your ambitions, your sense of personal identity and free will, are in fact no more than the behaviour of a vast assembly of nerve cells and their associated molecules. As Lewis Carroll's Alice might have phrased it: 'You're nothing but a pack of neurons' (p. 3).

In assessing where Crick stands on the relationship between consciousness and the brain, it is important to note that he is not as dismissive of the phenomenon of consciousness as some other contemporary figures. Dennett (1991), for example, seems not so much to want to *explain* consciousness as to persuade us that, if we would only straighten out our ideas, we would see that there was nothing to be explained. He seems to see talk about qualia as a lot of misleading nonsense that could be dispelled by a strong dose of clear thinking. Crick, in contrast, takes 'qualia' seriously as phenomena, and is intrigued by how they arise from brain processes.

As with qualia, so with the soul. When Crick talks about, '"You", your joys and your sorrows, your memories and your ambitions, your sense of personal identity and free will', he is talking about the aspects of the human person that are roughly what people have referred to when they have talked about the soul, and he is apparently taking them seriously. He does not seem to be denying the reality of soul phenomena anymore than qualia. Though he has tendentious points to make about how the 'you' relates to neurons, he is not – if I understand him – denying the reality of the 'you'.

Part of the attraction for Crick of his astonishing hypothesis seems to be that it constitutes an alternative to the dualistic or religious idea of the soul. Crick is opposed to dualism, and thinks that the only way to vanquish it is to persuade people to come over to the strong reductionism of his astonishing hypothesis. What is particularly unsatisfactory about this approach is the way it sets up dualism and strong reductionism as the only alternatives. They are both extreme and unsatisfactory positions, and by no means the only ones possible. What the debate needs is more subtlety and precision in examining the philosophical alternatives.

One puzzling thing is that Crick actually seems to have reasonably good insight into the possibility of a more subtle philosophical position than that of the 'astonishing hypothesis': it surfaces in some statements of the hypothesis itself. For example, in one version he says that '"You" are *largely* the behaviour of a vast population of neurons...' (p. 93, my italics). This is a very different from the initial version because that little word 'largely' radically modifies the astonishing hypothesis. If we are only 'largely' the behaviour of our neurons, clearly we are something more. There follow difficult questions about what that something more is, and how it relates to our central nervous system. However, the initial claim that we are 'no more than' our nervous systems has clearly been abandoned. It is not even clear that Crick himself notices the difference between the two ways of stating his astonishing hypothesis.

The word 'largely' takes us from a strong and objectionable version of reductionism to weak and unexceptionable form. Strong reductionism assumes that one set of phenomena can be explained in terms of another *without remainder*. Once you assume this, it becomes almost unnecessary to talk about higher-level phenomena at all, except as a shorthand matter of convenience, because there is nothing to be said about higher level processes that could not in principle be translated into statements about the lower-level ones that wholly explain them. Moderate reductionism, in contrast, pursues in a pragmatic way the enterprise of explaining higher-level phenomena in terms of lower-level ones as far as possible, without necessarily expecting that this will be completely successful.

It is a central part of the scientific enterprise, as Crick would clearly agree, to try to explain higher-level phenomena in terms of more basic, lower-level processes. In recent decades the attempt in molecular biology to explain biological phenomena in terms of physics and chemistry has been one of the most striking reductionist scientific enterprises, and it has met with a significant degree of success. The important point, though, is that it has not been *completely* successful; it has not been possible to show that biology is 'nothing more than' physics and chemistry. Given the lack of any cases of completely successful reductionism in science, it is hard to see where Crick's confidence comes from for his idea that we are 'nothing more than' our neurons.

Interestingly, he seems in two minds how confident to be. His inclination is clearly to think that the astonishing hypothesis *must* be right. However, as a well-trained scientist, he knows that you should not be confident of anything until you have proved it, so he calls his astonishing idea a 'hypothesis', and in Chapter 18 admits that it might be wrong. In an interesting passage (pp. 262–3), he holds out three possibilities, first that the astonishing hypothesis will be proved correct, second that 'some view closer to the religious one may become more plausible', and third that a third view will emerge 'that is significantly different from the rather crude materialistic view many neuroscientists hold today and also from the religious view'. This is reminiscent of his earlier remark that 'reductionism is not the rigid process of explaining one fixed set of ideas in terms of another fixed set of ideas at a lower level, but a dynamic interactive process that modifies the concepts at both levels as knowledge develops' (p. 8).

This is how pragmatic reductionism actually works in science, and you can see it in the most successful example of reductionism currently available, the reduction of thermodynamics to statistical mechanics. What emerges is a kind of 'two-way reductionism' which is prepared to examine both bottom-up and top-down explanations. If this has proved necessary even within physics, it will surely be all the more important in the biological sciences, where top-down explanations are very important alongside bottom-up ones. A scientific approach that integrated the nervous system with consciousness and personality would transform our understanding of both, just as thermodynamics and statistical mechanics have both been transformed by our growing understanding of the relationship between them. The result would be most unlikely to show that consciousness was 'nothing more than' the activity of neurons, but would transform our scientific understanding of both consciousness and the brain.

In one of the most sophisticated discussions of these issues that I know, Michael Arbib and Mary Hesse (1986) put it like this:

Two-way reductionism is a more realistic view of the relation between two sciences. According to this view, at any given time the higher level description is likely to contain laws and descriptions that cannot be identified with or deduced from lower level brain science at that time but that provides suggestions as to how brain science should be extended to include new concepts and new laws ... In a successful two-way reduction, the two sciences ultimately become one science that is not identical with either of its prereductive components. (p. 64)

Crick is obviously right to endorse the value of scientific research in moving towards such a view. However, it would be better to avoid simplistic phrases like 'proved correct'. We are talking here about background paradigmatic assumptions that are rendered more or less plausible by research. In this sense it is somewhat misleading to talk about his 'nothing more than' idea as a *hypothesis*. It is surely not the kind of idea that could be tested by scientific research in a direct way, and it is significant that he does not advance any scientific evidence whatsoever for holding the idea that we are nothing more than our neurons. Indeed, it is not clear how he could; it is not that kind of idea. The astonishing hypothesis is just a working assumption that guides the research of scientists.

If a new 'integrationist' view is more likely to win the day than Crick's astonishing hypothesis, in what he himself calls its 'crude materialistic' form, why is the astonishing hypothesis so attractive to him? Part of the trouble lies in the over-sharp contrast he sees between strong reductionism on the one hand and dualistic views on the other. The other important factor is his equation of dualism with religion. Indeed, one reason why he is attracted to the materialism of his astonishing hypothesis is that it is incompatible with religion. Espousing crude materialism, and claiming scientific authority for it, may look to be the best strategy for 'seeing religion off'. Unfortunately, as I have already argued, crude materialism seems very *un*likely to be where the scientific enterprise will lead us. It is also unlikely that a third, integrationist view, arrived at by 'two-way reduction', will be incompatible with religion.

Crick has a rather simplistic understanding of religious thinking about human nature and the soul. Certainly, some of it is dualistic, but much of it is not, and there has recently been something of a rediscovery of Biblical monism (Green, 1998). Just as a good number of neuroscientists have already abandoned crude materialism, so many theologians have already abandoned dualism. Both seem to be heading towards a middle ground on which there would be room for both scientific and religious approaches. Crick's effort to organize a war in which materialism would defeat religion seems likely to be thwarted by a spread of moderation on both sides.

God and Consciousness

Next, we will turn to the implications of the modern study of consciousness for how we should think about God, focusing particularly on the analogy that has often been advanced between the God and the human mind. Though many theologians have abandoned dualism about human beings, emphasizing that the human mind is an emergent property of evolution and the physical body, such an approach does not seem applicable to the mind of God. It thus seems as though God may be the exception to the principle that mind is grounded in the physical brain. As we will see, in as far as God can be thought of as a kind of mind, he is clearly not dependent on a body in the same way as human minds.

The analogy between the human mind and the mind of God is well brought out by Taliaferro (1994) in his *Consciousness and the Mind of God*. In dualist theology, the link between them tends to be taken both ways. If a dualistic view of the human mind has been accepted, then it is easier to conceive God as a kind of disembodied mind too. Equally, if the idea of disembodied mind has been accepted in the case of God, it is a modest further step to accept substance dualism in the case of human beings. Further, a dualistic view of mind may be attractive precisely because it links human beings to the mind of God. If the human mind is a substance, relatively independent of matter and additional to it, that appears to make human beings more similar to God, more open to him, more capable of becoming like him, than if an account of human beings is given in purely natural terms.

However, there is a danger of extrapolating too readily from human minds to the mind of God, or vice versa. I suggest that we should simply recognize that the mind of God and the human mind may have different ontological bases, and not try to force them into the same straightjacket. The theology of consciousness does not need to embrace philosophical dualism about human consciousness, either as a conclusion from the nature of God, or as the premise of an argument for the existence of God. God can be conceptualized without making dualist assumptions about human beings.

The argument has sometimes been advanced that the existence of human consciousness proves the existence of God. Some theologians, such as Swinburne (1979), have started from the assumption that it is not possible to give a satisfactory account of how consciousness emerges from matter and brain. That leaves a puzzle as to how consciousness arises. Swinburne then seeks to resolve the puzzle by introducing God as the source and origin of human consciousness. If the assumption is accepted that God is the source of the human mind, the existence of the human mind can then in turn be used as the premise of a further argument for the existence of God. By that stage, of course, there is a serious risk of circularity.

The argument has a long lineage. In the seventeenth century, John Locke (1690/1960) argued in his *Essay Concerning Human Understanding* that matter by itself could never produce thought, any more than it could produce motion. Thought must therefore come from an eternal source, which must necessarily be a 'cogitative' being. This is taken to be an argument for the existence of God though, as with all such arguments, there is a big gulf between the assumption of a cogitative being that is external to humanity, controversial as that is, and the assumption of the Christian God.

My first objection to this kind of argument is that, though it is true that we do not yet have a fully specified account of how consciousness might have emerged from brains of increasing complexity, there is no justification for concluding that such an account could not be offered. Any account of the neural basis of consciousness will remain somewhat speculative until it has been elaborated more fully, and supporting evidence adduced. However, some kind of emergence view of the origin of consciousness is the one most likely to prove correct. I certainly would not want to build a theological position on the premise that material theories of consciousness have failed. With each year that passes, it becomes less appropriate to say that we have no idea how consciousness might arise from the brain. Admittedly, we do not have a complete account, and we certainly do not yet have one that we have sufficient reason to accept as correct. However, there are candidates in the field that deserve scientific exploration. We can no longer say that we have no idea how brain might possibly give rise to consciousness.

Incidentally, I would take Penrose's (1989) theory that the distinctive non-computable physical processes in the brain are the basis of consciousness as one specific kind of emergence theory. He contrasts his position with the kind of emergence theories that see the sheer complexity of the brain as the critical requirement for consciousness, and proposes a different kind of quantum basis for consciousness. However, that seems to me a disagreement about exactly what is required for consciousness to emerge, rather than a disagreement about whether or not consciousness has some kind of physical basis. Penrose, I suggest, is arguing for the non-algorithmic nature of consciousness, rather than its non-material basis.

So, while accepting that emergence theories remain to be substantiated in detail, I submit that it is at best premature, and at worst misconceived, to seek to build an argument for God's role in the origin of consciousness on the supposed failure of such natural, physical explanations. My general position, as indicated in the first chapter, is that theological and natural accounts should be seen as complementary rather than as alternatives. Applying this general principle, the relevance of God to consciousness does not depend on the failure of natural explanations of consciousness.

Though philosophical dualism has generally gone out of fashion, it retains particular attractions for some theologians. Swinburne's argument for the existence of God, based on the assumption that there is no adequate natural explanation of consciousness, is an example of this. It involves, I suggest, an over-close analogy between the mind of God and the human mind. Of course, all talk about God is analogical, and the analogies are always rather inexact. So let us now consider the adequacy of mind as an analogue for God, in the light of contemporary scientific and philosophical understandings of mind. Though it is a helpful and appropriate analogy up to a point, it has serious limitations if pressed too far.

The human mind is selective. Attention is by definition selective; we attend to some things at the expense of others. Memory is also selective. We do not at any one time consciously remember all the things that we are capable of remembering. Specific memories are reconstructed as they are required. One of the implications of speaking of God as omniscient is that this kind of selectivity is not a feature of the divine mind. He knows all, attends to all, remembers all. In this, the mind of God is so fundamentally unlike a human mind that the analogy comes under severe strain. It is not just that God's mind can be thought of as like a human mind, but with enhanced power. On the contrary, the way the human mind works is very largely organized around the fact that attention and remembering are selective. An omniscient mind would be organized on such radically different principles that it would be nothing like the human mind.

Some of the classical attributes of God, such as omnipotence and omniscience, seem designed, in part, to be warning signs about the inadequacy of the analogy between human minds and the mind of God. Though human beings know and act, they are not omnipotent and omniscient. Attributing those qualities to God serves to emphasize the dissimilarity between the human mind and the mind of God. Indeed, a good deal of what may appear to be the classic description of God can actually be seen, not so much as description, but as a warning about how *not* to think and talk about God. As Lindbeck (1984), among others has argued, many theological statements are best taken as grammatical, even when they appear on the face of things, to be descriptive. They can be seen as regulative, setting boundaries to appropriate talk about God, and warning against inappropriate, idolatrous talk.

Those who have thought about God as a mind have probably been thinking of the mind as a seat of consciousness, as a focal point of awareness. This corresponds to seeing the human mind also as a centre of consciousness or, in Ryle's (1949) famous phrase, as a 'ghost in the machine'. Implicit in this view is the image of sensory processes eventually reaching the 'little man' at the centre, who then makes decisions and sets in train motor actions. One of the philosophical problems with this view is that it is hard to see how to formulate the causal connections required to establish consciousness as the end point of an otherwise physical causal chain. What I particularly want to emphasize is that this is not the only way of thinking about consciousness. Consciousness can be seen, not as a homunculus, but as an emergent property of a distributed system.

Unfortunately, there has so far been very little theoretical work on how consciousness might relate to a distributed cognitive architecture. There are two reasons for this. One is that the dominant scientific interest is currently in how the brain gives rise to consciousness. While this is a perfectly legitimate question, my hunch is that it might be more fruitful for the time being to concentrate on the intermediate question of how a cognitive architecture might give rise to consciousness. The other important reason for the neglect is that, until quite recently, the dominance of the mind-computer analogy in psychological theorising distracted attention from the theoretical problem of consciousness. Because computers are not conscious, psychological theorising in the tradition of classical artificial intelligence (AI) has had a vested interest in assuming that consciousness is nothing more than an unimportant epiphenomenon.

That is now changing, and there is growing interest in how consciousness might arise within the cognitive architecture. Teasdale and Barnard (1993) have set out one approach to cognitive architecture that embodies explicit assumptions about where and how consciousness arises within the system, and we will return to their approach in connection with religious consciousness in Chapter 6. More generally, the introduction of connectionist modelling in psychology (Bechtel and Abrahamson, 1991), while not in every respect the holy grail, has at least given us a general approach that is better adapted to handling emergent properties of the mind.

This developing notion of human consciousness as an emergent property of a distributed system makes it very unlike what theologians have traditionally wanted to say about God. Though there are pantheistic theologies that would see God as some kind emergent world mind, this is a long way from classical theism. The move away from thinking about mind as a central seat of consciousness in human beings

– first general and philosophical, but now more specific and scientific – should thus bring caution to any tendency to think about God as a seat of consciousness like the human mind.

Another important development in thinking about the human mind, along with seeing consciousness as a property of a distributed system rather than as a homunculus, has been to emphasize how closely intertwined are passive and active mental processes. Homunculus-type conceptions always left a gap between awareness and action. The assumption seemed to be that all impressions and information had to be received by the 'ghost in the machine' before it decided how to respond. The reality is that active and passive processes are intertwined throughout, both neurologically and psychologically. There has been a move to embrace what has called a 'motor theory of the mind' (Weimer, 1977). As Varela *et al.* (1991) have put it, the human mind is not only embodied, it is also 'enactive'.

Such lines of psychological theorising converge with the insights of European philosophers such as Gadamer, who would also see the mind as actively bringing forth meaning out of a background of understanding. Up to a point this is helpful theologically. Dualistic theology tends, as Lash (1984) has caustically put it, to see God as 'either an idea or a ghost'. He suggests that it is better to see God as a 'thinker' than as a thought. The modern emphasis on the enactive mind would accord well with this theological emphasis.

It would also provide an analogy for how the omniscience and omnipotence of God might be closely intertwined, rather than being quite separate attributes. Action is inherently cognitive; knowing is enactive. This is how we currently think about the human mind, and it also provides a theologically congenial way of thinking about the mind of God. In this view, God's knowledge of the world would not be detachable from his sustaining activity within the world, and similarly that his activity in the world would be intertwined with his knowledge of it. This seems to be one of the points at which the analogy between God and mind has become *more* fruitful in the light of contemporary, scientific concepts of mind. Nevertheless, most of the points I have made emphasize how distant and loose is the analogy between the human mind and the mind of God. It is not an analogy that can be pressed too far.

From this vantage point it is interesting to look back historically at the rise of the analogy. As Edward Craig (1987) brings out in *The Mind of God and the Works of Man* there was a period of about a hundred years in the early modern period, the Enlightenment, when philosophers were particularly preoccupied by the analogy between the human mind and the mind of God and took it much more literally than it had been in classical theism. The same period came to see God as a 'person' in a new way (Webb, 1919), another analogy that was pushed much further than it had been previously.

It is an interesting matter for discussion in the history of ideas exactly why these analogies were so appealing at the beginning of the modern scientific era. Craig points out that it was a period that sought a path to absolutely secure knowledge, and laid great store by human rationality, and by objective observation as the means to achieve that. It was perhaps in keeping with this intellectual mood that God should be conceived as a being who represented the ideal of completely secure knowledge, the ideal to which the human mind aspired.

However, with the wisdom of hindsight, each interlinked element in this early-modern intellectual enterprise has come to seem misconceived. It no longer seems tenable to think of mind as a substance that is wholly separate from the physical body. Equally, it does not seem tenable to see knowledge as wholly objective and 'spectorial', independent of the person who arrives at it. Equally, I suspect that theology needs to draw back from the theistic aspects of this intellectual project. As Buckley (1987) has suggested, modern atheism may have arisen in part as a reaction to relatively new, but scarcely tenable, ways of thinking about God. Among them is the idea that there is a close analogy between the mind of God and the human mind.

Immortality

Finally, and briefly, let us consider how the hope of immortality intersects with these debates about the relationship of consciousness to brain and to God. Immortality has often been thought of as the continuation of some kind of mind or consciousness, which is why it links with debates about consciousness. Immortality might be formulated in terms of a disembodied soul, but it is not necessarily wedded to the concept of soul (which will be discussed more fully in Chapter 5). Concerns about immortality seem to have had a substantial influence on the assumptions people have wanted to make about consciousness. In turn, the way in which hopes of immortality have been framed has been influenced by changing assumptions about consciousness. This is not the place for an exhaustive discussion of the complex issues involved, but it is worth indicating how questions about consciousness and immortality intersect.

There are at least three broad approaches to the problem of immortality in the Christian tradition. One is based on a dualistic view of human nature. It assumes that there is some aspect of human nature, the soul or mind, that can be dissociated from the physical body and can survive after death. Indeed, one of the chief attractions of such an idea of the soul for many people is probably that it seems to make immortality possible.

However, there are severe problems associated with this approach. The idea that the soul can continue to exist without the body or brain, strains scientific credibility. Though that is not, of course, a decisive argument against it, it is enough to lead people to explore alternative approaches. The dualistic approach is also unattractive theologically. It sits very uneasily with the Christian tradition about immortality to suppose that human beings are so constituted that their souls can survive, without the body, without God, without any resurrection by him, but simply because human souls are inherently immortal. More generally, the dualistic approach to immortality makes a claim (that soul survives death), but does not give a satisfying account of how that is achieved, beyond just stating that souls are immortal by their very nature.

What are the alternatives? There is increasing interest, in some circles, in the resurrection of the body (for example, Polkinghorne, 1994; Peters, 1999). It is true that the Apostles' Creed focuses on the resurrection of the body rather than the survival of a disembodied soul. In this, it is more holistic than many people imagine. Also contemporary neuroscience clearly espouses some form of physicalism, the doctrine that we are essentially physical creatures in whom the complex functioning of our physical nature gives rise to whatever mental powers we have. It may thus look as though there is some kind of convergence here. However, it would be a mistake to exaggerate the similarity between the holism of the Christian belief in bodily resurrection and the physicalism of current science.

Theologically, there is no classical theologian, not even Aquinas, the most holistic of theologians, who entirely dispenses with the survival of the soul in some form prior to the resurrection of the body. In the mainstream Christian tradition, there is certainly an emphasis on the resurrection of the body, but this complements a doctrine of the survival of the soul rather than being an alternative to it. Also, the Christian tradition of the resurrection of the body is a long way from anything that contemporary neuroscience could accept. The best source for the idea of physical resurrection is St Paul (especially in 1 Corinthians 15). However, St Paul makes a clear distinction between *soma* (body) and *sarx* (flesh), and it is doubtful whether St Paul envisaged a resurrection of the flesh, but of some different kind of transformed, spiritualized body. That raises interesting issues, but it takes the doctrine a long way from the kind of physicalism that neuroscience generally assumes.

There is a yet another approach to immortality, one that begins from the assumption of an eternal God. In this view, people would not have any kind of immortality were there not an eternal God; such immortality as human beings may have is entirely secondary to God's eternity. Thus, it is only in so far as people come to share in God's eternity that they can hope to have immortality themselves. There are still, of course, further questions to address about how such unity is bestowed by God on human beings, and whether it is bestowed universally or selectively, and such questions are not easily answered. However, it is enough in the present context to suggest that the possible unity, or resonance, that can exist between the human mind and the very different 'mind' of God provides a coherent basis for the hope of immortality. The suggestion is thus, not that the human mind or soul can exist without any kind of substrate, but that it can co-inhere in the eternal God when its original basis in the brain is no longer available. It may be that our soul life can develop properties that become relatively independent of the natural existence out of which it has emerged. When new properties emerge, their operation is often not predictable from lower-level laws. Though soul comes into being from a natural basis, once it has come into being it may to some extent operate in radically new ways that are not fully explicable in material terms, and come to transcend its original natural basis.

Chapter 4

Computer Intelligence

Few scientific topics raise such fundamental religious and ideological issues as artificial intelligence (AI). In considering scientific work on AI, it will be important to distinguish the scientific work itself from the rather grandiose claims with which it is often, though not necessarily, associated. It is these grandiose claims that sometimes bring AI into conflict with religious insights; if AI is pursued in a more humble spirit the sense of conflict disappears. Because of the grandiosity that often surrounds AI, religious thinkers have often felt threatened by its claims. Though that threat needs to be evaluated, it is important for theologians to move beyond the rather negative approach that it represents, and to ask whether they can enter into constructive dialogue with AI.

Before considering the religious issues raised by AI, it is important to understand what scientists working in this area are trying to achieve. Recent decades have seen enormous strides in the development of AI, and its implication can be divided into the practical and the theoretical. At the practical level, computers are revolutionizing industrial production, and an increasing number of expert tasks are now being performed by computers. At best, computers are able to improve their performance through learning and experience. For example, a computer that is programmed to recognize speech gets more accurate with experience of the speech of a particular user. Much computer technology is developed for strictly practical purposes, and any theoretical significance it may have is incidental. There is no specific requirement that computers should perform tasks in the same way as people do.

Computer Simulation of Human Intelligence

Alongside the technological applications of AI, there has been a more basic theoretical enterprise of using the computer as an aid to understanding the human mind. Strictly, that should be referred to as 'computer simulation' rather than 'artificial intelligence'. Much work has been done on programming computers to simulate various different mental functions.

Computer programs provide a very precise mode of theorizing. For example, to program a computer to perform the same kind of logical reasoning as people forces scientists to put their ideas about human reasoning in a clear form. The computer simulation of human thinking has thus, at the least, been a stimulus to a more precise form of theorizing in the scientific study of human cognition, and has produced cognitive theories that are testable in a new kind of way. When you have programmed a particular mental function on a computer you can run the program and see how the results match up against human performance. At this point there needs to be a to and fro between careful observation of the performance of people and computers, and this is a feature of the best scientific work in the field.

Testing how well computer and human mental functions match each other is actually a rather subtle business. For example, in doing logical reasoning, people make mistakes and there is a lot to be learned about how people think from seeing exactly what kind of mistakes they make. If the programming has been well done, and the computer really is doing things in the same way as people, it will make exactly the same kind of mistakes, and for the same reasons. That is quite a stringent scientific test to apply.

There is no need, so far, to make any particularly strong assumptions about how close the overall similarity may be between a computer and the human mind. It is only necessary to assume that it is possible to simulate at least some mental functions on a computer. The assumption is that the analogy between minds and computers is close enough to get started on the computer simulation of intelligence, but there is no need to make any strong assumptions at the outset about how close the analogy will turn out to be. Even if the analogy turns out to be less close at some points than people originally hoped, quite a lot will probably have been learned about human minds by pressing the analogy to the limits and finding out what the dissimilarities are.

Up to this point, there is nothing that raises any particular philosophical problems, and nothing that should worry people who have a religious view of the human person. It is important to emphasize this at the outset so as to not reject all work on computer intelligence on theological grounds. Most scientists concerned with computer intelligence work in the kind of modest, exploratory way that I have indicated so far. What they do is not controversial, from either a philosophical or a religious point of view.

The AI Creed

However, there are people working in AI who *do* make strong claims for the scope and potential of what they are doing, claims that often go under the name of 'strong AI'. The creed of strong AI is essentially two-fold: first that it will eventually be possible to capture *all* aspects of human intelligence in computer form, and second that the human mind is, to all intents and purposes, just a computer program.

The first claim is about the future, and consists of a strong prediction about what computers of the future will be able to do; that they will be able to perform all intelligent activities. We can call this part of the AI creed 'eschatological'. The other claim is about what the human mind really is; that it is like a computer program. Note that this is not a straightforward descriptive statement about the human mind, certainly not something that you could check out by making the necessary scientific observations. It is more a basic assumption about the nature of mind, a 'metaphysical' assumption.

In the creed of strong AI, the belief that the human mind is essentially a computer program (the metaphysical claim) supports the vision of the future in which computer intelligence will match or exceed human intelligence (a kind of AI eschatology). Generally these two claims go together, though there is probably no necessary connection between them. In Christian thinking the metaphysical belief that the world is essentially God's supports the eschatological belief that His kingdom will eventually be established. It is intriguing to find metaphysics and eschatology supporting each other in a similar way in the quasi-religious AI creed.

The first general comment to make on the strong AI creed is that it floats some way above the actual day-to-day scientific work done in the field. Some scientists working on AI would hold this creed; others would not. It seems to make very little difference to their actual scientific work whether or not they are adherents of this grand vision of AI. Equally, the strong AI creed is in no sense a conclusion from scientific research. There is sometimes a tendency to assume that all the claims made by scientists are the result of their research, but in actual fact many of them are basic pre-research assumptions. The strong AI creed is that kind of basic assumption, rather than a scientifically justified conclusion from research. The creed of strong AI is neither a necessary assumption of AI research, nor a conclusion from it.

Some have sought to refute the strong AI creed with an argument of principle. The most interesting argument of this kind comes from an application of Godel's theorem, and claims that computers could never achieve consciousness. Godel's theorem states that there could never be a sound system of mathematics that enabled you to prove all the propositions of ordinary arithmetic. However, that is a theorem about mathematics; the question is whether it has any implications for human beings and AI. The most enthusiastic current advocate of the relevance to AI of Godel's theorem is Roger Penrose, who believes that Godel's theorem shows that consciousness could not be computable, just as arithmetic is not mathematically provable (Penrose, 1994). However, this may be just too big an extrapolation from mathematics to people to be convincing, though Penrose's arguments are complex and rigorous, and not easily dismissed.

What Computers Can Do

In the absence of any wholly convincing arguments of principle about the strong AI creed, it may be best to look at what computers are able to do. Given the track record of AI so far, does it seem likely that computers will eventually be able to simulate all intelligent activities? Bold predictions about the potential of computer intelligence have been around since the beginning of modern AI in the 1960s. Partly there have been specific predictions, such as that within so many years a computer would be able to play chess so well that it would have the status of a grandmaster. Partly there have been more general claims that *any* intelligent activity could eventually be programmed.

One of the key issues here is what is meant by an 'intelligent' activity. What is clear is that any rule based intelligent activity can be programmed into a computer. Once the rules that underpin some particular intelligent activity are understood, it is a mere technical task to write the program. The problem arises over how far human intelligence is rule based. It may be, but the rules are often not easy to discern. For example, it is now clear from empirical research that when people do reasoning tasks, they are not following the rules of formal logic.

One very obvious point about the track record of delivering on these predictions is that progress has always been slower and more difficult than was expected

(Dreyfus and Dreyfus, 1986). It was a long time, for example, before chess
programs became really successful. Now they are. Real progress is being made, and
it is no part of my purpose here to deny it, but there has been a consistent tendency
to underestimate the problems. Computers are now of course, enormously more
powerful than in the early days, and a great deal cheaper. There is a very impressive
technological success story here, but the scientific success story of capturing human
intelligence in computer form has not been quite so good.

Indeed, it is tempting to say that there are certain *kinds* of intelligent activity that
computers will never be able to simulate. We need to be wary of that view, because
there are signs that at least some progress is being made, even with the more
difficult things. It has been tempting, for example, to say that computers cannot
learn, that they can only do what they have been programmed to do. That would no
longer be correct. Computers can, in effect, be programmed to *re*program
themselves on the basis of experience. Again, it is tempting to say that they could
never be creative, but there are some forms of musical composition that computers
can be programmed to do, and it is not yet clear what the limits are to computer
creativity. So, we need to be very careful about pontifications of the form
'computers could never ...'.

Nevertheless, there are some things that seem such major challenges for
computers that we simply do not know how to tackle them, and perhaps never will.
We do not know how to give a computer the kind of fluid intelligence that would
enable it to work out from scratch how to solve a problem quite unlike anything it
had ever encountered before. We also do not know how to program it to recognize
when the boundaries of a particular rule governed activity have been transgressed.
For example, if a computer is giving someone non-directive counselling, which it
can do reasonably convincingly, it simply cannot recognize when the person breaks
off the counselling and switches to some other kind of conversation.

Computers and Consciousness

One of the main problems for the computer simulation of human intelligence is
consciousness. Computers cannot easily simulate human consciousness. Indeed,
that fact has perhaps been one of the reasons why cognitive scientists have been
inclined to the view that consciousness is of no great functional importance to
human beings. It has enabled them to conclude that the lack of consciousness in
computers is no great problem.

It will be helpful here to refer back to what was said in the last chapter about
the different meanings of 'consciousness'. Taking the basic sense of consciousness
as sensory experience, there is no particular problem about claiming an equivalent
sensory consciousness for computers, especially robotic computers. Computers
can even go some way towards simulating reflective self-consciousness. It would
be possible, in principle, to construct a self-describing computer, that is, a
hierarchical computer which monitored what it knew. However, as Philip Johnson-
Laird (1988) points out, this would still fall short of human self-reflection. We also
have no idea how to give a computer consciousness in the sense of having the
subjective 'feel' of something.

We do not know how to give computers emotions, though we can take some steps towards that. Computers can recognize when a particular kind of emotional reaction, such as anger, would be appropriate. They could even be programmed to utter angry sentences through their voice box, and perhaps even to do angry things, like scrambling your data. However, we have no idea how to get them to *feel* anger. At this point, some people are inclined to redefine emotions in such a way that computers *could* have them. However, I am not impressed by the suggestion that there is nothing more to anger than the components that computers *can* replicate. Angry feelings, on any common sense view, are an essential part of what we mean by anger. Neither am I impressed by the argument that you can never know what another person is feeling, and that, for all we know, computers may be feeling angry. It is true that there is never absolute certainty about other people's feelings, but there are reasonable grounds for assuming that people have feelings and that present day computers do not.

In correspondence that followed an article I once published in the Catholic weekly, *The Tablet*, Edmund Furse (1993), claimed that prayer was an intelligent activity, and so computers could be programmed to pray. It is a problem rather like programming emotions. They could perhaps be programmed to recognize when a particular kind of prayer was appropriate, thanksgiving, confession or whatever. They could no doubt be programmed to compose prayers. Prayers are, after all, a fairly predictable, rule-governed 'art-form'. They could also utter prayers using a voice box. However, it seems that they do not have the kind of inner life that would allow us to say that they really were praying. There is much more to praying than simply formulating and uttering prayers.

The simulation of human consciousness on computers thus represents one of the greatest challenges in AI. Conscious cognitive processes probably proceed rather differently from non-conscious ones. Most conscious thought, as we all know from introspection, is couched in symbols, usually words or pictures. However, it seems that non-conscious cognition proceeds in a different kind of code (Johnson-Laird, 1988), and thinking that goes on in the rather compressed code used outside consciousness needs to be translated into a more accessible one of words or pictures before we can become conscious of it. If this is correct, one of the big challenges for any computational theory of mind is how to capture these two kinds of code, and the transformations between them.

There is overwhelming evidence that remembering something involves reconstructing it, not just bringing it within the spotlight of consciousness, and in this human memory is quite unlike computer memory. Modeling the transformations that take place when material is accessed in consciousness is perhaps one of the key challenges that now face computational theories of mind. There is no reason in principle why scientific progress should not be made with this enterprise, though it is not likely to be quick. Even if it were successful, it would be an entirely different question whether a computer in which these cognitive processes had been successfully modelled would actually be conscious.

Minds and Persons

This brings us to the metaphysical part of the strong AI creed, that the human mind is essentially a computer program. The idea is that minds can be defined in terms of the 'functions' they perform, and that the ways in which those functions are carried out in minds and computers are essentially the same. The claim is that in one case the program runs on the brain; in the other it runs on silicon, but the programs are essentially the same in each case. This view that the mind is essentially a computer was advanced by the American philosopher, Hilary Putnam (1975), at the dawn of the AI age. (Putnam, 1998, has now changed his position, but his original view remains historically important.)

However, there are some key differences between people and computers. One is that, when we think and talk, we know what we are referring to; our concepts relate to things in the world. Even when computers are successfully manipulating symbols in a way that is passably similar to human thought, they do not know how their symbols relate to the world. This shows up in translation, for example. In a sentence such as 'the box was in the pen', it is very difficult to decide which of the two meanings of 'pen' applies in this context without knowing what in the real world the sentence refers to.

One famous way of making the point that computers lack knowledge of what their symbols refer to is due to the philosopher, John Searle (Searle, 1989). Imagine a room in which you are alone. You are being asked questions in Chinese, which are passed in to you, and you have to pass answers in Chinese out again. The problem is that you know no Chinese. However, it is not an impossible situation. You could be supplied with a massive and complex set of rules which enabled you to get from a question to an appropriate answer without understanding anything about what the Chinese symbols meant.

Searle's point is that this is essentially how computers work. The rule books correspond to the programming of the computer. The fact that correct answers can be arrived at in no way implies that you understand them. In fact, a computer is in the same situation as you would be in if you understood no Chinese. Neither you nor the computer would know what in the world the symbols related to, what they actually meant. This is not what ordinary human thought is like. We *do* know what our words refer to. Sometimes it is pointed out that the Chinese Room parable does not show that computers cannot understand, but only that successful performance does not necessarily presuppose understanding. There have been many attempts to refute the Chinese Room argument (Copeland, 1993), though none of them seems wholly convincing. The fact that there are many different refutations in circulation perhaps makes the point that none of them really works.

A central problem with seeing states of mind as equivalent to computational states is that it involves looking at them in an abstract way, removed from the actual context in which they occur. No two human beings have the same history, and even when they hold what appear to be the same beliefs, their different histories cannot be entirely ignored. To take the ultimate religious example, the statement 'I believe in God' could never be defined in a completely abstract way that left out of account the different resonance that statement of belief had for people of different backgrounds. Yet that is what is assumed by the equation of mental and computational states.

Many of the problems with work on computer intelligence seem to rest on a mistaken and simplistic idea of how human intelligence works. Though AI has often been unconcerned with human cognition, it may well be the case that radical advances in AI will depend on understanding better how people think, which could lead, in turn, to better computer simulation of such thinking. One of the clearest statements I know of this radical approach to AI is by William Clocksin. He calls for a 'social constructionist' approach to AI which recognizes that 'an individual's intelligent behaviour is shaped by the meaning ascribed to experience, by its situation in the social matrix, and by the practices of self and relationship into which its life is recruited' (Clocksin, 1998, p 102).

Central to Clocksin's understanding of human intelligence is the role of narrative. We understand ourselves and all our experience in relation to narratives. Indeed, human action is itself a kind of narrative. In our actions, we are telling a story about ourselves. An approach to AI that was based on this understanding of the key role of narrative in human intelligence would no longer see intelligence as the manipulation of symbols relating to arbitrary and externally defined problems. Clocksin's vision of a narrative form of AI would be very much more congenial from a religious point of view, partly because, in recent years, theologians have also come to realize how central narrative is to theology. The Bible is essentially telling a narrative about the actions of God. Indeed, to understand anything in religious terms involves placing it in the context of a religious narrative.

As things stand at present, there are serious problems with the view that human minds and computer programs are essentially the same. In saying this I am not doubting that the analogy between minds and computers has been very fruitful scientifically. It has sharpened up our thinking about human minds, and has also helped to make technological advances in computer programming. However, it is a big step from the idea that there is a useful analogy between minds and computers to saying that they are essentially the same. Whether computers of the future become more like the human mind depends on how far it is possible to make progress with the kind of view of narrative intelligence that Clocksin has outlined.

Brains and Bodies

The philosophical argument about whether the mind is essentially a computer continues to run. Meanwhile, back in the labs, things have been moving on. The hard line view that mind is essentially a computer program and that it makes no difference whether it runs on the biological stuff of the human brain or on a silicon computer, is definitely on the way out.

Recent years have seen an upsurge of interest in how the physical structure of the human brain affects the way we think. This has led in turn to a great deal of interest in finding ways of programming computers so that they are more like the human brain in how they do things. Considerable progress has been made in developing this new generation of more biologically realistic computers, and this has led in turn to advances in what computers can do. In particular, it has led to computers that are much better able to learn than the computers of ten years ago. On the one hand this has probably fuelled the fantasy that computers will eventually be able to do everything. However, the metaphysical support for this confidence, based on the assumption that it was irrelevant that the human mind ran on a biological brain, is being cut away.

The key technical change in programming computers in a more biologically realistic way has been the move from a sequential approach in which one operation is carried out at a time, to a parallel approach (parallel distributed processing or PDP) in which multiple operations are carried out simultaneously in a massively interconnected network that in some way resembles a network of neurones, an approach to programming known as 'connectionism'.

However, there is disagreement about how biologically realistic this connectionist approach to programming is. Gerald Edelman (1992), who has been at the forefront of asserting the importance of the physical brain in human cognition, has been rather dismissive of such parallel processing, saying that a connectionist computer is really nothing like the brain. However, this approach to programming is just a first pass at getting something biologically realistic. No doubt we will gradually get better at it. The important thing is the change in intellectual climate involved in taking the physical brain seriously. It is an important step towards conceptualizing people as integrated wholes, rather than as minds that can just as well be realized in computers as in bodies.

Of course, there are dangers in this new emphasis on the brain. History gets forgotten quickly, and it is worth remembering one of the reasons why the idea that the mind is essentially a computer was so attractive in the first place. We had been through a period in which it had been fashionable to say that mind states and brain states were identical. When you described what was on your mind, you were really just describing the state of your brain, albeit it in a useful shorthand. To talk about minds as being like a computer program helped to get us out of the deadend idea that the mind was nothing more than the physical brain. Having extricated ourselves from that view, I do not want us to go back there.

There are also arguments about whether computers, made of silicon, and with nothing resembling a human body, could possibly simulate human intelligence. This leads on to the question of whether it would further the AI project if computers were given bodies. The way humans think is profoundly influenced by their bodies. Many of our concepts, even apparently abstract ones, come from metaphors that originate in our physical experience. We would not think as we do if we had no bodies. A computer that had no body, or had a non-biological body, could not think in exactly the same way as we do. The idea that minds can be abstracted from bodies is part of the inheritance from philosophical 'dualism', the separation of the human person into quite distinct minds and bodies. Though most philosophers have now abandoned dualism as an untenable view of the human person, it is strange to find it surviving in AI (Cotterill, 1989). The basic mistake is to say that it is minds that think. It is people who think, and people have bodies as well as minds.

These arguments have been accepted by some scientists working on AI, and a new movement of 'Embodied AI' has grown up as a result. It began with the development of artificial insects, but at MIT there is now a humanoid computer called Cog that has many of the elements of a human body (Foerst, 1998a, b; Reich,

1998; Gerhart and Russell, 1998). Moreover it interacts with the world through its body, and learns from that interaction, having been programmed to develop through its interaction with the world.

Such a computer is not open to many objections that have been raised against classical AI. Cog has a body, it interacts, it learns, and thus it potentially has individuality. The weakness of Cog at present seems to be that it cannot actually do very much. Even its insect-like computer forebears do not seem to have had the intelligence of insects, and Cog is clearly nowhere near having human intelligence. Some may hope that Cog's successors will get closer to that goal. However, it is equally likely that the long term impact of computers such as Cog will be to remind us of the huge gulf between human and computer intelligence.

One of the limitations with computers might be that they are made out of silicon. Searle has claimed that consciousness could only arise out of the biological stuff of the brain, not out of silicon (Searle, 1989). Though that might turn out to be a correct view, it is not clear that there is any convincing argument to support it. Even if he was right, computers may not always be made out of silicon. There might be a new generation of computers made of biological material to which Searle's argument would not apply.

The AI Vision of the Future

I have tried to give a balanced indication of the current boundaries of computer competence. Compared to this, some of the confident predictions made about what computers will be able to do are quite extraordinary. Take, for example, *Mind Children* by Hans Moravec (1988). He has a grand vision, that the computers of the twenty-first century will be 'entities as complex as ourselves', but 'transcending everything we know'. Whereas we are limited by the constraints of our bodies, we will create successors in computer form that will take us into a new phase of 'postbiological' or 'supernatural' existence. These computer successors will be able to exist in hostile climates in space that would be impossible for us, and in this sense will be superior to us. They will, Moravec says, be entities 'in whom we can take pride when they refer to themselves as our descendants'.

One of the puzzles about this kind of vision of the future is to see what it is based on. It is not, apparently, based on a particularly rosy view of our present computers. Moravec comments that 'the best of today's machines have minds more like those of insects than humans'. A lot of Moravec's optimism seems to be based on the expected continuing improvement in computer power, though it is not clear that all problems in AI require only additional power for their solution. Moravec is relying on a marriage between robotics and AI. What AI can deliver in the marriage he envisages may turn out to be a disappointment to him.

Morover, it is doubtful whether Moravec's vision is really a scientific one at all. It is more an article of faith than a secure extrapolation from how computers are currently developing. His vision of the future seems to be a quasi-religious one, and he is unusually explicit about it. The frank borrowing of theological terms like 'immortality' and the 'supernatural' to characterize the world of his envisaged new entities makes this pretty clear.

Frank Tipler (1994) has also made use of AI to provide the basis for a scientifically based form of immortality. The essence of his idea is that the unique personality of each person could be preserved in computer form, not subject to the vagaries of the human body. Then, through some rather suspect cosmology about the Omega point, these preserved intelligences become fully immortal. However, we are so far from being able to simulate individual differences in computer form that this project is, at best, massively speculative. It is also very doubtful whether human personalities could be captured at all in the disembodied form of a computer program. It is very strange that AI is perpetuating the dream of immortality as some kind of disembodied existence, and that this should be fashionable at the same time as neuroscience is emphasizing the closeness of the link between brain and mind. Many of the same scientists are interested in both neuroscience and AI, and sometimes seem scarcely aware of their discrepant assumptions.

There is something rather naive and unbalanced about strong AI as a quasi-religious vision. It is also, to my mind, rather distasteful in its assumptions about what kind of immortal life will be desirable. There has, of course, long been a strand in Western thought which has postulated a sharp dichotomy between minds and bodies, and seen the indefinite existence of the disembodied mind as something to be hoped for. However, the Christian tradition has generally taken a much more positive view of the physical side of our existence than this, rightly so in my view. I do not believe that the mind can be disentangled from the body and given an independent life of its own, and I would not want it to be so disentangled. The Judeo-Christian tradition values the bodily existence of human beings.

Unfortunately, like many of the secular eschatologies of the last century or so, AI eschatology is not good eschatology. It represents a naive application of some half understood concepts in a new context in which they do not work properly. Christian eschatology has worked hard to hold different strands together. There needs to be a place both for what God will do and what we can do; Moravec dispenses with this. There is also, in classical eschatology, a balance between whether the vision is of a distant goal, or something that can be expected imminently. Moravec's AI eschatology is rather like that of a fringe religious sect confidently predicting the second coming during the next century.

It is hard to know quite how to place some of the wilder predictions coming out of strong AI, such as those of Moravec and Tipler. It is the sort of vision that is found in much science fiction, though Moravec is not claiming to be writing fiction. Stephen Clark (1995) has argued persuasively that the central theme of science fiction is in fact how to achieve immortality, and various different schools of science fiction approach it in different ways. Among them, there is a prominent stream of science fiction, such as William Gibson's 'cyberpunk' novels, that speculates about immortality achieved through overcoming dependence on the human body. There is probably no area of contemporary science where the boundary between science and science fiction becomes as blurred as it does in AI.

Many of the fears of the humanoid computers that might arise from AI seem to involve a confusion about whether or not they would really be like us. I sense that the fear aroused by AI is not of creatures that were genuinely like ourselves in all important respects, but of computers that were *un*like us, with no moral and spiritual attributes, being passed off as though they were like us, or somehow taking over from us. If they were like us, they would generally have good moral intentions, but be unreliable about carrying them out. Computers that were wholly evil, or wholly good, would not be like humans. This also raises the question of how far the computers of the future would be under the control of the computer scientists who created them. Would they have the capacity to make their own decisions or not? If they did not, then they clearly would not be equivalent to human beings. If they did, they would not be under the control of scientists.

Theology and AI

A central religious suspicion of AI comes from the idea that creating computers that are like human beings would be 'playing God'. To create something that is effectively like a human being seems to place us in the role of God, and to challenge the unique role of God as creator. However, I think this is a mistake. Talk of God as 'creator' is, like all talk about God, an analogy, and the analogy can't be pressed too far. God's creative work is not like ours. One of the traditional ways in which this point has been made is to say that God creates 'out of nothing', that he is not dependent on any prior existence for his creative work. Clearly, when humans make something they are not creating 'out of nothing'; they are making use of preexisting materials. As Donald Mackay (1991) has put it in his Gifford Lectures, making a computer is more like an act of 'procreation' than the creative work of God, and it no more challenges the doctrine of God as creator than does the more usual biological form of procreation.

John Puddefoot (1996) has developed an interesting comparison of the work of God in creating human beings with the task of scientists in AI, in a way that illuminates the nature of both. He suggest that the three problems faced by God in creating human life, and of AI scientists in creating humanoid computers, are essentially the same:

(a) how to create the kind of free life God wished to see,
(b) how to prevent it from becoming monstrous, and
(c) how to hide himself from it sufficiently that it will relate to him for the right reasons.

Puddefoot suggests that God's solution to this was essentially to 'grow' life rather then to make it according to some pre-specified plan. This is essentially the view of creation that we took in Chapter 2 in the context of evolution. Perhaps the ultimate success of the attempts to create humanoid computers will depend on whether we are willing and able to pass on to them the kind of freedom that God has given us. Puddefoot suggests that a key criterion of success will be whether the resulting computers are able to surprise us. If so, they may be accepted by God as part of his human-like creation. As Foerst has put it, they may, like humans, become part of the *imago Dei* (Foerst, 1996).

One of the most fruitful of recent theological uses of AI of which I am aware concerns the nature of sin. The question of whether a computer could sin forces us to clarify the concept of sin in a helpful way. It is clear that computers can do bad things, in the sense of doing things with harmful consequences. Whether or not these ought to be called 'sin' is another matter. Bull has used this question to substantiate a definition of sin as 'freely willing a state of affairs that is known to be contrary to the will of God' (Bull, 1998). The question of whether or not a computer could sin thus turns out to depend on how far computers could have free will, and how far they could know the will of God.

This leads back to distinctions rather like those we have already discussed. Whether a computer could know the will of God is rather like whether it could pray. There seems no reason, in principle, why a computer, on the basis of scripture and tradition, should not have at least some knowledge of the will of God. However, discerning and experiencing the will of God in particular situations might not be possible. Also, if sin is taken to involve, not just a lack of knowledge of the will of God, but a deliberate turning away from such knowledge, then it seems unlikely that a computer could sin.

Anne Foerst (1996) has offered a rather different reflection on the relationship between AI and sin, drawing on Tillich's concept of the sense of sin as involving the estrangement that comes from unresolved polarities. For example, we wish both to be an individual but also to be in community; we wish to be free while also acknowledging the necessity of working within causal laws. For Tillich, the sense of sin arises from such polarities. Foerst suggests that AI resolves these polarities by treating them in mechanistic terms. Thus, for example, 'in the worldview of AI, freedom is actually nonexistent because everything that happens can be explained in a mechanistic and functional fashion' (p. 689).

It is surely debatable how effectively this resolves the polarity. It seems to be more a matter of collapsing it than resolving it. If the sense of estrangement that comes from such polarities is how sin is to be defined, it seems that computers cannot be said to have such a sense. Foerst acknowledges that AI introduces its own polarities, for example the hope that computers will come to have subjectivity, which coexists with an objectifying view of human beings. However, these are human polarities about AI, rather than polarities in the experience of computers.

Many theological issues about the computers of the future could be summarized in the question of whether or not they will have 'souls'. The question of what we mean by souls is one that I will treat more fully in the next chapter. However, to anticipate briefly, I suggest that we see soul, not as an entity, but as a set of capacities that have arisen from our natural nature, and which allow us to relate to God. In this sense, the question of whether or not computers could have souls cannot be settled by the fact that they are made by human beings out of silicon. It is a matter of whether they have the capacities that would justify us in saying they had souls. While I think that is highly unlikely, I do not see that it can be ruled out in principle.

If computers were constructed that really were like human beings, I do not see that they would represent any threat to religious beliefs. Indeed, if they are really like us, it would be inappropriate to exclude them from the fellowship of the Church, or from playing their part in building the kingdom of God. Keith Ward of the University of Oxford took a similar view in a radio interview. Though he is also doubtful about whether computers will be created that really are rational and spiritual creatures, he said that, *if* it happened, he would be 'prepared to baptize them' (Stannard, 1996, p. 118).

Religious Attitudes to AI

There is a tendency among religious people to be suspicious of AI. However, I believe that these instinctive suspicions are misplaced, and that the dialogue between theology and AI needs to move onto a new and more constructive level.

An example of concern in religious circles about AI is the report of the Church of England Doctrine Commission, *We Believe in God* (1988). The report suggests that there is a debate about human personality going on between those who 'claim that the model of artificial intelligence explains the physical and mental phenomenon so fully that it can be regarded as having scientific warrant' and those who 'know that there is more to people than this model allows'. This strikes me as a very polarized way of framing the issues. Most detailed scientific work on artificial intelligence does not make any strong or controversial assumptions about human personality. Actually, most work in AI is not about *personality* at all, but about more specific mental functions, often relatively low level ones, such as vision.

I see no reason why the rigorous way of thinking about mind, introduced by AI, but shorn of the more bizarre metaphysics and eschatology of the strong AI creed, should not help Christian thinkers to make *their* points about human personality. Though most AI scientists hold that there need be no essential difference between humans and computers, I do not see that AI as a discipline need be committed to that view. On the contrary, AI may eventually help to locate and define the essential differences between computers and humans much more precisely.

Back in 1967, H.C.N. Williams, a far sighted Churchman and the first Provost of the rebuilt Cathedral in Coventry, took a similar view in a lecture on the Christian faith from the standpoint of cybernetics (one of the sources of modern AI). He said:

> I have come in recent years to welcome cybernetics as a discipline which defines more clearly than any other I know the limits of a mechanistic approach to life and values, and makes more definable the area of existence which is broadly the concern of religious belief (Williams, 1967, p. 36).

It is my hope too that the language of computer simulation will increasingly be seen as a philosophically neutral way of framing a broad range of issues about human nature, including religious ones, in a rigorous and helpful way.

Chapter 5

Persons, Souls and Selves

In this chapter, I want to argue the case for taking a broad approach to human persons, including both biological and spiritual aspects of human nature. Psychology is both a biological and a social science and needs to hold these different aspects of human nature together. However, I suggest that theology also needs to see the human person in the context both of the physical body and the social body. It will thus emerge that psychology and theology are grappling with comparable issues in trying to integrate these different facets of human personhood. From both psychological and theological perspectives, we need a broad approach to the person that embraces both biological and social aspects.

The second part of the chapter will re-examine the concept of 'soul', which has historically been central to how the distinctiveness of human beings has been conceptualized. Though this has often been approached in a dualistic way, I will suggest that it can be rethought in a way that is more readily consistent with an integrative view of human nature. However, the concept of soul is by now so encumbered with unhelpful associations that it may be better to abandon it than to try and rehabilitate it. The concept of 'self' has taken over many of the functions of 'soul', but is more attractive, both because it is better embedded in holistic ways of thinking about human nature, and because it has currency in both psychology and theology.

Reductionism

Having considered the three most prominent reductionist approaches to the human person in the last three chapters, it will be helpful to draw the threads together. As we have seen, there has been a tendency for some psychologists to take a strong reductionist line, asserting that human beings are 'nothing but' something or other. Christian thinkers in contrast have wanted to claim the rootedness of human beings in a creator God, their unique receptiveness to his revelation, and the possibility of reconciliation between God and humanity. That has sometimes led them to neglect the natural aspects of the human person.

Because illegitimate forms of strong reductionism can be used as the launching pad for atheist polemic, it is important to see where to draw the line between first the moderate forms of reductionism that are scientifically plausible and are no threat to theology, and second the stronger forms that are theologically uncongenial and have no scientific basis.

One of the problems about discussing reductionism is that there are many different kinds. Everyone agrees about that, but there is no agreement about exactly what the different kinds are, or what they should to be called. I have come to think that the many alternative classifications of reductionism currently in circulation have brought more confusion than clarity to these matters, and so I will try to find an alternative approach.

There are a variety of interlinked claims in strong versions of the reductionist programme. Although, they tend to go together, they can in principle be detached from one another. The first is that higher-level phenomena such as mind can be explained completely in terms of lower level ones such as brain. It is worth emphasizing how hypothetical this concept of complete explanation is. In the human sciences, everything is so complex and interlinked that there are probably no examples of complete explanations of anything. In this situation, it is curious that so much debate is given to the implications of achieving a complete explanation, as if that would ever be possible. It is a debate about an entirely hypothetical scenario, one that is most unlikely to ever occur. Though it is complete biological explanations that are most often considered, similar issues arise about the idea of complete social explanations.

The hope of the reductionist programme is that we will eventually get an explanation of human beings that is both simple and complete. However, the search for simplicity seems to be a distraction in the human sciences. In the physical sciences, a great theoretician like Einstein could be assisted by the insight that the truth about the physical world is simple and elegant. However, there is no reason to suppose that the truth about human beings will be like that. Human beings are inherently complex and multifaceted, and the truth about them seems certain to be complex too. If that is right, simple theories about human beings are not only objectionable theologically, they are also bad science. Multiple perspectives will always be needed, and there is nothing to encourage the hope that all accounts will be reducible to a single, basic one.

The second reductionist claim is that higher-level phenomena have no causal influence, that they are mere 'epiphenomena' that float on the surface and do no causal work. This is also a curious claim, though it is very difficult to assess empirically, it seems unlikely to be correct. For example, it *does* seem as though it makes a difference whether or not people become consciously aware of something. Of course, that is not conclusive, because it is always possible to claim that consciousness of something has particular effects because of the distinct brain processes associated with it.

This leads to another strange aspect of the idea that causal work is done entirely at lower levels, the attempt to divorce high and low levels completely prior to specifying at which level the causal work is being done. The problem here is that the concept of the person gets obliterated. As Midgley (2000) has emphasized, *we* do things, not our minds or brains; there is something odd about tying to suggest that our minds have no place in this causal work. Minds and brains are too intertwined for it to be reasonable to suggest that causal work is done entirely by brains, and not at all by minds.

Thirdly, in reductionism, there are suggestions that higher-level processes are in some sense not 'real'. It is never clear what is meant by this. What is meant by 'real' in any context depends on what it is being contrasted with, and it is not clear what might possibly be meant by saying that high-level processes such as mind or personality are in some sense not real. If this claim were spelled out clearly, it would be evident that our minds and personalities are not unreal in any obvious convincing way. This is probably the aspect of reductionism that is most relevant to the theology of the person; a Christian view would certainly want to maintain the reality of the higher aspects of ourselves.

Despite my scepticism about classifications of reductionism, it is probably worth emphasizing the distinction between how far something can be explained, and whether or not it can be said to exist as a distinct entity. The former could be called 'explanatory reductionism' and the latter 'ontological reductionism'. There is a tendency to move from one to the other. Thus if a higher-level phenomenon can be explained in terms of lower-level processes, then there is a temptation to question its independent existence. However, there is no need to make that move. Explanation need not be seen as having implications for ontology.

This leads on to an ambiguity about what is meant by higher-level phenomena having a distinct existence. If they are grounded in lower-level process, and in some sense emerge from them, they are clearly not completely independent. However, it is still possible that they take on a life of their own, with their own processes, laws, function and significance, and in that sense can be said to have a distinct existence, even if not one that is totally independent of lower-level processes.

It is interesting to ask just what is the appeal of these strong 'nothing but' ideas about human beings. Notice that the appeal is not universal. Some people are clearly excited at reducing human beings to some basic, easily understood principles. This is perhaps, in part, just an aesthetic attraction to simple elegant theories, but there may be something more grandiose in the urge to understand human nature completely, and the associated hope that it would then be under our control. Others are appalled at these trends and want to preserve a sense of mystery about human beings. That comes from a different set of ethical priorities, one that values openness to the unexpected and a capacity to respond to it more highly than the ability to understand and control.

Though we now instinctively assume that the sense of mystery is a natural ally of Christianity, it is worth recalling that it has not always been so. If we go back to the early days of modern science, the assumption was that a sense of mystery about nature left the door open to a dangerous kind of pantheism (Midgley, 1991). In contrast, early science with its mechanistic approach, was seen as being against pantheism and on the side of Christian orthodoxy. Also, because the mechanistic approach to nature was assumed to be clearly inadequate and in need of being supplemented by something broader, it was assumed to provide an argument for the existence of God. It is hard to exaggerate how radically different the relationship between science and religion has been in the 'early modern' (Enlightenment) and 'late modern' (post-Darwinian) periods. Among the many important differences is the way in which the sense of mystery has changed from being seen as the enemy of Christianity to being its friend.

Part of the problem in the debate about reductionism is that both sides tend to assume that the attempt to find a complete explanation of human nature will be carried through successfully. Some hope this will be so while others fear it, but they often seem to agree that it is likely. In fact, it seems to me highly *un*likely that we will succeed in explaining human beings completely. If that is so, both the excitement and the alarm are misplaced. I am happy for reductionist lines of scientific enquiry to be pursued as far as they will go. There is nothing against 'methodological' reductionism. In the course of pursuing reductionist approaches, I expect us to learn much that is genuinely interesting about human beings, but I see no prospect of our arriving at a complete account of human beings in terms of evolution, neuroscience, or anything else. That means that I share neither the excitement nor the alarm that are so prevalent, though I regret the way in which enthusiasts for these scientific approaches exaggerate how far they are likely to get. Their optimism is surely more the expression of a scientistic ideology than a sober estimate of scientific prospects.

Psychology as a Biological and Social Science

Within psychology, there are strong forms of both biological determinism and social constructionism. It is the strong forms that are problematic; their weaker counterparts present no obstacle to a broad biological/social discipline. The phrase 'nothing but', or its equivalents, gives the game away and indicates that strong forms are being espoused. In both the biological and the social case, I am happy to accept the non-exclusive claims of the weak reductionist positions, but firmly reject the more exclusive claims of the strong positions.

Take social contructionism (Greenwood, 1994). There is a weak form that points out that all the categories with which we understand human beings are social constructions, and in this sense are contingent. However, there is also a strong form of social constructionism that goes further and says that our personal life is 'nothing but' a social construction. That makes it irrelevant, misleading and illegitimate to study other aspects of emotions such as the biological ones. However, there is no basis whatsoever for asserting that our thoughts and feelings are 'nothing but' social constructions.

At the opposite end of psychology, there is biological determinism; one of the most influential forms of this at present is neurological determinism. Of course, the brain is involved in every aspect of human functioning. Except in the most basic reflex-like reactions, it is not bypassed. However, there is a strong form of neurological determinism that would go further and say, with Francis Crick (1994), that our emotions, thoughts and personalities are 'nothing but' what goes on in our brains, that we are 'just a bundle of neurons' (p. 3).

I would also reject claims to 'primacy' for any particular aspect of human beings. Such claims to primacy arise, for example, in relation to depression, which is an interesting example of a complex multifaceted human phenomenon. Some people think that the social circumstances within which depression arises are primary; other people think that the biological aspects are primary. To say that one aspect of depression is primary is to claim that it comes first, and that it explains all the others. However, this is not how human beings work. Our social circumstances affect what goes on in our bodies; equally our physiological state and brain processes affect our social functioning. I suggest that all claims to primacy are spurious, and that human beings are too systemic for any of them to be credible.

Within psychology, the study of human emotions illustrates well the importance of holding together biological and social aspects of being human. Any attempt to deny either the biological or social aspects of emotions leads to a very impoverished account of them. Our physical being is critically involved in emotional reactions. In fact it is doubtful whether there could be anything that could properly be called an emotion that did not have a physiological substrate. There have been those who have tried to argue that the biological aspects of emotions are primary. For example, William James tried to argue that emotional feelings are just the way in which we become conscious of the bodily changes which are the core of emotional reactions, though this is a view which has proved too simplistic (Oatley and Jenkins, 1996).

Emotions are socially embedded too. They nearly always occur in an interactional context, and represent a response to another person. There are important social rules that influence how we interpret the situations that give rise to emotions. Though there are fundamental emotions such as fear and anger that occur with only minor variations in most cultures, there are many more subtle emotions which depend heavily on the social and cultural context. Emotions like guilt, embarrassment and resentment depend on the moral order (for example, Harré, 1986). Moreover, emotions have powerful social effects; our relationships are heavily dependent on our emotional response to those with whom we interact. There is no place for either biological or social imperialism about emotions.

Psychology has included a variety of rather narrowly based approaches that have had pretensions to 'take over' the discipline, and to provide a complete psychology. Religious suspicion about psychology is often held most strongly by those who do not appreciate the breadth of the discipline and mistakenly identify one particular approach to psychology with the whole of it. The problems come particularly from the reductionist traditions in psychology such as Freudianism, behaviourism, physicalism or evolutionism, none of which has been able to develop a complete psychology. There has always been a need for other psychological perspectives.

Indeed, psychology should be seen as a family of disciplines rather than one single discipline, and it covers a broad spectrum of approaches. At the social end, psychology is clearly a social science and has much in common with the social interactionist wing of sociology. At the other end, it is a biological science, concerned with the role of the brain and human physiology in psychological functioning, and with the evolutionary context of psychology. The challenge for psychology is to hold these two wings together. It is important, if we are to have a broad and coherent approach to human nature, that we should have an integrated scientific discipline concerned with human nature that stretches from the biological to the social. If we did not have such a discipline, we would need to construct one, but we have it already, and it is called psychology (Watts, 1992).

The need to integrate biological and social approaches within psychology raises general issues of how to relate naturalistic and social approaches within the sciences. Psychology is a particularly interesting case because of the diverse approaches to the human person that fall within it. At one end of the spectrum, psychology is a biological science, at the other it is a social science. There is always something of a tension between the two, and relatively few people conduct research on human functioning in a way that integrates both. I would want to take a broad view of the person, similar to that exemplified in Rom Harré's trilogy: *Social Being* (1979), *Personal Being* (1983), *Physical Being* (1991). Despite the strong reductionism that still lurks in some quarters, the human sciences are taking discernable steps, reflected in Harré's work, towards seeing the human being in broad terms, including the biological, personal and social.

Part of the difficulty in integrating the biological and social aspects of the study of human beings within psychology is the way in which psychology is both a natural science dealing with the biological aspects of human beings, and a social science dealing with the relational aspects of being human. In recent decades (stemming from Winch, 1958), there has been a developing philosophy of social science that emphasizes how it differs from the natural sciences, for example in being more concerned with reasons for actions than with causes. The distinction between natural and social science reflects the basic distinction (for example, Lash, 1996) between two different kinds of concepts, natural kinds (such as cabbages) and social constructs (such as cities).

Psychology is situated on the fault line between the natural and the social sciences. It is no surprise then that the discipline tends to fall apart, and some might argue that it is fruitless to try to continue with a discipline that is an uncomfortable hybrid between a natural and a social science. My own view is that human beings can never be understood if their natural (biological) and social (relational) aspects are kept separate, and that it is extremely important for the enterprise of understanding human nature that ways are found of pursuing naturalistic and social approaches in harmony with one another. The challenges psychology faces in holding its disparate wings together are of great importance in the broad intellectual context of our times.

The Theology of Personhood

An adequate psychology of human nature thus needs to take the biological and social aspects of personhood into account in a balanced way. Let us now see how this relates to theological concepts of personhood. On theological grounds, too, I would want to take a broad view of the human person that held together the social and the biological. Indeed, it would be helpful for the relationship between science and theology if strong links were forged between the naturalistic approach to the person of biological psychology and the more hermeneutic approach of social psychology. That could set helpful precedents for linking up the natural sciences and the hermeneutic discipline of theology.

At first blush, there is a contrast between the approaches of science and theology to human nature. Even where there is no clear incompatibility, their focus of interest shows very little overlap. One key difference concerns biology. Scientific approaches to human beings often emphasize biological aspects, whereas the theology of being human generally neglects biology. In contrast, moral aspects of being human are often emphasized in theological formulations, particularly as they bear sin and salvation (for example, Anderson, 1982), but are relatively neglected in psychology.

Though there is an apparent contrast in the emphasis on physical aspects of human nature in science and theology, there is currently a move to minimise these differences (Brown *et al.*, 1998). The claim is that Christian theology and contemporary science are at one in emphasizing the unity of the human person. It is held that both take an integrated view of body or brain on the one hand, and of mind, soul, personality or spirit on the other. This argues that science is not as reductively physicalist as it seems, and that the Judeo-Christian tradition is not as dualist as is sometimes supposed.

Clearly, there is a point here. The Hebrew tradition is, in the main, of an 'ensouled body', and does not take as dualist a view of soul as do many Greek thinkers in the Platonic tradition (Green, 1998). However, already within the wisdom literature of the Old Testament, there is a discernible move towards a more dualistic way of thinking. Of major theologians, Aquinas, who took as Aristotelian a view of soul as anyone, is a good touchstone of the more holistic strand of Christian thinking about the person. All that can be readily admitted. However, it seems to me that it is easy to exaggerate the similarity of Christian theology and contemporary science about these things.

It is true that Hebrew thought does generally assume an ensouled body (or an enspirited body), rather than a pre-existent soul that enters the body. On occasions, it even emphasizes the continuity between our natural being and that of the animal kingdom. However, even in passages such as Ecclesiastes 3: 18–21, that exemplify that theme, we are in a thought world that is a long way removed from what would be assumed by modern science: 'The fate of man and beast is identical; one dies, the other too, and both have the self-same breath ...Who knows if the spirit of man mounts upward or if the spirit of the beast goes down to the earth?'

There is often a tendency in contemporary theology to side with social imperialism, and largely to discount the biological aspects of human nature. Postmodern philosophy has tended to emphasize how much the individual is shaped by the culture and society, and much current theology has imbibed that emphasis on the primacy of culture, and neglected the personal and the embodied aspects of human existence. An admirable recent example of a theological view of human persons that emphasizes the relational context of personhood is McFadyen's (1990) *The Call to Personhood*. Though it is an excellent study of the social aspects of personhood, it completely neglects the biological aspects of human nature, as does much theological anthropology in this tradition.

However, there is a separate tradition of theological thinking that emphasizes the importance of physical embodiment to being human. Jim Nelson's (1979) *Embodiment* was an important early contribution to this line of thinking, and it has also been important in feminist theology (Coakley, 1997). It is very much to be welcomed that theology is beginning to recover a sense of the importance of embodiment. However, in theology as in psychology, there has often not been much contact between the different strands of theological thinking that emphasize the relational and the bodily aspects of being human.

The role of theologians in this warfare between biological and social imperialism should be to oppose extremism. The natural world from which we have emerged is God's creation, and we belong to it. There is nothing in the Christian agenda that wishes to minimize that. However, the social world in which we live is also enormously important, especially the moral community within which we learn how to conduct ourselves, and the community of faith within which we learn salvation.

Unfortunately, it has been relatively rare for theologians to seek to integrate social and biological aspects of the human condition. One important recent exception is Farley's (1990) *Good and Evil*. In Part One he develops a broad Christian anthropology which includes the personal, inter-human, social and biological aspects of human nature. The breadth of approach that Farley displays would be desirable in all theological reflection on being human. Perhaps those who are concerned with the scientific context in which theology must now operate, and who are aware of the importance of holding together the biological and social in the scientific study of human beings, can help to offer a corrective to the unbalanced view of human beings that often prevails within the theological community.

Soul

The second half of this chapter will examine the concepts of soul and self, and their role in Christian thinking about persons. Christian thinking about soul has often taken a dualistic form that conceives soul as a potentially disembodied entity. However, that is not the only possible Christian approach; it is also possible to conceptualize soul in more holistic terms. The question to ask about the soul, if we want to go on using the term at all, is *what* concept of the soul to have.

It is helpful to consider the implications of the philosophy of mind for how we should think about soul. Comparable points can be made about soul to those made about mind and brain in Chapter 3. If consciousness is an emergent property of physical brains, perhaps soul should also be thought of as an emergent property too. Philosophers of mind have been urging the advantages of thinking about mental powers, not about the mind as an entity. We have powers of mind that arise from our bodies and brains, and which interact with them. Similarly, soul is too often thought of as an entity, though it does not need to be conceptualized in that way. I would not want to say that we have a third kind of entity called a soul, separate from and additional to our bodies and minds, but rather that we have soul capacities. To talk about our 'souls' is to talk about ourselves from a particular perspective, not to talk about some entity that is distinct from the rest of us. This view of soul is similar to that of Keith Ward (1992) in *Defending the Soul*.

Sometimes the soul has been seen as an immaterial entity created by God before a person's natural birth, but this has by no means been universally accepted. That way of thinking goes back to Plato, but there is an alternative tradition, promoted by Aristotle, and very influential within the Christian heritage, that sees the soul as the form of the body, rather than as a separate entity. The soul is the person described from a non-material perspective, rather than a separate and distinct non-material entity. In the early centuries of the Christian era, there was a debate as to whether the soul should be seen as mortal or immortal; both views were well represented. Eventually, Aquinas attempted to work out a synthesis between the various traditions, but this was by no means a surrender to the dualistic view.

The pressures to see the soul as a separate entity grew in the seventeenth century, and came from various sources. People wanted to describe God in increasingly specific terms and, as we saw in Chapter 3, were attracted by the analogy between God and the mind. Also, it was thought that emphasizing the separateness of the body and the soul, and the limited nature of the body, would strengthen the argument that we are much more than our bodies. In the long run, that proved a counter-productive argument. Thirdly, it seemed that our potential for immortality could best be explicated in terms of the survival of the soul after death though, as we saw in Chapter 3, it is doubtful whether that is the classical Christian tradition.

It was with Descartes that the dualistic view of the soul finally won out, though his brand of dualism is more subtle than is often realized. He was not trying to defend an ancient view of the soul against the rise of science; he was refashioning the concept of the soul in a new way that he thought took account of early modern mechanistic science, in which he was himself a key figure. His idea was essentially that if you sharpened the difference between the soul and the mechanistic aspects of the body that science studied, then it would be clear that you needed both. It was never a good idea, and it did not work. In fact, science tended to remain mechanistic (modern materialistic neuroscience is a close descendant), and the soul was just lopped off Descartes' bipartite structure.

Francis Crick's (1994) attack on the concept of the soul in *The Astonishing Hypothesis,* discussed in Chapter 3, suffers from a simplistic understanding of the concept. Though he does not realize it, he is attacking one particular dualistic theory of what the soul is, rather than the very idea of soul. The concept of soul has a more complex history than people like Crick seem to realize. Objections to dualistic ways of thinking about the soul do not mean that the concept needs to be abandoned altogether. Certainly, the Platonic view of the soul was dualistic, but the Aristotelian view was not. Because Aristotle saw the soul as the 'form' of the body, it would have been problematic for him to think of the soul as separate form the body. It is entirely understandable that Crick should want to get rid of the kind of dualistic concept of the soul that sees it as completely divorced from the material body. However, it would be wrong to think that a crudely materialistic view of the person is the only alternative to a dualistic concept of the soul.

Crick also sees a close connection between the 'homunculus' (that is, little man inside the head) and soul, and he is against both. However, the soul is not necessarily to be seen as a kind of homunculus. It is possible to reject the idea of the homunculus (as I would), and still keep an Aristotelian concept of the soul as integrated facet of the human being. The biblical Christian tradition would similarly emphasize that the body and soul constitute an integrated whole. If we continue to talk about soul, it is probably unhelpful to reify it as 'the soul'; that already sets us off down a dualistic track. The question is rather how soul properties are emergent from the physical brain, and are supervenient on it, but nonetheless real.

If we were trying to capture a complete human personality in computer terms, I would not want to include a module called the soul, along with modules dealing with various other faculties. Neither would I want to have it as a kind of homunculus in the middle, monitoring and controlling everything that was going on. Rather, I would see soul as an emergent property of the whole system. The recent trend towards 'connectionist' modelling of the mind as a distributed system may eventually be helpful here. That way of modelling is leading us to see various mental and emotional properties as emergent properties of a distributed system (Eiser, 1994), and I believe this is the direction in which we should eventually look for thinking about how properties of soul arise within people, and affect them. AI might thus help religious people to think more clearly about what they mean by 'soul'.

Soul is best seen as a qualitative aspect of the person. As the Jungian psychologist, James Hillman put it, 'by soul I mean a perspective rather than a substance' (1975, p. x). I am as wary of talking about *the* soul as I am of talking about *the* mind. Perhaps we can see soul as a kind of emergent property of our whole beings, an aspect of us which, like our minds, is grounded in our natural being. If we were not natural beings with bodies and brains, we would not have come to have souls, any more than we would have come to have minds.

Yet there are some ways in which soul is not exactly parallel to mind. Consciousness is a universal property of human beings, apart from a few who are suffering from serious forms of damage or disorder. It is an interesting question whether soul is universal in the same sense. I see strong reasons for wanting to say at least that every human being has a *capacity* for soul life. This way of thinking has been an important foundation for the respect that we properly ought to have for each human being, and I would not lightly abandon it.

There is another point of view from which the soul life of some people remains more of a potentiality than an actuality. There is a hollowness and superficiality about many of us; and where there is little depth, there is little soul. Let me guard against any suspicion that soul is here being identified with intellectual powers. On the contrary, it is striking how people who are intellectually unsophisticated can have remarkable depth of personality and qualities of soul. I argued in connection with mind that our mental life involves separate and distinct powers, and that we could never capture what is important in our mental life by talking just about what was going on in our brains. That point would hold in an even more radical sense when it comes to talking about our soul life. Human soul-life is an even more remarkably emancipated flowering of our natural nature than our mental capacity for consciousness.

Soul and Spirit

There are important *both/and* things to be said about soul. On the one hand, I have suggested, our soul life arises from our natural nature. On the other it reflects our openness to God, our potential for becoming more spiritual creatures, for taking on something of the likeness of God. Because of this, it carries our hopes of eternal life. There is something Janus-like about soul. While still being grounded in the natural, it is pointing beyond the natural towards God.

This raises the complex question of the relation of soul to spirit, something about which there has been a good deal of ambiguity in Christian anthropology. Sometimes, soul is used as part of a three-part scheme in which soul and spirit are distinguished. In that case, there is a good deal of similarity between soul and psyche, and psychology can be seen as the study of the soul. At other times, and increasingly since the Council of Constantinople in 869, soul has been used as part of a two-fold scheme in which soul encompasses spirit. That tends to take soul outside naturalistic discourse, and away from psychology.

On this point, I am again inclined to follow James Hillman, in suggesting that there are important psychological reasons to make the distinction between soul and spirit (Hillman, 1979). The soul instinct is to go deep, the spiritual impulse is to soar. In some ways, they are polar opposites. Certainly, it is helpful to distinguish between psychological and spiritual aspects of the human person. However, that distinction can be made without treating either soul or spirit as separate entities. It also needs to be stressed that it is only a matter of conceptual distinction between soul and spirit that is being proposed; there is clearly no watertight division between them.

It is of considerable help in conceptualizing the personal issues that arise in counselling to have a clear distinction between issues that arise within the life of the soul, as opposed to more strictly spiritual issues. Some who have made the distinction between the spiritual and the psychological have suggested that personal problems belong to just one domain or the other. In fact most personal problems seem to be *both* psychological *and* spiritual, and can be approached from either perspective; the two aspects are distinct but complementary (Bennan, 1988).

It is also helpful to be able to make the distinction between psychological and spiritual aspects of spiritual practices, such as prayer. There is certainly a psychology of prayer, which is able to give an account of the impact of the various aspects of prayer, such as petition, thanksgiving and intercession, on the person who prays (Watts, 2001a). However, there is more to prayer than that. In considering religious experience in the next two chapters, it will also be helpful to bear in mind that there are both psychological and spiritual aspects. It is a moot point whether or not it is helpful to hang those distinct but complementary perspectives on the distinction between soul and spirit.

Self

The concept of 'self' seems in many ways a successor to that of 'soul' and to have inherited many of its functions. Even though soul and self are certainly not synonymous (Crabbe, 1999), self is probably now the main heading under which discussions take place about what used to be called soul. The critical difference is that the idea of soul, largely because it is old fashioned, is easily misunderstood. It is often thought to be incompatible with contemporary psychology, though in fact it is capable of being rehabilitated in a way that would render it more compatible. Self, in contrast, has the attraction of already being extensively used in contemporary psychology (see, for example, Yardley and Honess, 1987; Breakwell, 1992; Hampson, 1988, Chapter 7).

The dialogue between theology and psychology about the self could be a very rich one, but so far it is largely unexplored. There is a rich theological and philosophical inheritance which has helped to shape the modern concept of the self, which is admirably discussed in Charles Taylor's (1989) *Sources of the Self* (see also Habgood, 1998). The older theological discussion has often used other terms, such as person, but has nevertheless been an important source of the current concept of self.

There has been considerable interest in how the sense of self has developed in recent centuries. Logan (1987) has offered a five-stage scheme which is a helpful integration of such work. He begins with the self as a 'newly autonomous subject' in the late middle ages, and follows the story through the self as 'assertive subject' in the Reformation period, the self as 'competent subject' in the Enlightenment, the self as 'observed subject' in the modern period, and concludes with the self as 'alienated' in the postmodern period.

Unfortunately, there is considerable confusion surrounding the concept of self, something that needs to be acknowledged straight away. It is perhaps a reflection of the richness of the concept of self that it can be handled in many different ways. In fact, there seem to be several related but distinct concepts going under the same term of 'self': that can cause a good deal of misunderstanding. Worst of all, it can lead to debates between different, apparently competing theories of the self, when those theories really apply to different meanings of self, and so are not in competition with one another. It is therefore important to have some kind of classification of different meanings of 'self'.

Harré (1998) has made a valiant effort to sort all this out, and has proposed three different meanings of self:

1   self as the totality of our unique attributes,
2   self as a unique point of view, the centre of action and experience,
3   self as how we seem to others.

The distinction between the first and second senses of self seems the most fundamental one. Self can be used descriptively for the attributes of the person, or it can be used to focus on the processes by which people interact with the world around them. There is, then, a further distinction of a different kind to be made between the individualistic sense of self (that is, how we seem to ourselves) and the more social sense of self (how we seem to other people). This distinction between individual and social aspects of self can also be applied to how the sense of self arises, with some people emphasizing personal, intra-individualistic sources of the sense of self, and others emphasizing its social origin.

There are different emphases in different traditions of social psychology. American social psychology, with its strong emphasis on social cognition, has tended to focus on the self as a centre of cognitive processing, whereas European social psychology has tended to focus on the self in social and interactional context. British social psychology often functions as a meeting place for these two rather different traditions. Each of these approaches to self seems legitimate, and I suggest that no good comes of arguing what self 'really' means. Neither does any one approach tell us all we want to know about self; different approaches are complementary. Indeed, it is one of the attractive things about the psychology of self that it provides a meeting point for various different strands of psychology, social and individualistic, cognitive and psychoanalytic (Westen, 1985).

People's self concept is central both to much of their interaction with the world, and to themselves as centres of processing. Human emotions, for example, can be divided into a handful of primary ones that are relatively universal, and a larger pool of secondary ones that are elaborations of them, and which arise from people's sense of themselves (Oatley and Jenkins, 1996). Guilt is one important secondary emotion that depends of the sense of self, and which has played a large part in religious life.

Memory also arises out of the self-concept. There has been increasing psychological interest in personal aspects of memory. What we remember best, and the gloss we put on events when we remember them, are much influenced by our self-concept. The self-concept seems to be a more coherent and effective centre of processing in some people than others. For example, there are some indications that, when people become depressed, their self-concept no longer operates so effectively in facilitating memory. The fact that there seem to be such differences between people raises the interesting question of whether there is anything distinctive about the way religious people relate experiences to their self-concept. There are also important issues about the role of the transformation of memory in the Christian life (Elliott, 1995).

There is another set of questions about how people see themselves, that is, what set of attributes they see themselves as having (Harré's first sense of self), and again there are interesting differences between people. Consider 'self-esteem' (how good an opinion people have of themselves). The question of what kind of self-esteem it is right for Christians to have is a subtle one, as there are considerations that could steer things in apparently opposite directions (McGrath and McGrath, 1992). Christians could well come to have a sense of their limitations in relations to God, and a strong sense of humility. On the other hand, their sense of being empowered by God might lead to a strong self-esteem, even to a kind of religious narcissism (Pruyser, 1991). The empirical evidence suggests that there is actually a positive association between religious belief and self-esteem (Hood *et al.*, 1996) though, with more subtle empirical measures, things might turn out to be more complex than the empirical evidence has so far suggested.

There are further questions about whether people will see themselves in simple or complex terms. There are increasing indications that people have 'multiple selves' (Markus and Nurius, 1986), and that these different selves can arise in different contexts and social roles. That raises the question of what kind of self-concept is relevant, for Christians, in the context of their relationship with God. Will that God-grounded self-concept be relatively encapsulated, or will it interact with self-concepts that arise in other contexts? Some Christians will probably have a distinctively Christian sense of self that arises from a religious construal of their pattern of social interaction, whereas in others it will arise from a more private sense of relationship to God. These are just a few of the questions about the self that could be pursued in the dialogue between theology and psychology.

Though different strands of the psychological literature give weight to both the individual and social aspects of selfhood, there has so far been relatively little interest in the embodied self, and how people's experience of physical health and illness, and physical pleasure and pain, contributes to their sense of self. Emotion is, again, a helpful corrective, and it is clear that people's personal feelings are influenced to an important extent by their physical experience of themselves. The relative neglect of the embodied self in current psychology seems more a deficiency in the present literature than any inherent limitation in the psychology of self.

It is one of the potential advantages of the concept of self that it can encompass the different strands of experience, personal, social, somatic, and spiritual, from which selfhood arises. The interaction of social and embodied experience seems likely to be a fruitful theme in future psychological work on the self, and one that could be fruitful in theology too. Both psychology and theology, in their different ways, find it difficult to maintain an appropriate balance concerning the social and physical aspects of human personhood. They might find it fruitful to link hands and to collaborate in tackling this enduring problem, and in formulating a sufficiently broad concept of self.

Chapter 6

Religious Experience:
Cognitive Neuroscience

So far the book has concentrated on how central aspects of human nature and functioning are approached in general psychology. In this chapter, and the next one, we turn to a central topic in the psychology of religion, religious experience. It is a topic that will enable us to apply in a fresh direction some of the issues about reductionist approaches to human nature that have been explored so far. It will also prepare the ground for a broader engagement with Christian doctrine from a psychological perspective.

Both 'religious' and 'mystical' experience will be considered. The distinction between the two is not very clearly established, though there are differences of emphasis in how the two terms are used. Sometimes the emphasis is placed on the way experiences are interpreted, and the suggestion is made that any experience can be deemed religious if it is interpreted in a particular way, drawing on a framework of religious belief. Here 'religious' experience is the more appropriate term. At other times, the emphasis is placed on the distinctive phenomenological quality of the experience, or perhaps on assumptions about the kind of spiritual realties that are the object of the experience, and here 'mystical' experience is the more appropriate term.

However, it would be unhelpful to contrast the two concepts too sharply. There is a core set of experiences that meet both criteria; experiences that both have a distinctive phenomenology, and also are interpreted in a particular religious way. There are also secondary experiences that meet one criterion and not the other, either having a distinctive phenomenology but not being interpreted in a religious way, or lacking any distinctive phenomenology but being interpreted from a religious point of view. I will not attempt in what follows to make a sharp distinction between 'religious' and 'mystical' experience, and will often use 'religious experience' as a general term for both.

My approach to religious experience here will be broad, similar to that of Wildman and Brothers (1999), who also emphasize the importance of holding together different approaches. They emphasize, as I would, that the phenomenological, neurological and social-psychological approaches sit side by side, and it is good practice to consider the relevance of each of these non-theological approaches. However, the various approaches may differ in their importance in any particular case; for example, the social-psychological approach may sometimes be of great importance, sometimes of relatively little significance.

Reductionism and Religious Experience

There are three main reductionist critiques of religious experience in psychology. The oldest, stemming from Freud, sees it as a reflection of personal needs. The suggestion is that people believe in a good and powerful God because they have a psychological need to do so. That Freudian critique will not be discussed here, beyond making a few basic points. One is that Freud's views on religion are highly speculative and need not be regarded as having scientific authority. The other is that a psychoanalytic approach to religious experience need not be as reductionist as Freud himself was. Recent psychoanalytic approaches to religion, influenced by Winnicott (see Meissner, 1984) have been much more sympathetic, at least to the adaptive value of religion, if not to its truth. Also, Freud's critique of religion, can be a helpful indication of how inauthentic religious experiences might arise, and how people's ideas about God can be constrained by their personal background and outlook. That need not be taken to imply that all religious experience is nothing but a reflection of psychological needs.

Probably the most vigorous reductionist critique of religious experience at the present time is the social constructionist one that emphasizes how religious experience is shaped by social, cultural and linguistic context. I will consider that in the next chapter. There is also a neuropsychological critique that is rapidly gaining ground, concerned with the explanation of religious experience in terms of brain function. That is what I will consider in the present chapter.

The approach I will take to reductionism about religious experience will parallel that taken already to reductionism about human nature. I will avoid being simply for or against it, but will set out where the boundary is to be drawn between proper, moderate forms of reductionism and pernicious, extreme forms ('greedy' reductionism, as Dennet 1991, called it). A critical move in greedy reductionism is to suggest that a particular approach provides a complete account of religious experience, and that no other factors are relevant. The next step is to suggest that religious experience is 'nothing but' the product of whatever particular factors are the focus of current interest. That involves a form of genetic fallacy in which the *nature* of religious experience is equated with particular explanatory factors. That leads, finally, to the conclusion that there is nothing authentically religious about religious experience.

These pernicious reductionist moves can be made in terms of each of the three critiques of religion mentioned above, the Freudian, social constructionist and the neuropsychological. Religious experience can be seen as 'nothing but' a reflection of personal needs, cultural influence, or brain processes.

I shall give particular attention in my discussion of these debates to the cognitive processes by which meaning and understanding arise. The cognitive approach to religious experience is, so far, relatively under-developed, though it is currently the focus of active consideration (Andresen, in press). The social and neuropsychological critiques of religious experience will be evaluated in terms of the developing scientific understanding of human cognition. I shall suggest that considering what is cognitively plausible helps in finding a sensible path through often polemical debates.

In this chapter, I will extend the general approach to mind and brain issues already developed, and apply it to religious experience. Again, I will want to avoid the extremes of reductionism and dualism. One extreme to be rejected is the reductionist idea that physical processes can explain religious experience so fully that, in some sense, it is not 'real'. Another position to be rejected, at the opposite extreme, is the dualistic assumption that religious experience can be divorced from our physical nature.

Now that the neural basis of religious experience is beginning to be studied scientifically, many people are too ready to assume that neuropsychological explanations will be sufficient, and so to conclude that religious experiences are not experiences of God, or do not reflect his initiative. However, there is no reason to assume that divine action and natural causes are mutually exclusive. Applying that general point to the present case, the fact that religious experience has a neural basis does not exclude the possibility of such experience also reflecting divine action, though of course many detailed questions remain about how to reconcile divine action and the neural substrate in relation to religious experience.

Neuroscience and Divine Action

There are theological reasons for including the physical brain in our concept of the person when we think about how God acts in relation to people. From a theological point of view, the physical brain must be seen as part of God's creation. Like everything else in creation it should be seen as existing within the life of God and being dependent on him. When God seeks to reveal himself to people, it would be bizarre to suppose that he would wish, or need, to bypass this aspect of his creation in order to do so.

As cognitive neuroscience gains increasing understanding of the cognitive and neural processes subserving religious consciousness, it will probably become clear which brain processes are particularly involved in religious experience. However, this need not lead us to ask the question whether religious experience is caused by the brain *or* by God. The two cannot properly be set up against each other in that way. God can be expected to relate to people as the composite physical-mental-spiritual creatures that they are. In short, it is as *persons* that God relates to us, not as mere minds, brains, souls or spirits.

As I indicated in the first chapter, the complementarity of mind and brain accounts can be seen as in some ways like the complementarity of naturalistic and theological accounts. One does not exclude the other. Theological and naturalistic perspectives are different in character but complementary. A theological perspective can illuminate how human processes and events can be seen as being in tune with the will and purpose of God. In contrast, a naturalistic perspective elaborates the cognitive and neurological processes by which this arises. This approach in terms of complementarity implies there need be no incompatibility between first talking about God's influential presence in our thought processes, and second looking at the cognitive and neurological processes by which our thought processes are drawn into resonance with God's will and purpose.

Asking whether something comes from God *or* has a natural cause would involve the mistake of seeing God as one cause in a series of possible causes. It would 'naturalize' and limit God in a way that classical theism has always been careful to avoid. In their broad and comprehensive approach to religious experience,

Wildman and Brothers (1999) introduce the theological perspective as yet another approach to religious experience alongside those of the human sciences. However, it is important to emphasize that the theological approach is not just one more approach in a list of approaches, but an approach of a rather different kind that focuses on ultimate meaning and significance.

Many human processes need more than one account to describe them adequately. Similarly, it is often necessary to consider more than one causal factor and to offer multiple explanatory accounts. The modern, scientific mind tends to ask, 'What caused A? Was it X or Y?' It is a question that has its uses in scientific investigation, especially in the physical sciences. However, in the human sciences, the answer is usually that there are multiple causes, none of which is sufficient. Theories that 'go for broke' on a single cause are usually wrong. For example, the question 'is depression caused by physical *or* social factors?' has not proved a fruitful one. The answer is 'both'. Methodologically, there may be value in pushing a single explanation as far as it will go and discovering its limitations, but the lesson from the history of psychological research is that you generally don't get very far before you need to bring in a complex network of causal factors.

Nevertheless, you can still ask which explanatory account is most relevant and helpful. If someone has strange experiences associated with an epileptic seizure, it would generally be agreed that an explanatory account in terms of brain processes was the key one. But there are other occasions where, despite the fact the brain processes are involved, an explanatory account in terms of mind or person is more relevant and appropriate. For example, if you are seeking an explanation for why someone did well in an examination it is most appropriate to explain that in terms of the effectiveness of their preparation for the examination, and to couch that in terms of their thought processes, even though the physical brain was also involved. The key question is which explanatory level is 'in the driving seat', or most relevant in a particular context. Which explanatory account is most appropriate is, of course, dependent in part on the purposes for which an explanation is being offered.

Though religious experience is always potentially open to both theological and naturalistic accounts, it is appropriate to ask about any particular experience whether it really is of God. The Christian tradition has worked out some helpful rules of discernment, looking for example at the effects of experiences, as Murphy (1994) has pointed out in relation to Catherine of Siena. Essentially, the Christian tradition has often asked whether an experience has led to an enhancement of Christian love, and only accepted it as an authentic experience of God where the consequences of the experience confirm that. Such criteria will always be relevant in discerning whether particular experiences reflect the mind and will of God in a special way.

One interesting case where this issue has been focused is in terms of Ignatius of Loyola's concept of 'uncaused consolation'. A 'consolation' is essentially an experience that has brought the person closer to God, and it is 'uncaused' if no natural explanation is available. W.W. Meissner (1992) has provided an excellent analysis of this concept in relation to the human sciences, noting some of the available theories of religious experience in the human sciences, from the neurological to the psychoanalytic. He concludes by rejecting the antithesis of natural and divine causes that underlies the concept of uncaused consolation. This kind of antithesis between natural and divine causes has influenced how the Roman Catholic Church has examined miracles in relation to candidates for sanctification. For something to be established as a miracle, natural explanations have to be excluded. Such an approach is theologically misconceived in the way it sees natural causes and divine agency as alternatives to one another.

The issue here is similar to that which arises in connection with the explanation of new species in terms of evolution and natural selection. The array of species and their adaptedness does not constitute an argument for the existence of God, because there is an adequate naturalistic explanation that does not invoke God. However, as we saw in Chapter 2, it is perfectly possible to see evolution as reflecting the will and purpose of God; the facts of the relationship between species and their adaptedness to their environments are in no way incompatible with such an assumption. In the same way, religious experience is readily explained in terms of the influential activity of God, but it does not need to be explained in that way.

Religion and Epilepsy

We will now review some of the main theories currently being advanced about how brain processes give rise to religious experience. I will have criticisms to advance of these theories, from the perspectives both of science and of theology, and will then try to show how this critique points towards a new generation of theories. First, we will consider approaches which have localized religious experience in particular areas of the brain. Religious experience has been identified with two broad areas of the brain, one is the part of the temporal lobes involved in epilepsy, the other is the frontal lobes.

Probably the most widely canvassed neurological theory of religious experience is based on the idea that there is a relationship between religious experience and Temporal Lobe Epilepsy (TLE). Work on this link has attracted a good deal of popular interest, though I will argue that a critical examination of the research indicates that the link is much more tenuous than is often assumed.

The claim is that people suffering from TLE have more religious experiences and preoccupations than others. This leads on to the idea that the neural basis of TLE may lead to understanding the neural basis of religious experience. However, there is some doubt about the basic assumption of increased religiosity in TLE. A clear distinction needs to be made between religious experiences *while* people with TLE are undergoing seizures, and experiences and preoccupations *between* seizures.

Seizure experiences are sometimes rather like religious ones, but caution is needed because the religious aspects of seizure experiences are in many ways *un*like religious experiences. The emotional tone of seizure experiences is often disturbing, being associated with anxiety (Fenwick, 1996). In contrast, it is a standard feature of powerful religious experiences that they result in a positive emotional tone, even when people have been severely stressed before the experience (Hay, 1987; Hood *et al.*, 1996). Also, patients undergoing seizure experiences generally know that what they are experiencing is no more real than say a dream (Fenton, 1981). In contrast, people who have powerful religious experiences are generally convinced of the reality of what they are experiencing. Finally, the sense of the presence of God found in many religious experiences is notably undramatic, and usually does not have the rather weird quality of seizure experiences.

As far as between-seizure aspects of personality are concerned, it has become the received wisdom, on the basis of accumulated clinical reports, that people with TLE are unusually religious. However, this conclusion has often been reached without using any formal comparison group, and is not supported by more careful research. When Tucker *et al.* examined a series of 76 people with TLE, and included two comparison groups, they found no evidence to support the supposed religiosity of people with TLE (Tucker, 1987). Other studies that have controlled for brain damage, psychiatric illness and so on, have also not found a link between religious experience and TLE (see Fenwick, 1996).

In the early 1980s M.A. Persinger started the trail off again with some studies claiming a correlation between (a) the frequency of epileptic signs and (b) the frequency of paranormal and mystical experiences, and a sense of the presence of God (Persinger, 1987). However, the finding of a correlation between the two sets of signs is almost worthless scientifically, because the two sets of questions on which it is based (about seizure experiences and religious experiences) overlapped so much that it was inevitable that a correlation would be found between the two.

Unfortunately, this rather unpromising line of research seems reluctant to die, and it recently reappeared in some newspapers; one carried the headline, '"God Spot" is Found in the Brain'. The report arose from recent research by V.S. Ramachandran (1998), showing that epileptic patients who also had religious preoccupations showed strong physiological responses to religious words. However, the same might well have been true of any religious people, and it does not prove anything about the supposed link between religion and TLE.

There are currently no strong scientific reasons for thinking that religious experience and TLE have a common neural basis. It also seems most unlikely that a neurological theory of religious experience based entirely on the supposed link with TLE will be adequate. Nevertheless, a multi-component neurological theory in which TLE-like mechanisms are just one strand, such as that of Wildman and Brothers (1999) may still have promise.

Another broad area of the brain which has more recently been linked to religious experience is the frontal lobes. They constitute a large area of the brain that is notably well developed in human beings, and which does not seem to be much involved in basic sensory-motor functions. The frontal lobes seem to subserve a variety of high-level cognitive capacities. While there is no question of their being exclusively devoted to religion, it is very likely that religious cognition and experience is among the range of things that they support.

McNamara (in press) has identified some of the non-religious functions of the frontal lobes that are sufficiently close to religion that they suggest the frontal lobes might be linked to religious experience too. They are 'theory of mind' (the attribution of mental powers to another person), the processing of emotional experience, and the capacity for empathy and moral insight. More tentatively, the high-level self-consciousness that seems to be distinctively human, and a fixated adherence to particular beliefs, may also be linked to the frontal lobes.

So far, there is little direct evidence to link the frontal lobes to religious experience, but it is highly likely that there is such a link, and more direct evidence for it will probably be available before long. However, that would not show that the frontal lobes are the exclusive key to religion, and it would certainly not show that religion is 'nothing but' a matter of frontal lobe functioning.

D'Aquili's Theory of the Cognitive Operators

Though ideas about TLE and religion have had the greatest exposure, and ideas about the frontal lobes are coming into fashion, I believe theories that link religion to a particular area of the brain are likely to prove simplistic in the long run. Ultimately, we will probably need a multi-component theory that links different aspects of religion to different parts of the brain. At present, the approach to the neurological basis of religious experience taken by Eugene d'Aquili (1998, 1999) and his colleagues is probably the best example of this kind of approach. Though I will have criticisms to make of his theory, I will begin by recognizing the important ways in which it represents an advance on the idea of a link between religion and epilepsy.

First, d'Aquili has a considered theory, of some sophistication, about the nature of religious experience; he knows what he is trying to explain. Second, his neuroscientific theory is grounded in a comprehensive analysis of the functions of the human brain, in terms of what he calls its 'cognitive operators'. Third, his theory is on the right lines in trying to see how brain processes that subserve more general cognitive functions also have a particular application in the context of religious experience. From an evolutionary point of view, it is more likely that the parts of the brain involved in religion should have other functions as well. Fourth, unlike Persinger, d'Aquili does not see religious consciousness as arising solely from a malfunctioning of the human brain; it would certainly sit uneasily with a theological perspective to suggest that God was dependent on neurological abnormalities to reveal himself.

D'Aquili sees two different cognitive operators as being involved in different facets of religion, the Causal Operator and the Holistic Operator. They subserve different aspects of religion. The Causal Operator is involved in the perception of the world as being controlled by God, and subserves that part of religion that seeks to influence the world through the relationship with God. The Holistic Operator subserves the altered states of consciousness that are an important part of religious experience, especially the sense of unity that is central to mystical experience. These two will need to be considered separately.

In introducing the terms 'Causal Operator' and 'Holistic Operator' we already encounter one of the problems with d'Aquili's approach, as these are not generally accepted terms in neuroscience. In a sense, that is not as worrying as it sounds. There is no generally accepted, comprehensive theory of human cognitive architecture and its neural substrate. Most researchers in cognitive neuroscience are not even interested in formulating a comprehensive model; their interest is only with the neural basis of highly specific cognitive functions. Because of the early stage of scientific work in this field, the functions that have been the chief focus of concern are relatively low-level cognitive ones.

When we turn to looking at the basis of religion in cognitive and neural processes, it is clearly not going to work to consider just a highly specific, localized system. Religion is clearly a high-level aspect of human functioning that involves a broad array of cognitive processes; it seems clear that only a broad and fairly comprehensive theory of human cognitive architecture will provide an adequate account of the neural basis of religion. As there is currently no generally accepted theory of that kind, it is not surprising if researchers, such as d'Aquili, who are grappling with high-level functions, find they need to make up their own comprehensive theory of the cognitive architecture. The relatively unconstrained nature of such theorizing is unattractive scientifically, but currently there is no alternative.

Moreover, I suggest that there is nothing particularly idiosyncratic about d'Aquili's theory of cognitive operators. There are seven of them, the holistic operator, the reductionist operator, the causal operator, the abstractive operator, the binary operator, the formal quantitative operator, and the emotional-value operator. It is a speculative theory of cognition, but it seems as defensible as any other at the present early stage of modelling how the cognitive system works as a whole.

Of the two parts of d'Aquili's theory relevant to religion, I think his treatment of the Holistic Operator is sounder scientifically. One of the more convincing aspects is the way it handles the ceremonial rituals that are an important part of religious practice in many different cultures. D'Aquili draws attention to the way in which rhythmic activity of some kind, whether visual, auditory, tactile or proprioceptive, plays a key role in inducing a mystical sense of unity. He suggests that this leads to a high degree of activation of the sympathetic nervous system, with some spillover into the parasympathetic system, leading to activation of the parietal-occipital region of the non-dominant hemisphere, which is where d'Aquili locates the Holistic Operator. An alternative route by which the Holistic Operator can be activated is the use of meditation. Here it is the parasympathetic system that becomes highly activated, with spillover into the sympathetic system. It is the neurological specificity of this theory that makes it convincing.

The other half of d'Aquili's theory concerns the role of the Causal Operator in subserving the perception of the world as being controlled by God, which he suggests gives the religious practitioner a sense of control over the world. Whereas the Holistic Operator is located on the non-dominant side of the brain, the Causal Operator is located on the dominant side, specifically in the anterior convexity of the frontal lobe, the inferior parietal lobule, and their interconnections. However, this half of d'Aquili's theory seems less well developed, and less impressive in the range of considerations it can handle.

Also, I have serious doubts about the plausibility of a single 'Causal Operator.' The perception and ascription of causality is very varied in the level at which it proceeds. While I am happy to accept that the part of the brain d'Aquili labels the Causal Operator is involved in the ascription of causality, it seems much more doubtful that a single system is responsible for *all* ascriptions of causality. Someone ascribing a 'cause' to a ball they see coming over the garden fence is doing something very different from parents worrying over where they went wrong in bringing up their children, though both are in different ways seeking to ascribe causality. Religious ascriptions of causality are more like the latter, yet I suspect that the more complex the causal ascriptions, the less satisfactorily they can be localized in the Causal Operator.

Perhaps the chief concern about d'Aquili's theory is the range of 'religious experience' to which it is applicable. One of the problems here is that religious experience is so diverse it may indeed be inappropriate to look for a single neural theory of such diverse phenomena. As far as unitive experience is concerned, d'Aquili's theory deals with experience that is deliberately induced by ceremonial ritual or meditation; it does not deal so explicitly with spontaneously occurring mystical experiences, though it has become clear from surveys that such experiences occur to a substantial proportion of the population.

An even more serious limitation of d'Aquili's theory is that mystical experience may not be central to religious beliefs or practices. Much religious practice and experience is concerned neither with causal influence over the world, nor with unitive experience. This is perhaps a point at which the umbrella term 'religious experience' can mislead, because it includes such disparate cognitive and social phenomena.

The ascription of causality to God, and the accompanying sense of control over the world, is perhaps most clearly a feature of the sort of primitive religion studied by social anthropologists. However, it is not clear that this is really what is going on in contemporary Christianity. Belief in God's providence may look and sound like a belief in God's control of the world, and intercessory prayer may look like an attempt to influence this 'controller,' but there are many features of how these 'language games' are played that suggest they are not quite what they seem. Most theologies of prayer generally do not see it as an exercise in controlling the world by influencing God (Brummer, 1984).

It should be noted that I have presented in very condensed form the detailed theory that d'Aquili and his colleagues have evolved over 20 years. It derives much of its scientific credibility from making sense of a wide range of circumstantial considerations surrounding the occurrence of mystical experience. His theory seems to give a plausible account of the neural basis of mystical experience, and is probably the best such theory we have at present. However, these are early days in the investigation of a difficult and complex question, and no one would suggest that we already have the definitive scientific account.

Towards a Multi-level Cognitive Theory

I want now to suggest how theories of the cognitive processes subserving religious consciousness might evolve. In tackling this, there are useful lessons to be learned from theories of the cognitive processes present in emotion. Emotion is a 'high-level' phenomenon of comparable cognitive breadth and generality to religion, and there is a useful scientific analogy to be drawn between religious and emotional experience (Watts, 1996). By 'cognitive' I mean here primarily the structures and processes that shape attention and memory, by which our responses to experience are mediated, and from which our understanding of the world arises. Cognition in this sense is not necessarily conscious, though some cognitive processing may be carried out consciously.

The first generation of cognitive theories of emotion were single-level theories. For example, Gordon Bower developed a theory of the semantic networks subserving emotion (see Williams, Watts, Macleod and Mathews, 1997). The network idea is essentially that each concept is a node in a semantic space, with links to semantically related nodes. Bower suggested that when a particular emotion (for example, anxiety) is activated, the node concerned leads to a degree of activation of associated nodes. Tim Beck developed a similar, but rather less precise theory of emotional 'schemata.' A schema is here a kind of template through which experience is filtered and which may distort it, and from which memories and automatic thoughts may arise (see Williams *et al.*, 1997).

However, it became clear that such single level theories were inadequate. For example, it was unclear whether the emotion nodes in Bower's network theory were concerned with emotional concepts or emotions themselves, and a multi-level theory seemed necessary to handle that distinction better. Also, single level theories were quite unable to handle the clash between different levels which is a common feature of emotions, for example *knowing* that there is nothing to be frightened of, but nevertheless *feeling* frightened. It thus became clear that only multi-level theories would prove adequate, and I suspect that the same will prove to be true of cognitive science theories of religious consciousness.

There are now several multi-level cognitive science theories of emotion in the field (see Williams *et al.*, Chapter 11) and a consensus about them has not yet been reached. However, there is emerging agreement about the different levels of the cognitive system concerned with aspects of cognition relevant to emotion, and I want to suggest that the distinction between them is also relevant to the scientific analysis of religious consciousness.

In the first multi-level cognitive theory of emotion, Howard Leventhal distinguished three basic levels; sensory-motor, conceptual and schematic (Leventhal, 1984). Sensory-motor aspects of emotion are very important; this is reflected, for example, in the way in which people with specific animal phobias develop remarkable perceptual tuning for the relevant stimulus and show a reflex-like response. We are coming to have a good grasp of the neuropsychological processes underlying this lowest cognitive level of emotion, for example in the work of Joseph LeDoux (1996).

The distinction between Leventhal's other two levels (conceptual and schematic) has probably now been made more clearly in terms of John Teasdale and Philip Barnard's model of the cognitive architecture, 'Interacting Cognitive Subsystems' (ICS) (Teasdale and Barnard, 1993). This model is in turn a development of an earlier version of a model that Barnard proposed to handle psycholinguistic data. It is one of the attractive features of the model that it has spawned a very diverse range of applications. ICS is a general model of the cognitive architecture, though it is not yet concerned with the neural substrate. It is often a good scientific strategy to get a fairly clear idea of the requirements of a cognitive model at a functional level before going on to consider brain mechanisms.

ICS proposes a distinction between two different systems in the central engine of cognition, called the Propositional (PROP) and Implicational (IMP) systems. The Implicational system is concerned with abstracting meanings or regularities from various lower level subsystems, and it is from the meanings coded in the Implicational system that emotion arises. These meanings are not coded in conceptual or propositional form, and so cannot be articulated directly. For that, they have to be translated into the different code of the Propositional system. The

Implicational system in humans is presumed to be a development of a similar but less developed subsystem in other species. However, the propositional system seems to be a more distinctively human one, associated with the special human capacity for language. There are many obvious benefits in this human capacity to translate meanings into a form in which they can be articulated.

In terms of this distinction, I would want to argue for the importance in religious cognitive processing of the Implicational system, a subsystem concerned with meanings, albeit at a non-propositional level. Indeed, the discernment of such meanings seems to be at the heart of religion, though it is probably not unique to religion. Another context in which similar cognitive processes seem to operate is the development of insights about oneself in psychotherapy. It is not unusual for important but difficult insights to be glimpsed initially at the level of inarticulate meanings before being recoded in a propositional form capable of articulation.

The suggestion that religious consciousness comes into being initially at this level is consistent with much traditional theology, especially with the apophatic tradition of the unknowability of the transcendent God. However, in the light of what I am proposing here, the apophatic approach to theology takes on a new significance. It can be seen as reflecting, not only the transcendence of God, but also how the cognitive system works in arriving at an understanding of God. When mystics have spoken of the ineffability of God, perhaps they have been talking not only about God's nature but also, at a human level, about how there is a sense of loss as the felt meanings of the Implicational system are recoded in a form in which they can be articulated. The Implicational system is in this sense always somewhat 'transcendent'.

Of course, words and phrases may play an important role in revelatory experience, and the intrinsic ineffability of religious consciousness in no way denies this. Even when a phrase from the scriptures strikes home with revelatory power, there is often a further task of discerning exactly what its significance is for the person concerned in their particular situation. This leads to a kind of 'cross-talk' between verbal, scriptural material encoded in the Propositional system, and the more intuitive grasp of its significance that emerges in the inarticulate code of the Implicational system. Far from calling the distinction between the two systems into question, the role of particular words and phrases in revelatory experiences helps to elucidate the contribution of the two systems and the inter-relationship between them (Watts, 1997).

The Implicational system is essentially concerned with meanings and interpretations, which is likely to include the processes of interpretation that are central to religious consciousness. This relates back to the debate referred to earlier about whether religious experience is to be defined in terms of qualitatively distinct experience, or in terms of the religious style of interpretation of any experience. My own view is that this is a false dichotomy. While accepting the crucial role of interpretation, which I would locate in the operation of the Implicational system, I do not see this as ruling out the possibility of religious experience sometimes having a qualitatively distinct character.

The distinction between the Implicational and Propositional systems may be helpful in formulating discrepancies between different aspects of religious life, just as it is helpful in formulating discrepancies between different aspects of emotion. It seems to be quite common for people who reject religion at an intellectual (propositional) level to be drawn to it at a more intuitive (implicational) level. For example, people who do not 'believe in God' may find themselves praying at times of severe stress. It is perhaps one of the current features of much of Christianity in the developed world that it shows a split between different cognitive levels, with religion making sense intuitively but not intellectually.

These remarks on the role of the Propositional and Implicational systems in religious consciousness clearly do not amount to a complete account of how the cognitive system is involved in religious awareness. Nevertheless, I hope they point towards a new kind of theory that sees religion as hierarchically organized, and recognizes the to and fro between different parts of the overall cognitive system. My guess is that, within a generation, we will have a fairly precise understanding in cognitive science of what Teasdale and Barnard call the Implicational system, and its neural substrate. We might even begin to understand how the Implicational system can operate in accordance with the mind of God. That would be a major step forward in the scientific understanding of religion.

Let me emphasize again that I see this kind of theory as being neutral as far as the reality of religious belief is concerned. A theory of the basis of religious consciousness in the meaning-generating processes of the Implicational System could be coupled with a non-realist view of God; religion could be seen as nothing more than a spin off of the way that our Implicational system functions. On the other hand, it can be taken, in conjunction with a realist view of God, as indicating how we are receptive to revelation of the nature and purpose of God, and his significance for people's lives.

Chapter 7

Religious Experience: Interpretation and Social Context

In this chapter, we will turn from approaches to religious experience from the perspective of cognitive neuroscience to issues about the social construction of religious experience, and the processes of interpretation involved. There have been some vigorous debates in this area, though one of the weaknesses in the way the discussion has been conducted is that no attention has been paid to scientific considerations. I want to suggest that it helps to take the relevant scientific evidence into account, though we are dealing here only with what is judged likely, not with what scientific evidence can prove.

In considering the role of social factors in religious experience, it will also be important to make a distinction between different kinds of religious experience not sufficiently emphasized in the literature. Prepared and involuntary experiences are likely to arise in quite different ways. Some religious experiences arise from deliberate preparations such as those associated with meditation. Such prepared religious experiences are very different from those that appear to arise spontaneously.

Of course, it would be unwise to assume that these apparently unprepared experiences are absolutely unprepared, even though there has been no attempt to prepare for them. They may well arise from unconscious precursors, just as 'sudden' conversions can arise from a long process of gestation, and apparently spontaneous panic attacks can arise from unconscious worries. However, at least they come as a surprise to the people concerned. It seems that involuntary experiences tend to be more powerful than prepared ones. They are also in some ways more difficult to explain, and certainly the social constructionist approach works less well with them.

Social Constructionism

Social constructionists have challenged many of the assumptions about religious experience of 'perennialists' such as William James (1902/1960) and Aldous Huxley (1946) who assumed that religious experiences provided direct insight into the true nature of reality. The debate is complicated because there are actually three distinct issues here that tend to be associated with one another, but are not logically connected.

The first issue, already referred to in the last chapter, is how religious experience should be defined. Social constructionists generally want to define it in terms of the religious interpretative frame of reference, whereas perennialists tend to define it in terms of the distinct content of the experience. That latter approach subdivides further into those who emphasize the distinctive phenomenological quality of the experience, and those who define the experience in terms of the spiritual being or realities experienced.

Next, there is the question of the shaping of religious experience, with social contructionists wanting to emphasize the crucial role of the social context in giving rise to religious experiences. Perennialists, in contrast, often wish to claim that religious experiences are in some important sense 'pure', 'direct', or unmediated, a kind of experience in which people break free, in an exceptional way, from the normal constraints on experience.

Third, there is a debate about universalism, with social constructionists emphasizing that different faith traditions give rise to different patterns of religious experience between, while perennialists emphasize the common elements in religious experience across, traditions. Of course, this is largely a matter of emphasis. There are both common elements and divergencies between the characteristic religious experiences of different traditions, and either one or the other can be emphasized for a particular polemical purpose.

The advocates of a constructionist approach to religious experience such as Steven Katz and Wayne Proudfoot have many good points to make, though they have not gone unchallenged (Forman, 1990). Unfortunately, the debate has become over polarized, largely because people have assumed linkages between positions that are not logically connected (Short, 1995). It seems clear that religious experiences are influenced by cultural background. Everyone seems to agree that there are different emphases among faith traditions in the way experiences are described, and that these reflect, in part, different traditions about religious experiences. The question is how far such points should be pressed, and at what point they lead to a pernicious form of social reductionism. That is not always easy to tell from how views are presented.

The touchstone formulation of the constructionist approach is Katz's (1978) essay in the volume he edited on *Mysticism and Philosophical Analysis*. He makes his main assertion clear:

> There are No pure (that is, unmediated) experiences. Neither mystical experience nor more ordinary forms of experience give any indication, or any grounds for believing, that they are unmediated. That is to say, *all* experience is processed through, organized by, and makes itself available to us in extremely complex epistemological ways (p. 26).

This assertion seems likely to be correct, given what we know in general about cognitive processes.

Katz emphasizes the radical differences between reports of mystical experiences in different faith traditions, something that would be widely accepted as correct. He also emphasizes the methodological importance of attending fully to the context in which religious experiences occur, not just to the reports of those experiences. Again, the merit of doing so would, I think, be generally accepted. Katz is right to challenge the over sharp division between experience and interpretation made by many theorists, and to emphasize that interpretative processes are often integral to experience itself. By the time something becomes an experience it must already, to some extent, have been interpreted.

Despite the merit of Katz's point about the normal role of interpretation in experience, his position about religious experience is unnecessarily extreme. He fails to consider at all what seems a likely possibility, that religious experience, though not wholly unmediated, is *relatively* unmediated. It may arise from an attempt to free oneself from the usual processes of cognitive mediation. Religious experience may be less subject to background contextual factors than most ordinary experiences. That possibility is much more difficult to refute than the extreme claim that religious experience is absolutely unmediated.

Thus, the debate about whether or not religious experience is unmediated tends to go to extremes. Some claim that it is absolutely unmediated; others claim that it is as much mediated through background cultural and cognitive processes as any other experience. The real possibility that religious experience, especially the prepared forms that arise in the context of meditation, are less constrained by background cultural and cognitive and processes than most experiences, though not absolutely free of such influences, is a plausible one that deserves to have more advocates than it has had.

The key question is just how much influence contextual factors have on religious experiences. In at least one place, Katz is commendably cautious about this. He says that a Hindu mystic does not have an experience of something or other that is subsequently interpreted in a Hindu way, but rather the experience 'is itself the, *at least partially*, preformed, anticipated Hindu experience of Braham'. Similarly, the Christian mystic 'has the *at least partially* prefigured Christian experience of God' (p. 26, my italics in both cases). If that is indeed Katz's position, it is clearly not the extreme social constructionism that would assert that religious experiences are 'nothing but' the product of social circumstances. Such a position is taken up by Gimello (1978) in an article in the same book as Katz's own essay, which claims that mysticism is 'simply the psychosomatic enhancement' of religious beliefs. Katz's more cautious formulation of 'at least partial' predetermination by religious context leads to the question of just what other factors apart from that context he is allowing, and how they interact with the religious context. He gives no guidance on that.

Wayne Proudfoot (1985), in another influential discussion of these matters, adopts elements of Katz's position, but in a less extreme way. He shares Katz's critique of a totally unmediated core of religious experience, but disagrees with him about the separate issue of common elements in religious experience across cultures, '... there do seem to be expressions, experiential reports and practices that are sufficiently similar across different traditions to warrant the use of the term *mysticism* and attention to some common characteristics' (p. 24). He goes on to emphasize that the questions of commonality and mediation are different. 'One can employ the results of phenomenological analyses without subscribing to the conviction that these represent some fundamental uninterpreted experience' (p. 124).

Proudfoot also differs from Katz over how to interpret some of the classic ways of describing mystical experience, such as *ineffable* and *noetic*. Proudfoot steers a middle course between those like William James who regard them as describing a 'simple unanalysable characteristic of the experience' (p. 125) and those like Katz who dismiss such claims as simply misleading. Proudfoot suggests that they are quite precise and helpful terms, not to be simply dismissed, but that they serve to *constitute* an experience as mystical, rather than to *describe* it. In other words, it is because people regard particular experiences as being ineffable and noetic that those experiences are deemed mystical. Proudfoot dissociates himself from Katz's view that there is a causal link between antecedent beliefs and mystical experience. For Proudfoot, 'the connection between a mystic's antecedent beliefs and his experience is not a causal one but a conceptual one' (p. 123). Each of these differences between Katz and Proudfoot take the latter further away from strong social reductionism about mystical experience.

Another related critique, focusing specifically on William James's approach to religious experience, has come from Nicholas Lash (1988). I will not concern myself here with the intriguing question of how James, author of *Principles of Psychology*, and someone who understood perfectly well how experiences are shaped by cognitive processes, came to the view that religious experiences are 'pure', or what he meant by that puzzling claim (though see Watts, 1996). In the course of rejecting James's approach, Lash makes clear his own position that no experience can be pure religious experience, and regrets James's over sharp division between thoughts and feelings.

Like many of James's critics, from von Hugel onwards, Lash laments James's emphasis on the individual, and claims that what is primary is 'the public world of culture and its institutions' (p. 58). But in what sense is the public world primary? Certainly, there are powerful social and cultural influences on personal experience, but must it not also be the case that the public world is built up from how individuals function? James's emphasis on the individual certainly seems unbalanced on this question. However, in asserting the primacy of the public world, Lash is perhaps in danger of becoming unbalanced in the opposite direction. Claims of 'primacy' are notoriously difficult to defend. I would myself prefer to emphasize the 'to and fro' between private and public worlds rather than attempt to claim the primacy of either.

Yet another critique of the perennialist approach to mystical experience has alerted us to the danger of misreading classic mystical texts as being mainly a description of experience. Don Cupitt (1998) has provided an accessible statement of this kind of position, though much the most scholarly and subtle version of it is Denys Turner's (1995) *The Darkness of God*. Cupitt reminds us of the dangers of misreading the classic mystical treatises through the eyes of twentieth-century preoccupations with personal experience. Cupitt also emphasizes that we need to remember the mystics were writers and theologians of a particular kind, and we need to pay attention to the social function of their alternative theological tradition within the Christian world. All these are helpful points.

As is so often the case with such re-readings, the positive points about what has been neglected are more convincing than the negative ones about what is not to be found in classic mystical texts. There is a danger of replacing an anachronistic 'modern' reading, with its overemphasis on personal experience, with an equally anachronistic postmodern one with an overemphasis on language. However, the point is well taken that the path of spiritual development mystics such as St Teresa are describing in her *Interior Castle* is more than a path of *experience*.

There is an interesting ambiguity about whether 'religious experience' is the best term for what is being described. It could equally well be described as a religious 'reaction' or 'state'. Experience is no doubt part of what is being referred to, but that term describes it in a slightly unbalanced, and potentially misleading way. There is a similar ambiguity about whether emotions are experiences, reactions or states. In fact, they seem to have elements of all three. It is a shame that we do not have a noun for 'religious somethings', comparable to the noun 'emotions'. The fact that 'religious' is an adjective forces us all the time to link it to some noun or other, and whichever is chosen is not entirely appropriate.

It is also important to remember that the study of religious or mystical experience is not, in the end, constrained by classic historical texts. Even if it were shown conclusively that particular historical texts were not really describing a path of experience, there remain questions about the nature of religious experience in our own time. Human religious consciousness may have evolved, and there may be a kind of religious experience in our own time which, despite initial appearances, does not have an exact historical counterpart. There are other methods of studying mysticism besides the study of the classic mystical texts, such as the empirical research methods of the modern human sciences.

Empirical Research

The debate that has been reviewed so far is largely a philosophical one, though it contains assumptions about psychological processes. Indeed, the social constructionist approach really arises from a basic assumption about how, as a matter of empirical fact, all experience arises, including religious experience. It is therefore relevant to bring psychology to bear on the debate more explicitly, as a way of examining the prevailing assumptions.

A convenient place to begin is with empirical research that bears fairly directly on the debate about religious experience, even though, as we will see, that research is somewhat inconclusive. It is hard to get any empirical purchase on the debate about religious experience, largely because what is at issue are interpretations, even ideologies, rather than the facts. However, it is instructive in exploring what the debate is really about to see how far empirical research might be relevant.

One interesting issue is the relationship between religious belief and religious experience. Are people with strong religious convictions more likely to have religious experiences, or are such experiences independent of personal belief? Of course, it depends on how religious experience is defined; the narrower the definition of religious experience (that is, the more strictly it is defined as an experience that is described in religious terms), the tighter the link between belief and experience is likely to be.

One of the now classic surveys is that of David Hay (1987) at the Religious Experience Research Unit at Oxford, which took a broad definition of religious experience. Participants were asked 'Have you ever been aware of, or influenced by, a presence or power, whether you call it God or not, which is different from your everyday self?' Such a question is deliberately framed in a way that even an atheist could answer 'yes' to. In fact, 24 per cent of 'atheists and agnostics' said they had had such an experience. That was less than in the population as a whole (36 per cent), but still a sizeable proportion. It is a debatable point whether all the experiences reported in answer to Hay's question were 'religious'. It depends what is meant by a religious experience.

Some might be impressed by the lower frequency of religious experiences in atheists and agnostics than the rest of the population; others might be impressed by the fact the proportion was still substantial. That so many atheists and agnostics have 'religious' experiences, albeit broadly defined, might be thought to challenge social constructionists' assumptions. However, there is also the point that we live in a culture in which religious beliefs are prevalent, whatever the position of individual might be. On that argument, it might take a completely secular society before the frequency of religious experiences fell to zero.

Another line of research of potential relevance is that of Ralph Hood and his colleagues (see Hood *et al.*, 1996, p. 256ff.), who have examined the structure of responses to a questionnaire about mystical experience, the *Mysticism Scale*. The wording of the 32 items of the questionnaire was influenced by Stace's (1960) conceptualization of mysticism, and the factor analysis of responses to the questionnaire successfully recovered his conceptualization. It may be tempting to dismiss that as a case of researchers just finding what they had set themselves up to find. However, it should be noted that factor-analytic studies of questionnaire responses by no means always recover empirically the intended structure; it is a significant achievement when a factor-analysis produces the hoped for result.

Hood's research lends some support to the distinction between experience and interpretation. His original research found that the items in the questionnaire fell into two groups (or factors): one focused mainly on the experience of unity and reflected minimal religious interpretation; the other embodied religious and theological claims about the experience in a more obvious way. In subsequent research, the minimal interpretation factor was replaced by two distinct factors concerned with extrovert and introvert aspects of mysticism respectively (the unity of the world, and an experience of pure consciousness or 'no-thing-ness' respectively). However, for present purposes, the interesting fact is the questionnaire items fell into two clusters according to how obviously interpretative they were. This is consistent with a two-factor theory of a core of minimally interpreted experience, and another distinct element of religious interpretation. It is also interesting that churchgoing was more closely related to the obviously interpretative factor than to the less interpretative one.

Of course, such research is only suggestive, and how items in a questionnaire correlate with one another is only a pointer to the nature of religious experience. A questionnaire such as the Mysticism Scale may be a better guide to habits of describing experience than to the nature of the experience itself. Thus, the factor that looks as though it reflects minimal interpretation may actually reflect one particular approach to the interpretation of religious experience, and perhaps one that depends as much as anything else on cultural context and traditions of talking about religious experience. While such considerations may weaken the conclusions that can be drawn from the research, the structure of responses to the Mysticism Scale is at least consistent with the idea that mystical experience consists of a minimally interpreted core, and a religiously conditioned outer belt of interpretation.

Another possible way in which to explore these issues is to try to replicate something like mystical experience in the laboratory, and the most celebrated research of that kind is Arthur Deikman's (1966) 'blue vase' research. The research was conducted on 'naive' American college students, who entered a bare room with a blue a vase in it. They were asked not to think about the vase discursively, but simply to focus their attention on it. They reported a variety of strange perceptions such as the colour becoming intense, the shape changing, the vase becoming less separate from themselves, and so on. Deikman compares these reports to those in *The Cloud of Unknowing*, which is surely an exaggerated comparison. However, it is striking that such a simple procedure produced sensations that were at all what one might expect if the normal cognitive processes by which experiences are constructed had begun to break down. It lends credence to the claim that a more radical deconstruction might occur in experienced meditators.

Theoretical Psychology

We will turn now to implications of general theoretical psychology for current debates about the role of interpretation in religious experience. The first point to note is that psychology generally supports the point that experience is not raw or uninterpreted. This point, which has normally been made philosophically, can equally well be made in terms of what psychologists have learned about how experience is cognitively constructed. The points that cognitive psychologists make about the role of 'construction' in experience are parallel to those made by philosophers about the role of 'interpretation'. The information we gather about the world is not neutral 'view from nowhere' information, but selected and processed in terms of the kind of environment we have experienced previously, coloured by our memories, and so on. This role of cognitive processing in shaping experience is at the heart of contemporary experimental psychology.

Nevertheless, information is not always fully processed when it is first experienced. People often continue the process of interpretation well after the initial experience is over. For example, people sometimes experience powerful feelings they do not at first know how to describe. The best documented examples of this occur in psychotherapy where, at key moments of self-discovery, or when people are on the brink of recalling some critical repressed experience, they may experience powerful feelings before the content of them has become fully clear. Another somewhat different example is where people have had some very upsetting or threatening experience that calls for a good deal of 'emotional processing' or 'working through' before the experience can be assimilated. Again, a good deal of psychotherapy is taken up with such processing of difficult experiences. Here the nature of the experience is already clear, but the process of interpretation can be a long-term one.

The analogy between the processing of emotional and religious experiences is a helpful one. It is one of the interesting features of Wayne Proudfoot's approach that he draws on modern scientific theories of emotion in his approach to religious experience. The link between religion and emotion dates back at least to Schleiermacher (1768–1834), the so-called 'father of modern theology', and is also apparent in William James (1842–1910). It is perhaps worth emphasizing that what is being suggested here is not, like Schleiermacher, that feelings are the base from which religious experience arises or, like James, that feelings are the essence of religion. Rather, the proposal is the more modest one that there are helpful parallels to be drawn between the psychologies of emotional and religious experience (see Watts, 1996).

Proudfoot makes particular use of Schachter's (1964) 'two-factor' theory that emotional states arise from a conjunction of physiological state and social context. On this theory, physiology tends to determine *how* emotional people feel, whereas the social context of experiences affects *which* emotion is experienced. Thus, high levels of adrenaline can enhance whatever emotion is being experienced, whereas aspects of the context, such as what kind of film you are watching, can determine whether you feel anxious or euphoric. This line of theorizing, stemming from Schachter, has by now become considerably more complex, though it is still a helpful first approximation. Schachter's approach to emotion suggests a similar approach to mysticism, one in which social context plays a significant role, but is not all determining.

There are other aspects of the modern psychological approach to the emotions, not mentioned by Proudfoot, that are even more relevant to current questions about religious experience. Especially interesting is the debate stemming from Zajonc (1980) and Lazarus (1982) about whether emotional/affective states are shaped by cognitive processes *or* whether they precede them and are independent of them. This closely parallels the debate about whether there can be an unmediated core to religious experience. The fact that a distinguished psychologist like Zajonc has argued affect is independent of cognition implies at the very least the parallel position that religious experience is independent of cognition deserves serious consideration. It is not something so absurd as to be simply laughed out of court.

With hindsight (for example, Lazarus, 1999), and despite the vigour and quality of the debate, a number of confusions were obviously involved in this debate. One key one, as I argued in my own contribution (Watts, 1983) is what is meant by 'cognition'. It is a highly ambiguous term, that can mean either the processing of information that proceeds tacitly and without conscious awareness, *or* conscious, reflective thought processes. I suggest that Zajonc was right in arguing affective responses can arise with reflex-like rapidity, without any conscious reflection. However, Lazarus was also right to emphasize the extent to which emotional reactions are shaped by implicit processes of appraisal.

So, could religious experience be independent of cognition? It depends what you mean by cognition. It seems entirely plausible that religious experiences sometimes arise without conscious reflection, especially those that arise with apparent spontaneity. However, that is not to say either affective or mystical experiences can arise without being tacitly influenced by background concepts, assumptions or prior learning. Religious experience may be unmediated by conscious reflection, but it is much more doubtful whether it can avoid being shaped by tacit information processing.

This issue can be sharpened up in the light of the hierarchical approach to religious experience developed in the last chapter, in which a distinction was made between the deep-level 'implicational' meaning system, and the propositional system that can more readily be translated into linguistically encoded thoughts. It is very hard to see that any religious experience could bypass the implicational system. Indeed, much religious experience, the sense of unity for example, is clearly concerned with the kind of discernment of meaning that is characteristic of the implicational system. On the other hand, religious experience may well not initially involve the propositional system. In these terms, when the suggestion is made that religious experience is independent of cognition or mediation, the point is probably that the propositional system is not involved.

Seen in this light, the question is not whether or not cognition, or mediation, is involved in religious experience, but what kind of cognition is involved. In religious experience, there may well be a somewhat unusual, though not unique, decoupling of the levels of cognition represented by the implicational and propositional systems. If such decoupling occurs, it becomes even more important to make the relevant distinctions, so as to be clear which aspects of cognition are involved and which are not. The debate about the role of interpretation in religious experience has been vitiated by a failure to make the kind of distinctions about different levels of cognition that modern cognitive psychology is establishing.

The debate has also failed to make the equally important distinction between deliberately prepared and apparently spontaneous experiences. The significance of that distinction can now also be clarified. Though some powerful religious experiences arise without prior conscious reflection, it is very unlikely that they come from nowhere. The case is probably similar to apparently spontaneous panic attacks, which normally arise from cognitive processes that are not fully conscious. Similarly, the likelihood is that apparently spontaneous religious experiences arise from prior cognitive processes that have been proceeding outside conscious awareness, at some deep cognitive level, such as the implicational system. It also seems likely that such apparently spontaneous experiences are less powerfully shaped by traditions of interpretation than those that arise in the context of meditation, or at least that any such shaping proceeds at a different level in the cognitive system. The social constructionist approach has failed to argue its case convincingly in connection with apparently spontaneous experiences.

The predominant view that has emphasized the role of interpretative processes in religious experience has tended to take a reductionist turn. The tendency has been to argue, or at least imply, that because religious experiences can be seen as arising from social context and processes of interpretation, it need not be accepted as a genuinely religious experience. Up to a point, that is reasonable. If the claim is only that apparently religious experiences *need* not be seen as such, it is perfectly fair. Other explanations are available. However, it would be wholly unwarranted to go further and argue that, because of the role of social experience and human interpretation, apparently religious experiences *cannot* be seen as genuinely religious.

The point here is exactly parallel to that made in the last chapter about the role of brain processes in religious experience. The fact that brain processes are involved cannot be taken as showing that religious experiences are 'nothing but' the spin off of brain processes. Equally, the fact that socially grounded processes of interpretation are often involved cannot be taken as showing that religious experience is 'nothing but' a spin-off of them. In both cases, there is also a theological point to be made. The physical brain is part of God's creation, but so in a different sense are the social world and the human capacity for interpretation. There is no reason to think that God would seek to bypass them in revealing himself.

This raises the question of whether, and in what sense, religious experience can be regarded as a 'social construction'. It is clear, that religious experiences are shaped by social and cultural factors, and that accounts of them are especially influenced by cultural traditions about religious experience. In that sense, religious experiences can indeed be regarded as social constructions. However, it would be a completely different position to argue that they are wholly determined by cultural factors, or that no room was left for any other influences. Here as elsewhere, greedy, 'nothing but' forms of social constructionism are to be resisted.

The Interpretative Task

While resisting the view that religious experience is 'nothing but' a culturally conditioned way of interpreting experiences, the current emphasis on interpretation is highly significant. Though this emphasis has often been pursued in a reductionist way it has broader implications. If we suggest that religious experience depends to a considerable extent on interpretation, this interpretative process is of considerable practical, spiritual importance.

The process of interpretation has probably been of considerable importance for many of the classic mystical writers. Mark (2000) argues this in an interesting way for St John of the Cross. St John carried out several revisions of some of his texts, which gives the scholar the opportunity to study the process of revision and to garner clues about the process of mystical development. Mark suggests that mystical experiences elicit a process of interpretation. The experience, and its progressive reinterpretation, change the mystic and bring about mystical 'development'. That development in turn influences susceptibility to further experiences. It is a plausible and interesting hypothesis that emphasizes the important role that interpretation plays in mystical development.

Let us briefly try to put this emphasis on interpretation in long term historical context, anticipating points about the evolution of consciousness that I will discuss fully in Chapter 9. Some of the issues about religious experience that arise in our own time may stem from the fact that our habitual modes of consciousness are somewhat different from those that obtained when the classical religious traditions such as Christianity became established. It seems likely that there have been long-term historical changes in the nature of consciousness, and that these changes affect the kind of religious experience people have, or indeed to whether they have religious experience at all.

In particular, there seems to have been a gradual change in the extent to which the outside world has been *felt* to be distinct from an inner, subjective one (Watts and Williams, 1988, Chapter 7). Our present way of sensing and conceptualizing things, in which the inner world is seen as sharply distinct from an outer one, is not how things have to be, and probably not how they used to be (Combs, 1995). The sense of separateness from an external world seems to have increased sharply around the seventeenth century. At that time there came into being a 'spectorial' consciousness (Lash, 1996) or 'onlooker' consciousness (Davy, 1961). The story since then, though it has involved some complex twists and turns, is roughly one of a gradually increasing sense of interiority (Logan, 1987).

This increasing sense of separateness from the environment has been intertwined with linguistic changes that appear to go back much further than the dawn of the modern period. Many linguistic terms seem to have begun by being 'double aspect' terms, referring both to something in the external world and to an aspect of conscious experience. However, the tendency has been for words to come to refer to something inner or something outer, but not to both (Watts and Williams, 1988, Chapter 9). This is of considerable theological interest in view of the extent to which religious experience often links the inner and the outer. A word such as 'light' continues to function in religious discourse as a 'double aspect' term. The erosion of double-aspect language, and the increasing sense of separateness of inner from outer, seems to have made religious experience of the traditional kind much less available to us in the modern world. (There will be further discussion in Chapter 11 of the significance for contemporary theology of this erosion of double-aspect thinking.)

In addition, we also live now in what can be called the age of the 'enactive' mind (Varela *et al.*, 1991). We have become aware of how active our minds are in constructing our experience. This has become clear from scientific research in cognitive psychology. The continental philosophical tradition of 'hermeneutics' is making a similar point. Yet another facet of this change is the tendency, to which Craig (1987, p. 229) has drawn attention, for 'practical concepts to invade areas previously thought of as purely theoretical', something that he calls the 'practice ideal'.

Of course, it is hard to be sure whether some of the changes that have apparently taken place have been merely literary or philosophical ones, or whether they were more basic phenomenological changes. We can only infer the consciousness of past ages from the material they have bequeathed to us. However, I am inclined to suspect there really have been changes of consciousness. Indeed, experience is so much shaped by how we *think*, it is hard to see how changing ways of thinking could leave actual experience unaffected.

For those who value religious experience, the question is what forms of religious experience are available to a consciousness in which double-aspect thinking has been replaced by an enactive mind. In general terms, it will clearly be a kind of experience in which the work of interpretation plays a key place. I would suggest that it is a critical feature of religious consciousness that it involves a sense of close linkage between the inner and outer. However, in the contemporary world, this link will probably have to be achieved in a way that is quite different from that which obtained in old double-aspect thinking. For the enactive mind, such a link can probably only be achieved 'enactively', through a deliberate process of interpretation.

So I return to endorsing, in a rather different way from Katz *et al.*, the role of interpretation in religious experience. However, as I see it, enactive, interpretation-based, religious consciousness is largely a possibility or an ideal. It is not yet a widespread reality; the challenge is to make it one. It is an implication of the social constructionists' emphasis on the importance of interpretation in religious experience that such experience often needs to be deliberately sought and created. In this sense, the balance between prepared and unprepared experience may be changing.

Conclusion

This way of approaching the role of interpretation in religious experience is not reductionist. I have steered away from the strong social reductionism of Katz and Proudfoot, without going to the other extreme of postulating absolute pure religious experience. A likely position is that religious experience is less dependent on established constructions than most other experience. This view has at least enough empirical and theoretical plausibility to warrant being taken seriously. It accepts, in a moderate way, the social contructionists' emphasis on the importance of interpretation in some religious experience, especially that which occurs as the result of deliberate preparation.

I would not want to pit this view of religious experience as an act of human interpretation against theological accounts that see it as a gift of God. Rather, I would want to hold together, as complementary discourses about religious experience, a theological discourse about it being the awareness of the presence of God, and a more natural discourse about it arising from the human work of interpretation. It makes no sense to insist on choosing between these two discourses about religious consciousness.

Chapter 8

Divine Action and Human Experience

This chapter will carry forward the discussion of religious experience from the last two chapters, and examine its implications for revelation and divine action. It is the first of three chapters that will examine specific topics in Christian doctrine in a psychologically informed way.

There has recently been enormous interest in divine action, and the questions of whether and how it can be reconciled with modern science. It has been the focus of an important series of volumes edited by Robert J. Russell and his colleagues (Russell *et al.*, 1993; 1995; 1998; 1999). The relation between divine action and science has also been admirably reviewed by Nicholas Saunders (in press). A key question is how God could possibly act in the natural world, and in particular whether there is sufficient causal openness in the world for God to act without suspending the laws of nature. Some have seen quantum indeterminacy as providing the crucial justification for thinking this is possible. Others have based their position on a more general understanding of the 'laws' of nature not being absolutely determinative, and especially on the unpredictability of complex phenomena that has been the focus of 'chaos theory'. For technical reasons set out by Saunders, I think it is very difficult to hang divine action on quantum indeterminacy in a coherent way, and I would myself prefer to rely on more general considerations about the openness of the world.

An important general issue about divine action concerns the relationship between general and special providence (see Langford, 1981). A central task for theology here is to find an appropriate way of balancing God's general upholding of the world with God's influential presence through particular events. There are strategic choices here. There is no great difficulty in squaring at least a weak view of general providence, which emphasizes the orderliness of the world, with modern science. However, that leaves a great deal of work to be done in giving an account of special providence that is scientifically credible and theologically adequate. The general approach I would like to take to this problem is to try to develop as strong a view of general providence as possible, and then to see special providence as arising as far as possible (albeit not entirely) out of general providence.

For this proposal to have any kind of plausibility, a richer account of general providence will be needed than is sometimes given. It will need to be one that allows more scope for the purposes of God than, for example, just seeing his faithfulness reflected in the orderliness of nature. If we are prepared to postulate general propensities in nature that reflect God's creative, redeeming purposes, many of the events that appear to be specific providences can be seen as particular manifestations of those general propensities.

The distinction between general and specific providence is often made too sharply, as though God acted in two different ways. It is better seen as a distinction between different manifestations of God's continuing activity. In one case the emphasis is placed on the broad sweep of that activity, in the other case it is focused on particular events. It is more an epistemological distinction between different perspectives on God's activity, than a taxonomy of different ways in which God can act.

Of course, there is work to be done in reconciling an expanded view of general providence with modern science. However, there are strong theological reasons for challenging a view of the world as merely orderly, but purposeless. The 'fine-tuning' of the universe is one key place to look for scientific support for a strong, rich view of God's general providence. Another would be the underlying propensities of evolutionary biology. Though there is strong resistance to suggesting that evolution followed a fixed or predictable path, I argued in Chapter 2 that it is reasonable to see it as reflecting a general trend towards the capacities for information processing that have made possible the relationships of human beings to each other and to God.

Providence and Persons

Though it is important to keep a steady connection between general and specific providence, it may not be possible to sideline the problem of special providence in this way entirely. Theology certainly requires some scope for God to act in relation to specific events in the world. I wish to propose that all specific providences that really *must* be handled as such arise in connection with human beings, rather than with the rest of the created, natural world.

Some of the key events that Christians would wish to handle in terms of specific providence relate to the unique figure of Jesus Christ, others relate to ordinary human beings. Perhaps the strongest candidate in the Judeo-Christian tradition for an event in the *non*-human world that calls for an interpretation in terms of specific providence is the crossing of the Red Sea by the Israelites. However, it would perhaps not do violence to the core tenets of Christian belief to regard the crossing of the Red Sea as mythological, though that is not true for the salvific events surrounding Jesus Christ, I suggest that a rich view of general providence makes it unnecessary to offer any distinct account of non-human special providences; specific providence can be confined to God's influence on human beings.

The focus of this chapter will thus not be on God's action in the natural world, but on God's action in relation to people. There has often been a recognition that different issues arise when divine action is considered in different domains. For example, Austin Farrer (1967/1988) distinguished between action in physical creation, individual human minds, and public history. Sometimes, there has been a particular emphasis on God's action in relation to the human mind, on the assumption that it involved fewer problems of credibility than divine action in relation to physical creation (for example, Bartholomew, 1984, p. 143). Similarly, some commentators have seen the core miracles of Jesus as being those focusing on the human mind, and the 'nature' miracles as being later embellishments (Kasper, 1976). If the credibility of divine action in relation to minds is established, then the perception of divine action in physical creation could perhaps be handled as a particular psychological interpretation of physical events, perhaps even one inspired by God.

Why is it felt that God would be able to act more easily in relation to the human mind than to physical creation? Partly because, as we saw in Chapter 3, God has often been thought of as like a mind. Though that analogy has its problems, God is no doubt more like a mind than a physical object. It is also sometimes imagined, as Pailin (1989, p. 145f.) discerned, that the human mind is a safe refuge from the laws of nature. However, the idea that the human mind is somehow outside nature is an illusion that must be discarded (Polkinghorne, 1994, p. 69).

Given the close intertwining of mind and brain that we discussed generally in Chapter 3, and specifically in relation to religious experience in Chapter 5, God could not act in relation to the human mind without acting in relation to the physical brain, and the brain is part of the natural world. There may be doubt about how far the physical brain determines mental experience, and certainly about how far the latter can be reduced to the former, but that is really no help. The mind could only be regarded as a separate domain to which God had access, without involving the natural order in any way, if a very radical form of mind-brain dualism were adopted.

It is necessary to guard against a misinterpretation of what I am proposing here. There is no complete separation of the human world from the world of nature. Human beings arise within, and are part of, nature. I have already emphasized that all human experience is grounded in the brain, which is part of the material world. Nevertheless, in human beings, material processes are operating in the new context of the distinctive mental life to which they give rise. Narrowing the task of providing an account of special providence to human beings changes the scientific and theological nature of the task, and makes it more manageable.

The distinction I want to make in the discussion of divine action is not between mind and nature, but between people and the rest of the natural order. Though human beings have arisen from the natural world, and remain part of it, they have powers that transcend it, and so questions of divine action arise in a different form in relation to people. In some ways they come into sharper focus. When divine action is considered in relation to the physical sciences, or to evolution, we are grappling with the rationality of faith, with whether it is credible in our contemporary scientific world to believe in a God who is active in his creation. However, when we come to the relationship between divine action and people, we are also dealing with the credibility of daily religious life and practice, in particular with the prayerful relationship of Christian people to the God in whom they believe.

It is a bedrock Christian assumption that there is a God with whom people can have some kind of communion and that, through prayer and meditation, they can enter into some kind of relationship with God. It is assumed that people's thoughts can become attuned to God, that they can open themselves to God's influence, and that they can, in some measure, discern God's will. The question is how these assumptions square with the scientific study of mind and brain.

Another, more theological, way of putting the special issues that arise when divine action is considered in relation to people is to say that, in this context, divine action cannot be considered in isolation from revelation. Divine action in relation to the natural world would presumably not involve revelation. However, because human beings are capable of receiving revelation, it is to be expected that God would normally choose to act in relation to people by revealing himself to them. God would be expected to interact with each aspect of creation in a way that made use of the highest capacities available. That means that questions about the scientific credibility of God's *action* in relation to human beings are intertwined with questions about how he *reveals* himself to human beings.

It is not being suggested that God's action in relation to individual human beings is absolutely restricted to their conscious awareness of his action. God could presumably act in relation to people who, through incapacity, had no conscious awareness of anything. However, it seems that God's action in relation to people is particularly powerful and effective when they are conscious of that action and acknowledge it. The same point can be expressed differently by saying that God can act in relation to people more effectively when they believe in him, though disbelief does not take them altogether outside the orbit of divine providence.

I assume, on general theological grounds, that God would normally choose to influence people by revealing Godself in ways that they could understand. The experiences by which they become aware of God's nature and will can be called 'revelatory' experiences. Such experiences are likely to be extremely diverse phenomenologically. If the distinction is made between religious and mystical experiences (see Chapter 5), either might be involved. God might exercise influence through experiences that were in no way unusual phenomenologically, but defined by the religious mode of interpretation employed. Equally, God might work through powerful unitive experiences, though I would certainly not wish to suggest that God's influence on people was confined to such experiences. Of course, the diversity of religious or revelatory experience complicates the business of relating them to the psychological sciences because, if the experiences are heterogeneous, so also will be the cognitive, neurological and social processes that underpin them.

A more explicitly Trinitarian way of highlighting the distinctive issues that arise when considering divine action in relation to human beings is to say that when we are concerned with providence in relation to human beings, we are thinking primarily of the Spirit. In contrast, when divine action is considered in relation to the physical sciences or to evolution, we are focusing primarily on the activity of the Father; we see 'footprints' of the work of the Father in the created order. Enlightenment 'natural theologians' were even tempted to say that you could observe evidence of God. I think it would now be widely accepted that talk of 'observation' and 'evidence' in this context is not quite appropriate, because it discounts the crucial contribution of faith, reverence and prayerful reflection in discerning the footprints of God in the world (Lash, 1996, Chapter 4). However, it is interesting that the work of the Father Creator comes close enough to being observable for this mistake to be credible.

The work of the Spirit is known chiefly through human experience, both individual and collective. Indeed, the Spirit becomes known to people chiefly through their cooperation with him, and attempts to 'observe' or 'demonstrate' the work of the Spirit are even more misplaced here than they are with the Father. The Spirit is known primarily through obedient action. Acquaintance with him is primarily enactive knowing, and only secondarily propositional knowing. The cognitive neurosciences are especially relevant to understanding how this enactive knowledge of the Spirit might proceed. I will return to this in the final section of the chapter in which I consider the phenomenon of conscience.

Mind, Brain and Divine Action

I suggest, on general philosophical and theological grounds, that God's influence on people should be seen as operating holistically. One can conceive of God exercising some kind of highly specific influence on people, affecting their thoughts, actions or brain-processes in some discrete way. However, it seems both more likely scientifically, and more theologically congenial, that God would want to relate to us as the integrated physical-mental-spiritual creatures that we are. God's relationship to us should therefore not be seen as *purely* spiritual.

On the other hand, I would not want to go to the other extreme of suggesting that God somehow 'tweaks' people's brain processes, or controls their behaviour in ways that do not fully respect their personhood. That would be repugnant theologically and scientifically. When God acts in relation to people, or reveals himself to them, we should expect this to be reflected in, and mediated through, all levels of our personhood, including brain processes, cognitive processes, phenomenal experience, and observable behaviour.

Nevertheless, there are questions about how best to describe God's actions in relation to people. It is in the nature of human experience and action that multiple descriptions are always available. Let us now consider how best to describe those special experiences and actions through which God reveals himself to people, and acts in relation to them. Because mind and brain act as a unity, it never makes sense to ask which is responsible for a particular outcome, with the implication that the other was not involved at all. However, there is a useful sense in which some explanatory factors for any particular event can be regarded as primarily physical and others as primarily mental.

There is an important set of arguments here that is not always given sufficient weight by eliminative materialists. There are actions and interventions that occur primarily at the level of mind or action, and can only occur at that level if they are to have demonstrable efficacy. One interesting example arises in the rehabilitation of neurological patients and concerns the benefit of rehearsing particular actions. There are two possible discourses about such actions. The first is a discourse about mere bodily movement that could in principle be described in mechanical terms, the second is a discourse about human action, a discourse that is always implicitly intentional. The interesting fact is that it makes a great deal of difference whether rehabilitation patients seek to rehearse implicitly intentional actions or whether they merely rehearse the corresponding mechanical movements. As Marcel (1992) has pointed out, the former result in measurably better progress in rehabilitation.

There is a helpful analogy here with the relationship between natural and theological discourse. Though I reject the idea that some events fall wholly into the natural realm and others wholly into the theological realm, there may nevertheless be some events for which the natural discourse is primary and others for which the theological discourse is primary. Just as revising for an examination needs to be seen primarily as a mental activity rather than as a brain exercise, and just as rehabilitation needs to be approached as the rehearsal of actions rather than of mere movements, so there may be some events that particularly need to be conceptualized in theological rather than natural terms if they are to be described adequately. Indeed, it may be the case that there is a certain efficacy in seeing things theologically. Possibilities may arise when the world is conceptualized theologically that do not arise if it is conceptualized naturally.

This approach would yield a formulation of what might be meant by special acts of God's providence, even of 'miracles'. I would explicitly *not* want to suggest that natural explanations are irrelevant. In the past, there has been a tendency to see miracles as occasions when God overturns the laws of nature, though there has recently been a move away from seeing things in such terms (Polkinghorne, 1989). Scientifically, it is difficult to see how there can be events for which natural processes fail to operate at all. Theologically, if one assumes that the laws of nature are God's laws, it is problematic, to see God as overturning them. This leads to an alternative approach to miracles, which would see them as events in which the laws of nature operate in a special way, rather than being overturned.

One particular way in which this could be explicated, within the kind of complementary discourse approach I have suggested in the first chapter, is that special acts of God's providence are events for which the theological discourse is primary in an unusual and special sense. A natural account of miracles can still be offered, but they can be seen as events for which such a natural account is more radically incomplete than usual, and particularly needs to be supplemented by a theological account. Special acts of God's providence would thus be acts or events for which the theological account carried descriptive and explanatory primacy over the natural one.

It is important to distinguish what is being suggested here from another approach to divine action in terms of complementary discourses taken by Compton (1972). He also makes the point that divine action is to be described in theological rather than naturalistic discourse. However, he seems to assume that the theological account has no implications for the natural one. Such dissociation between accounts is only tenable if you take the discourses in a non-realist way. Once you assume that both natural and theological discourses are, in different ways, referring to the same real world, there must be constraints on their compatibility. Of course, there need not be an exact one to one mapping between the discourses, but what is said in one discourse must at least constrain what is said in the other.

The Metaphor of Divine 'Action'

Like all talk about God, talk of divine *action* is analogical, and the background metaphorical assumption is that human action provides a way of understanding God's influence within the world. However, when the analogy between divine action and human action is pressed too far it becomes misleading. It is another part of our inheritance from the Enlightenment, when the analogy between God's relation to the world and the soul's relation to the body was drawn more tightly than before (Craig, 1993).

Though every theologian would maintain the world's dependence on God, it remains the case that much theological talk about the 'world' seems to implicitly assume a degree of autonomy for it that is foreign to what is assumed in either Old or New Testaments (especially the Old), or indeed in the early Fathers, such as Origen. There have been at least two particular points at which Christian theology has taken a turn towards seeing the world as being separate from God. One was in the thought of Augustine, driven largely by the problems of theodicy; the problem of evil in the world seemed less acute if it was suggested that the world had in some sense fallen away from God (Knox, 1993). The other was the Enlightenment, when the growing tendency to see the world in mechanical terms again emphasized its separateness from God. Of course, early-modern thinkers assumed that the merely mechanical nature of the universe showed its dependence on God all the more clearly. However, the fact remains that mechanical science increasingly led to the world being seen as separate from God (Midgley, 1992).

Once we stand back from the religious thinking stemming from the Enlightenment period, it can readily be seen that it would be a theologically preposterous piece of idolatry to suggest that what we call 'the world' could exist independently of the 'maker of heaven and earth.' There is no pantheism lurking here. I am not saying that God cannot be separated from the world – only that the world cannot be separated from God. I share the conventional theological assumption that the world is part of the life of God, but God is not just the life of the world. To say that the world cannot be *separated* from God is not to imply that it cannot be *distinguished* from God. Expressed in these terms, the classic theological assumption is that the world can be distinguished from God, but cannot be separated from him (it would have no existence apart from him).

Those who have grappled with the problem of divine action in the modern dialogue between theology and science have generally seen the dangers of starting from the assumption that the world can be divorced from God. However, the phrase divine 'action' may in fact be a subtly misleading way of talking about God's influential presence in the world, and especially so when we consider his influence on people. One of the key problems is that it does not adequately suggest the *inter*active nature of God's involvement with people. To talk of divine 'action' conjures up the notion of God acting unilaterally and independently. In contrast, Christian theology has always seen God's influence on people as being interactive – as being dependent on God's initiative, but also on people's response. The free will of human beings, which has long been a core assumption of Christian theology, means that God should be seen as leading and influencing people, but not acting in a way that controls them.

In addition, the episodic nature of human action can also mislead us into thinking that God's influence in the world is similarly episodic. In some ways, divine 'activity' might be preferable to divine 'action' because it suggests a less discreet, episodic mode of God's influential presence in the world. Clearly, the metaphor of divine 'action' has its uses, and I would not propose abandoning it. However, we could do with alternative metaphors, so that we are less dependent on that of 'action'. Given that every metaphor for God's involvement in the world is bound to be misleading in some way or other, we can reduce the extent to which we are misled by using more than one metaphor. That weakens the grip of particular metaphors on our theological thought processes.

Resonance

I want to explore the contribution that ideas of 'resonance' or 'tuning' can make as additional metaphors to set along side that of divine action. In discussing how prayer can be understood in relation to science, John Polkinghorne (1989) refers to 'the tuning of divine and human wills to mutual resonance through the collaboration of prayer'. He explicates the notion of resonance by referring to the 'coherence' of laser light, in which oscillations are perfectly in step with one another, thereby affording maximum reinforcement. Alternatively, less technically, one might think of resonance in terms of people being 'attuned' to God, rather as a receiver can be attuned to a transmitter. Of course, the concept of resonance does not exclude all notion of 'action'; in physical resonance there is still a specific 'input'. However, the metaphors of 'resonance', 'tuning' or 'coherence' seem to point in helpful directions.

Above all, they suggest the interactive nature of God's influence on human beings, something which is especially important in considering how the Spirit acts in relation to people. For the Spirit to act, there has to be receptivity. In the Johannine metaphor, the Spirit comes to 'dwell' with believers; and this dwelling requires receptiveness. The metaphors of resonance, tuning, and coherence also suggest how God normally acts in relation to people, allowing them the freedom either to respond, or to go their own way. The notion of resonance is essentially an interactive notion, which is what is required when we consider God's action in relation to people.

Further, there is an implication of constancy in the way God seeks to bring us into attunement with himself. The Christian tradition has generally emphasized that God does not seek to reach out to people and guide them only at certain times, but constantly seeks to do so, even where there is no receptivity on the part of the people to whom he reaches out. The human world, reflecting as it does God's creative purpose, is one in which people's thoughts and actions are constantly being drawn into attunement with God's nature and purpose.

Nevertheless, the notion of resonance also implies that, on specific occasions, when we become attuned to God, new possibilities are opened up which might not otherwise arise. In this way, the resonance metaphor is not at all inconsistent with 'mighty acts of God' occurring, once resonance is established. Resonance thus implies a link between general providence and special providence. This is to be welcomed in view of the fact that the notion of special providence becomes particularly problematic when it is divorced from general providence.

Thinking about God's providence in terms of resonance and attunement is also helpful in suggesting the right kind of relationship between providence and other causal processes. There are two pitfalls to be avoided here. One is to see divine action simply as no more than a particular, religious way of describing events in the world, but one with no real explanatory power, and which reflects no actual divine influence. Liberal theologians have often been tempted by that kind of approach (for example, Wiles, 1986). The other is to see God's influence as real, but operating in a way that is totally divorced from all other causal influences in the world. If talk of resonance is to be fruitful, it needs to point us towards a way of conceptualizing God's influential presence in the world that recognizes it as real, but preserves an interactive compatibility between God's influence and other levels of explanation.

The metaphor of resonance is, of course, fairly close to talk about the input of 'information' from God (for example, Peacocke, 1999). This is an attractive idea, and has the possible advantage of not implying an input of physical energy. However, there are at least two potential problems with it. If 'information' does not involve physical energy, there remains a 'causal joint' problem of how it relates to physical energy. Also, at least in the form in which informational input has been proposed so far, it seems to place a less clear emphasis on human receptivity than does the idea of resonance. However, there may not ultimately be much at stake here. If the concept of information-input is adopted in preference to that of resonance, I suggest that it will be important to develop it in a way that is more explicitly interactive.

I put forward the concepts of 'resonance' or 'tuning' as metaphors; it remains to be seen how successful they will be as such, and whether eventually they become more than metaphors in guiding us to a scientifically congenial understanding of God's activity in relation to people. New metaphors take time to prove their worth (or to fail to do so). Too much should not be expected of or claimed for them at the outset. I am more committed to the theological principle of conceiving divine action in interactive terms than I am to these particular metaphors. The activity of the Spirit in relation to people should be conceptualized in a way that makes explicit the role of human receptivity in relation to his activity.

Moral and Religious Intuitions

Finally, I want to suggest that conscience is a fruitful topic around which to focus discussion of the activity of the Spirit of God in relation to people.

The cognitive processes underlying conscience can be understood in a hierarchical way, rather like that which has been developed for emotion, and which I have applied in Chapter 5 to religious experience. At the lowest level, some reactions to transgression (or possible transgressions) seem to involve an almost reflex-like internalization of prohibitions. Then there is a more propositional knowledge of what is held to be right and wrong, and a capacity for a discursive exploration of that. At the deepest level, there are moral intuitions arising initially at the inarticulate level of the Implicational system, and which are probably particularly powerful in guiding conduct, because we feel we owe them integrity.

Another interesting aspect of conscience is that it relates both to thoughts and actions, and that the two are intertwined. Discerning what is right to do seems to be a kind of enactive knowing. Conscience should not be seen as two sharply distinct steps that occur in sequence, first discerning what to do and then doing it. Often the discernment is enhanced or revised in the process of beginning to act. This reiterates, in a different way, the point made at the start of this chapter about God's action and revelation being intertwined in relation to human beings. God's influence on people normally arises from a kind of enactive knowing, in which understanding and action are held together.

Christian philosophy has often taken a rather naturalistic view of how conscience arises, emphasizing the importance of having a well educated conscience. Through steeping ourselves in the guidelines of a moral community, such as the Church, we develop reliable intuitions about how we should behave in particular circumstances. This emphasis on the importance of educating conscience can be found in many classic writings on the subject, such as those of Thomas Aquinas and Joseph Butler. It is also consistent with an important strand of contemporary moral philosophy, such as that associated with Alasdair MacIntyre (1989), which has emphasized the role of the moral community.

Alongside this, there has been another tradition which has seen conscience as the inner voice of God. There was a particular flowering of this tradition in some of the moralists of the eighteenth century. The interesting question is how we should understand the relationship between these two traditions about conscience. Some, such as Kenneth Kirk (1927), would deny that conscience is a special moral faculty, or in any special sense the voice of God, and would see it as simply ourselves taking moral decisions as best we can. Of course, on this view, conscience may still be in accordance with the will of God, but in as far as that is the case, it would be because people, through the education of their consciences, have come to hold intuitions that reflect the will of God. From this view, it would not be necessary to assume that God had any *direct* influence on people's consciences. Others, while admitting the helpful role of the moral community and the education of conscience, might wish to allow for the active and direct work of the Spirit in shaping our intuitions about how to behave in particular circumstances.

This raises, in different terms, the issue addressed in the last chapter, of the relationship between mediated and unmediated religious experiences. Our assumption was that there are no experiences that are *wholly* unmediated. All religious experiences, whatever their felt revelatory power, arise in the context of a particular cultural and social background, a particular personal developmental history and the memories arising from it, and a particular set of conceptualizations about the nature and will of God. William James's notion of 'direct' religious experience, if understood as experience that bypasses all these contextual features, is simply not viable. Also, as emphasized in Chapter 6, the physical brains of people are involved in their religious experience; there is no way in which 'unmediated' religious experience could somehow bypass the physical brain and, in that sense, stand outside the natural world.

However, that is not the end of the matter. Granted that all religious experiences and all intuitions of conscience are contextualized in these ways, the question still remains of whether there might not also be some direct influence of God on religious experiences and moral intuitions. Peacocke (1999) has rightly emphasized that thoughts and intuitions can arise entirely through the ordinary processes of social influence, reflection on memories and so on, but nevertheless be in accordance with the mind and purpose of God and be of great religious significance. This is similar to the way in which, through a well educated conscience, people can discern how to act in accordance with the will of God. But does it fully capture all that the Christian tradition would wish to say about God's influence on people? It is an important part of the Christian tradition that the Spirit can 'dwell' within people as a source of revelation and guidance. It is not clear that this influential presence of the Spirit is being adequately formulated if it is reduced entirely to externally mediated influences that simply happen to bring people into attunement with God.

The metaphors of 'resonance' and 'tuning in' to the Spirit of God may be helpful here. They seem to place us in the right kind of midway position between extremes of acceptance and denial of the direct influence of the Spirit on people. Resonance, with its interactive emphasis, does not imply a 'controlling' influence on people's thoughts, brains or actions; it is readily compatible with the recognition that all our thoughts inevitably arise out of our social and personal background. However, it also allows for the possibility of a more direct kind of facilitation or enhancement of thoughts and intuitions which are in accordance with the activity of the Spirit.

Chapter 9

The Fall, Christ, and the Evolution of Consciousness

The theory of evolution propounded by Darwin has always aroused mixed religious reactions. There were religious enthusiasts for Darwinism from the outset, such as Charles Kingsley, though initially they were in the minority. However, it was not long before the need to rethink theology in the light of evolution became widely accepted. There have been few more dramatic revolutions in Western thinking than the widespread acceptance that species, including *homo sapiens*, have evolved from one another. It has been a critical part of the background of modern theology over the last nearly 150 years, and there has been a significant programme of recasting theology in the light of its implications.

Integrations of theology and evolution have taken a variety of different forms, as Jim Moore (1979) points out in his thorough and scholarly book on *The Post-Darwinian Controversies*. On the one hand there were those who sought to link the evolution of species with a general doctrine of moral and spiritual progress. This synthesis, built around the intuitive but confident belief in progress that was one of the outstanding hallmarks of the period, involved placing Christ in the context of evolution as the pinnacle of natural evolution and the inauguration of spiritual evolution. The other main approach, that took natural selection much more seriously, involved a Calvinist belief in predestination. One of the most difficult theological challenges raised by evolution was to find a way of reconciling the extinction of many species with the creative purposes of God, and religious thinkers who already espoused a doctrine of predestination had a head start in doing that.

The nature of the relationship between evolution and Christian doctrine can easily be misconstrued. Karl Rahner (1978) is helpful here. He points out that the task is not merely to show that there is no incompatibility between theology and evolution, which he says would be too easy to be interesting. Neither is it to try to prove Christian theology from evolution, which would be impossible. Rather it is to 'coordinate' the two in a way that illuminates both. His assumption here, which I share, is that the scientific and theological approaches will remain separate, and that they provide distinctive and complementary perspectives. There has sometimes been a failure to keep the disciplines distinct. Coordination between the two perspectives does not imply the kind of integration in which they loose their distinct identities.

The particular focus of this chapter will be the relation between evolution and the Christian story of salvation history; the story of the 'Fall' of humanity, and the restoration of its relationship to God through Christ. It is one of the interesting features of evolution that it is the only area of science that has been coordinated with specifically Christian theology in any sustained way. Though the general sweep of evolution is relevant to the doctrines of creation and providence, it is the evolution of humanity that is most directly relevant to the Christian account of salvation history.

Efforts to coordinate evolution with Christian theology have often not focused sufficiently on the evolution of *humanity*. One fruitful attempt to focus on human evolution has been that of Gerd Theissen (1984), who – as we saw in Chapter 2 – examined the relation between natural and cultural evolution, and tried to relate the work of Christ specifically to cultural evolution, seeing him as a cultural mutation that ameliorated the severity of natural selection. Another potentially fruitful focus, and the one that will be taken here, is to focus on the evolution of mind or consciousness.

The coordination of evolution and salvation history has been too much influenced by a background belief in progress. It is tempting to see both evolution and Christian salvation history as representing two different kinds of progress. However, in both cases, the assumption that we are dealing with examples of progress is debatable. As we saw in Chapter 2, evolutionists have been divided about the concept of evolutionary progress. There are also problems with construing salvation history as some kind of progress. I approach the coordination of evolutionary with salvation history in a spirit that is critical of the excessive reliance on the concept of progress in effecting their coordination. However, even if the idea of progress is discounted, the task of relating evolution to theology remains an important one.

The evolution of humanity does not seem to represent any linear progress towards salvation. Rather, it seems that each stage of human development is ambiguous as far as humanity's relationship to God is concerned. At each moment, there are both opportunities to be taken, and dangers to be avoided. Humanity may draw closer to God, but in other ways may draw further away. It seems that God's way with humanity is constantly to present such 'cross-roads'. Each point presents its own 'kairos'. Indeed, this is perhaps the essence of a Christian approach to change and progress. Things are not going straightforwardly uphill, or downhill, nor even round in circles. Rather, at each point, there are critical choice points.

The Evolution of Human Consciousness

Because the approach taken here to coordinating evolution and salvation history will focus specifically on the evolution of consciousness, it is necessary to say something general about that aspect of evolution before proceeding to the task of coordination. First, it should be acknowledged that the evolution of consciousness is not an easy matter to study; the available data is limited. Further, it has only recently begun to be given the sustained academic attention that it deserves, and there is not yet any well worked-out consensus about it. We will have to make do here with the best approaches currently available, while hoping that the quality of background work will continue to improve.

One problem in studying the evolution of consciousness is the familiar one in psychology, that the more scientific approaches achieve their more secure methodological status by severely narrowing the range of questions they consider. For example, the main focus of the scientific literature at present is on how consciousness might have originated in evolution; there has so far been less attention to how consciousness has developed and changed. There is also a broader, less scientific, literature on the evolution of consciousness that at the present time has greater theological relevance. One can hope that, in due course, the two rather different literatures on the evolution of consciousness will merge and there will be a more secure approach to the broad questions of greatest theological relevance.

There is now a wave of interest in the evolution of mind from the perspective of evolutionary psychology. One of the pioneering books, still worth studying and particularly interesting for its attempt to relate the evolution of consciousness to Buddhist psychology, was John Crook's (1980) *The Evolution of Human Consciousness*. Others, such as Steve Mithen (1996) in *The Prehistory of Mind*, have used the perspectives of archaeology and anthropology to approach the subject. His central idea that developments such as art and religions depended on the partial dissolution of boundaries between different modules, or components, of the mind is plausible and attractive.

Hegel was the founding father of modern work on the development of human consciousness. His pioneering work in the *Phenomenology of Spirit* (Hegel 1807, 1977) has influenced everyone who has worked on this topic subsequently, whether directly or indirectly. Bergson (1907/1983) also had an important influence, not least upon Teilhard de Chardin, one of the key figures in the coordination of salvation history and the evolution of consciousness. The evolution of consciousness was also a central concern of the cultural philosopher, Jean Gebser (1905–1973); his monumental book, *The Ever-Present Origin* remains one of the best treatments of the subject. He describes five different stages of consciousness, the archaic, magical, mythical, mental and integral – though he is uneasy about applying the term 'evolution' to this sequence. A recent popular and readable integration of some of these approaches can be found in Ken Wilber's (1983) *Up From Eden*, and there is another accessible introduction to this literature in Allan Combs's (1995) *The Radiance of Being*.

Two people whose approach to the evolution of consciousness will be considered carefully here are C.G. Jung and Rudolf Steiner. There is an interesting, specifically psychological approach to the evolution of consciousness stemming from C.G. Jung. The most important Jungian contribution is Eric Neumann's (1954/1973) *The Origins and History of Consciousness*. The evolution of consciousness was central to the work of Rudolf Steiner (1861–1925), the founder of anthroposophy. His approach has influenced others, such as Owen Barfield, who based his work chiefly on etymological evidence. Steiner, and those influenced by him, have also been explicitly concerned with the relation of Christ to the evolution of consciousness. We will return to the contributions of Jung and Steiner in the context of relating the Fall and Christ to the evolution of consciousness.

The Fall

We will begin with a key topic in Christian doctrine that can be illuminated from a psychological perspective, the story of the Fall in Genesis 3, and the related doctrine of original sin. In particular we will try to place the Fall in the broad context of evolutionary thinking, and especially of the emergence of our distinctively human form of consciousness. Any evolutionary account of salvation history would do well to start from an analysis of the human predicament, and so the story of the Fall is a logical place to begin. We will then proceed later in the chapter to the relation of Christ to the evolution of consciousness.

I will not attempt here to defend a literal reading of the story of the Fall, though those who are interested in how a more conservative reading of Genesis 3 can be integrated with biology will do well to consult Berry (1999, see also Addinall, 2000 and Berry, 2000). I assume that the story of the Fall was never intended to be read literally, and that to do so is a modern form of misreading. The near consensus in twentieth-century theology has been to take the Fall, not as describing a change that took place, but as describing a static ontological view about the inherent sinfulness of human beings. The paradisal Garden of Eden is often taken, not as describing as a state of bliss that once actually existed, but as depicting a possible redeemed state that can be hoped for; it has thus become part of eschatology rather than salvation history.

Clearly, this is one way of rescuing the ideas of the Garden of Eden and the Fall, in the light of the realization that Genesis 3 is myth, not history. Taken literally, Genesis 3 cannot be squared with evolution. However, I am not sure that it is right to opt exclusively for an eschatological reading of paradise and a static way of reading the Fall, though I have no doubt that these are important elements in a proper reading. In this chapter I want to explore an alternative way of reading the Fall that reintegrates it with current assumptions about evolution. There are relatively few who have even attempted such a task. Among them are Daly (1988), Hefner (1993), Lash (1985) and Polkinghorne (1991), though they have tackled the task in slightly different ways.

As I see it, there is no problem, from a scientific point of view, in taking the myth of the Fall as having some kind of historical reference. Even if you do not think that it describes changes that took place in a moment of disobedient apple eating, it can be taken as relating to a gradual development in the evolution of human beings from their primate origins. We can assume that human beings have a moral consciousness that is of a different order from that found in any other species, a new capacity to reflect on right and wrong. If you make that assumption, you will be led to the conclusion that humanity's moral consciousness evolved gradually.

The evolution of moral consciousness makes it possible to do wrong with a new kind of deliberateness. Indeed, whatever view is taken of the Fall in theology, it is hard to avoid supposing that human beings must, over a period of time, have come to have, in a new way, what Genesis 3 calls the 'knowledge of good and evil'. There is thus no problem at all in taking at least some aspects of the myth of the Fall as having historical reference of a general kind. It is plausible that one of the origins of the myth of a Fall was a folk memory of such a change in moral consciousness, or a supposition about what must have occurred.

Now it might be objected that the doctrine of the Fall is not about the development of a new moral consciousness, but about human disobedience against God, and the source of original sin. It is true that the Fall has usually been taken in that way in Christian theology, chiefly due to the influence of St Augustine. However, it is not obviously the correct reading of Genesis 3. It is also worth noting that the Eastern churches, and the Jewish tradition, have not read the story of Genesis 3 in conjunction with the idea of the original sin in the way that Western Christians have. As James Barr (1992) points out in *The Garden of Eden and the Hope of Immortality*, the main changes that are actually described in the text are the knowledge of good and evil, and the loss of the prospect of immortality.

I will return to mortality later. So far as morality is concerned, note that there is no reference in Genesis 3 to sin at all. The moral change described there is one of moral consciousness, knowledge of good and evil. Even the reaction to the awareness of nakedness, Barr claims, is not one of guilt or shame, but apparently just the milder one of shyness of embarrassment (p. 62). Here too the story is more about a new consciousness of nakedness than about wickedness. I take Barr's point that Genesis 3 is not really about guilt though, as I have suggested elsewhere (Watts, 2001b), it can more readily be understood as being about shame. Indeed, Genesis 3 can reasonably be taken as being, not just about mild embarrassment, but as one of the touchstone stories in our culture of the experience of deep shame.

Various interpretations have been advanced about what is meant by knowledge of good and evil, from the highly specific to the very general. Thus it has been variously assumed to refer to practical know-how, like choosing good foods or, at the other extreme, to 'knowledge of everything'. This is not an easy matter to settle, but let me just say that I will assume that Barr's suggestion that what is meant is 'the power of rational and ethical discrimination' is a reasonable one. Thus, the myth of the Fall as found in Genesis accords reasonably well with what, on the basis of general evolutionary thinking, one would suppose to have occurred.

One attraction of this way of taking the Fall is that it does not make strong assumptions about the inherent, ontological wickedness of human beings. Theological anthropology has sometimes become exceedingly gloomy, and some religious thinkers pile on pejoratives about how deeply wicked human beings are in a way that seems excessive. What worries me about this is not so much the content of what is said; it is clear that human life is in many ways tragic and fraught, and that human beings perpetrate many dreadful things. It is the rather hysterical tone of some Christian material about the wickedness of humanity that is the greater concern. A more measured and matter of fact approach to the moral qualities of human beings would be preferable. It is one benefit of interpreting the Fall primarily in terms of the development of moral consciousness, rather than a descent into sin and wickedness, that it may assist in that.

Seeing the Fall chiefly as the acquisition of moral consciousness leads us to reconsider the nature of the state that existed before it. This is where the predominant Augustinian interpretation of the myth comes most adrift from the text. Barr has argued that the assumption that Adam and Eve were immortal before they ate the apple has no real support. The notion that the pre-Fall state was paradisal, a state of original perfection, is also suspect. The traditional assumption that the Fall was into sin, rather than into the knowledge of good and evil, goes hand in hand with the idea that the pre-Fall state was one of paradise. Both are reading back into the text things that are not really there.

It is, of course, generally recognized that the text is an edited version of two prior stories, each with their own trees, and making rather different points. For example, Ricoeur (1967), proposes that, in one of the sources, Adam cultivated the soil intelligently before the Fall, and that it was the Yahwist who 'suppressed all the traits of discernment and intelligence connected with the state of innocence and ... assigned all of man's cultural aptitudes to his fallen state' (p. 246). Be that as it may, let us work with the text as we have it; there was presumably a point to it being edited in the way it was.

The pre-Fall state seems an ambivalent one, innocent in the sense of not having enough awareness of the distinction between good and evil to sin deliberately, rather than being paradisal in the sense of being perfectly good. It is true that occupancy of the Garden is lost, along with a general ease, and enjoyment of a harmonious intimacy with God. However, it is not clear that it was really better to lack the knowledge of good and evil, and the awareness of nakedness. The pre-Fall state was not obviously a perfect one. This is one reason why I am uneasy about an eschatological interpretation of the innocent pre-Fall state, of the kind that is now common. It is also not clear how consciousness, once gained, *can* return to innocence, nor that this would be desirable, something to be hoped for eschatologically. What would be the point of ending up back in the place where, according to the myth, we are alleged to have started?

Some might object that I am misunderstanding the nature of myth. It might be argued that it is a mistake to see the events described in the myth as being truly sequential at all. Ricoeur, amongst others, makes this point. 'The possibility arises of interpreting the two states of innocence and sin no longer as successive, but as superimposed' (p. 251). Lash (1985) makes a similar point about the 'aboriginal' nature of the Fall. From this view, the point about paradise preceding sin in the story is, not to assert that it actually occurred first, but to accord it ontological primacy of a more general kind. The point is not so much that we were originally good, but that we are basically good.

No doubt, this primacy is, in part, what the sequential story is intended to signify, but Ricoeur chooses his words with care. The 'possibility arises', he says, of reading the story as making non-sequential points about the relation of the states of innocence and sin (or moral consciousness). However, it is not clear that recognizing the mythological character of the story rules out any kind of sequential, historical reference in it. Granted that the story of the Fall should not be taken as literal history, it is at least arguable that it can still properly be taken as describing in a mythological way events that *could* in principle be described in a historical sequential way.

The Fall and the Evolution of Consciousness

It is not difficult to map the more differentiated consciousness indicated in the story of the Fall on to a more general account of how consciousness has evolved. In terms of Gebser's five stages in the evolution of consciousness, the Fall marks the transition from the first (archaic) stage on to the next (magical) stage. Gebser explicitly recognizes the analogy between Biblical paradise and archaic consciousness. He suggests that the main hallmark of the archaic stage was the lack of differentiation between humanity and the universe, though I suggest there may have been a more general lack of differentiation. Coombs (1995) speculates that *homo habilis* was an example of this archaic consciousness, and possibly also *homo erectus* – though that may have been a transitional case.

Ken Wilber (1983) also relates the Fall to emergence from a primitive state in which 'environment, consciousness and body were all largely undifferentiated' (p. 298). Wilber calls this the 'scientific fall', and distinguishes it from the 'theological fall', by which he means the sense of separation of people from God. He perhaps makes too sharp a distinction between the two. The distinctions between good and evil, person and nature, person and God all seem to be manifestations of the same basic change of consciousness. What is at issue is whether these new distinctions are *just* matters of consciousness, or whether they represent anything more.

Wilber seems to want to say that the new *sense* of separation from God was just that, only a sense, and that it did not mark any actual change in people's relationship to the spiritual. In his terminology, the scientific fall is mistaken for a theological fall. Though these matters are very difficult to assess, I would be less confident that we are dealing *only* with a new sense of separation from God. It seems to me entirely possible that the new sense of separation from God inaugurated a new era of actual separation from him.

Theodosius Dobzhanzsy (1967) makes the interesting suggestion that the development of a new, differentiated consciousness may have involved a new awareness of death. He speculates that this may correspond to the Fall (p. 79), and certainly it would shed light on the loss of immortality described in the story. However, an issue arises here about how to frame this, that is rather similar to that raised in connection with Wilber. Are we dealing here with a new consciousness of mortality, or with an actual loss of immortality?

Julian Jaynes (1976) also makes some interesting remarks about the Fall in *The Origins of Consciousness in the Breakdown of the Bicameral Mind*. It is Jaynes' general thesis that there was a time when people could not think as we do. They would have had consciousness in the minimal sense of being aware of what was going on, but not in any higher sense. In particular they would not have been able to introspect in the way that we do. However, they would have had some conscious phenomenal experiences that we do not have, in the sense of hearing 'hallucinatory' voices. Jaynes theorizes that these cognitive and phenomenal changes arose from a changed relationship between the two hemispheres of the brain. That is, to my mind the least plausible aspect of his theory. However, his descriptive insights into the evolution of consciousness can be detached from his neurological speculations, and I believe are likely to be roughly correct.

Jaynes interprets the Fall in terms of the 'groping of newly conscious men to narratize what has happened to them, the loss of divine voices and assurances in a chaos of human directive and selfish privacies' (p. 444). He emphasizes that the serpent, the source of the temptation, is described with a Hebrew word used rather rarely in the Scriptures, 'arum' ('crafty' and 'deceitful'). The capacity to deceive is, for Jaynes, one of the hallmarks of the new consciousness which he associates with the breakdown of the bicameral mind. He also sees the new consciousness as central to the development of morality. Though he doesn't elaborate this aspect of his interpretation of the Fall, he makes the point elsewhere that 'Consciousness and morality are a single development. For without gods, morality based on a consciousness of the consequences action must tell men what to do' (p. 286).

A Jungian View of the Fall

To advance the discussion about the relation of the Fall to the evolution of consciousness, I want to look at ideas developed with a tradition of twentieth-century thought that stands outside mainstream theology, that stemming from C.G. Jung. Let me emphasize that I am not purporting to offer a correct exegesis of the views of Jung on the Fall; his remarks are too brief and fragmentary for that to be possible. Rather I am offering a Jung*ian* approach to these matters.

It can be developed in terms of the relationship between ego (the centre of consciousness) and the Self (the complete person that we have the potential to become when the unconscious is integrated with the conscious). Note that 'Self' is a technical term in Jungian thought; it is the state of wholeness that is the goal of individuation, but also the state of undifferentiated wholeness from which we come. The Self is the centre of both the conscious and the unconscious aspects of mind, whereas the ego is only the centre of consciousness.

The fullest Jungian interpretation of the myth of the Garden of Eden is in fact to be found in Edward Edinger's (1972) *Ego and Archetype*. The Garden is seen as representing an original state of psychic wholeness and is, in a sense, an image of the Self. A clue to the Garden as an image of wholeness is the four rivers that divide it into a kind of mandala, with the tree of life at the centre. In the Garden, there is as yet no self-consciousness, no distinct ego, no conceptual contrasts, and no conflict. Eric Neumann (1954/1973) has written extensively about this original undifferentiated consciousness in *The Evolution of Consciousness*.

In Jungian theory, the move towards a more differentiated consciousness, an 'ego' consciousness, is accompanied by inflation, the tendency of the ego to overreach itself and identify with archetypes of the collective unconscious. On Edinger's account, the passive inflation of original undifferentiated consciousness gives way to a more active form of inflation as ego consciousness is born. The appeal of eating the fruit of the tree of knowledge, succumbing to the appeal of 'being like God', can be seen in terms of active inflation. It was very different to be in a state of unconscious union with God (passive inflation) than to become consciously aware of the possibility of becoming like God, and to act to bring it about (active inflation). The inflationary act of eating the fruit also arises, Jung himself suggests, from inferiority. He remarks:

> There is deep doctrine in the legend of the Fall; it is the expression of a dim presentiment that the emancipation of ego consciousness was a Luciferian deed. Man's whole history from the beginning is a conflict between his inferiority and his arrogance (Jung, CW (9i), para. 420).

The consciousness of inferiority is thus another aspect of the developing ego consciousness, and issues in the new experience of nakedness.

I am not sure that this interpretation of the motivation to eat from the tree of good and evil in terms of inflation, and its shadow of inferiority, is faithful to the text. It is perhaps reasonable as an exegesis of the post-Augustinian interpretation of the Fall, but it is not clear that inflation is to be found in Genesis 3 itself. Despite the serpent's remark to Eve, it is not obvious that being like God was what actually attracted her to eat the apple. Barr (1992) suggests that it was rather that she saw the tree was good for food, nice to look at, and excellent for giving wisdom.

Anyhow, the fruit is eaten, the fruit that marks the inauguration of ego consciousness and the loss of the old state of undifferentiated consciousness. The new ego consciousness is marked by a differentiation of opposites, including specifically the differentiation of good from evil. Ego consciousness also leads to a new state of alienation. Though the ego has the new prize of consciousness, it is alienated from the Self. Note that, in Jungian thought, the Self is seen as the image of God in the psyche. This implies that alienation of the ego from the Self symbolizes the separation of humanity from God. Such alienation leads in turn to the journey of individuation, in which the ego reestablishes a relationship with the Self. The ego remains distinct as a centre of consciousness, and does not identify with the Self, but it reestablishes a relationship with the Self. The journey of the ego back into relationship with the Self parallels the journey of humanity back into relationship with God.

This raises an aspect of the Genesis myth that lends itself to Jungian interpretation, though I have not seen the point made elsewhere. It concerns the relationship between the tree of knowledge of good and evil, and the tree of life. If eating from the tree of knowledge of good and evil is a symbol of the birth of the ego, then the tree of life can be seen as corresponding to the final individuated state, centred on the Self. Note that this tree of life would bestow immortality in a way that the knowledge of good and evil does not. There seems a natural progression from one tree to another. After knowledge of good and evil, the tree of life comes next. There is, similarly, a natural progression from ego to Self. However, the path from one to the other, the path of individuation, is not a straightforward one. It is a long, hard journey that cannot be rushed.

It is here, I think, that we find an element of inflation in the story, not in eating from the tree of knowledge of good and evil, but in wishing to go on too quickly to eat from the tree of life. Attempting to move too quickly, without due preparation, from an ego-consciousness to a Self-based, individuated consciousness, is what really represents inflation, a premature attempt to snatch immortality. Such inflation is, in Jungian psychology, always disastrously counterproductive, and it is to prevent this premature act of inflation that, on this account, God would have to bar Adam and Eve from the garden. Note that this is done more in sorrow than in anger; I would suggest that it be seen more as prevention than punishment.

One striking feature of this Jungian account of the Fall is that it does not see it as all bad. Indeed, in a very important sense the Fall represents an achievement, an advance. In a phrase that has often been used, it is a fall *upwards*. The achievement of consciousness described in this account creates new possibilities. Opposites can now be differentiated; right can be distinguished from wrong; people can have a sense of their own distinct identity. However, these advances are bought at a cost, and the task is then to consolidate these advances, which once made cannot be undone, while restoring in a new way something of what was lost. This idea of achievement at a price is, of course, central to all Christian soteriology. There is nothing new or strange about such a position in Christian theology, though it is not often associated with the Fall.

The essence of the Jungian method is to proceed by seeking parallels in different kinds of material. We are in fact dealing here with several types of material:

(a)   assumptions about how consciousness actually developed during the evolution of homo sapiens, in terms, for example, of the development of a new kind of ego consciousness,
(b)   a recapitulation of that in the development of ego consciousness in infancy in each individual, and
(c)   a mythological salvation history that begins with the alienation of humanity from God.

Edinger also draws in other types of material, such as clinical dream material that partakes of some aspects of the myth of the Fall, and has a particular significance in the individuation process of the person concerned.

As always with Jungian thought, it is hard to know quite how this kind of interpretation ought to be taken. However, it is less an exercise in psychological reduction than might at first appear. The parallelism helps in the interpretation of both sets of material. It is not the intention to 'reduce' one kind of material to another, but to elucidate *both* kinds of material by means of the relationship that is shown to exist between them.

Steiner and the Fall

There are parallels with Jungian thought about the Fall in the ideas of Rudolf Steiner about the evolution of consciousness, though here again I am working with a Steiner*ite* view of the Fall, rather than one found fully worked out in Steiner himself. Winkler (1960), for example, presents a Steinerite interpretation of the Fall in terms of the evolution of consciousness. It is an approach that has many features in common with the Jungian one presented above. A prior dreamlike mode of consciousness was lost, and a new more analytical consciousness was born.

Steiner sees the intuitive consciousness that was lost as having been characterized by an effortless communion with the spiritual world, and seems to take that aspect of the Genesis myth more historically than Jung. In that, his approach is similar to that of Jaynes. Like Jung, Steiner saw this loss of spiritual communion as having had advantages as well as disadvantages. He particularly stressed the sense of individuality that a more differentiated consciousness makes possible. He also emphasized that perception took a more detached, 'spectorial' turn, and became less spiritual and more material. The new sense, recorded in Genesis 3, of the skin being naked could be seen as a marker of that change.

Steiner foresaw the continued development of consciousness towards a point that will, in some ways, be a return to its unitive origin, but in a new and transformed state. Jung was concerned with the reestablishment in individuals of a healthy axis between the ego and the Self, but it is not clear that he anticipated anything comparable in the continued evolution of the consciousness of humanity as a whole. Steiner is, at this point, more explicitly Christian and eschatological than Jung. For Steiner, it is the calling and destiny of human consciousness to be reunited with both the spiritual and natural worlds, overcoming the separation between them. However, this will be achieved through a transformation of analytical consciousness rather than a regressive abandonment of it.

Within the Steinerite tradition there is an explicit recognition that what is helpful at one stage of human evolution may be unhelpful at another. This, I think, is sound, both empirically and theologically. It would be widely recognized that evolutionary fitness cannot be defined in absolute terms, without reference to the environment. What is adaptive in one context may become a handicap after, say, climatic change. Similar points can be made about the moral and spiritual evolution that comes to the fore when evolution is brought into dialogue with salvation history. What is, so to speak, 'adaptive for salvation' at one point may become a handicap at another point, and vice-versa.

The birth of ego-consciousness, recounted in mythical form in Genesis 3, is thus not an absolute turning away from God. It marks a development that represents a disruption of one kind of relationship with God, but in order that a new and better relationship may eventually be born. On this Steinerite view, an important correlate of the knowledge of good and evil is the new sense of self-identity that accompanied it. The development of such a new sense of self at one stage in salvation history may have disrupted one form of relationship between humanity and God. Nevertheless, it can lay the foundation for new and different relationship to be established later. For Steiner, the Fall made possible a new kind of human freedom and individuality.

Evolutionary Christology

Having considered how the Fall relates to the evolution of consciousness, we will now see how the broader story of Christian salvation history can be placed in that context. The chief issue is, of course, how Christ relates to evolution. The twentieth century has seen the development of a rich diversity of contextual theologies, each of which has incorporated its own approach to Christology, including a liberationist Christology and a feminist Christology. Evolutionary Christology can be placed among these specialist approaches to elucidating the work of Christ. Work on evolutionary Christology goes back to the nineteenth century. It was initially largely a British endeavour, and Peacocke (1985) has told the story of the key early contributors, such as Henry Drummond, Frederick Temple, Charles Gore, F.R. Tennant, Lionel Thornton. A key publication was the influential *Lux Mundi*, (Gore, 1889), in which several authors, J.R. Illingworth among them, took an evolutionary approach.

It may be helpful first to set out one version of might be called the conventional approach to evolutionary Christology, and I will select for this purpose that of the major Catholic theologian, Kahl Rahner, in his *Foundations of Christian Faith*

(1978). His approach is representative of the mainstream approach, though Peacocke (1993) would also have served as a good example. Rahner's formulation is theologically sophisticated, and in many ways clear and impressive. However, the potential weaknesses of the kind of approach that he represents can still be discerned in his formulation.

Rahner assumes that there has been evolutionary progress towards life, humanity and spirit. He identifies 'spirit' in humanity with self-consciousness, and the associated capacity for self transcendence. He further assumes that the universe is now moving onwards towards its ultimate fulfilment, which is to be found in the spiritual creatures who are the goal and high-point of the universe, and in whom the ground of the universe is revealed.

Given those background assumptions, what is the role of Christ? He is both an end and a beginning. As an end, he is the 'climax of God's self-communication'. Christ also embodies the promise of God to humanity as spiritual creatures, and calls for acceptance of God's self-communication to them. Rahner looks forward to the 'divinisation of the world as a whole' and suggests that Christ marks the 'necessary and permanent beginning' of that process. Christ is an, 'absolute saviour' in that he is the person who marks the beginning of God's 'absolute self-communication', and in whom that revelation becomes irreversible.

Rahner himself is quick to make one obvious comment on this proposal, which is that it does not see Christ as undertaking a rescue of humanity. Rahner does not think that the incarnation of Christ was made necessary by the Fall, but rather that the incarnation of Christ was part of the eternal destiny and purpose of the world. He is thus 'the summit and height of the divine plan of creation'. This is a minority way of understanding Christ, albeit an established one, and Rahner places himself in the Scotist tradition. However, it is not clear that Rahner is consistent about it. He also says that Christ brings about the 'restoration of a divine world order destroyed by mankind', and that sounds as though it is slipping the idea of rescue in again.

It is also notable that there is no engagement with the details of evolution in Rahner's approach. There is nothing about natural selection, about how consciousness has evolved, or about the relationship of natural to cultural evolution. There is simply a grand view of evolution as an onwards and upwards process, with no hint of caution about such an approach. There is also nothing about how spiritual creatures came about. The concept of 'spirit' is used rather loosely, and in a way that enables Rahner to link together several rather different ideas, such as the distinctive self-consciousness of humanity, God's revelation in Christ, and the ultimate goal of the universe. It is also not clear what justifies Rahner's assertion that Christ marks the 'necessary and permanent beginning' of the process of divinisation that he anticipates.

This is a recurrent problem in evolutionary Christologies, as Polkinghorne (1996) complains in his discussion of Peacocke's evolutionary Christology. It is reasonable to claim that Christ marks the culmination of evolution up to that point. It is also reasonable to claim that Christ reveals the meaning and purpose of the universe, including the evolutionary process. What is much more difficult to explain, from the perspective of evolutionary Christology, is how Christ makes any difference to anything; and that is something that an adequate Christology has to tackle. If Christ simply marks a staging point in evolutionary progress, why could that progress not have continued without Christ?

Though Rahner's style is sober, his approach to evolutionary Christology is indebted in many ways to the more florid and expansive work of his fellow Jesuit, Teilhard de Chardin, set out in *The Phenomenon of Man* (1959). One marked difference is that Rahner does not try to say anything about the details of the evolutionary process, whereas de Chardin, a paleontologist, knew a great deal about it, and could comment knowledgeably. Teilhard de Chardin seems never to have doubted the basic process of evolution, though he yearned for an expanded understanding of it. His approach to evolution was a visionary one, indebted both to his scientific work and to his deep faith. However, it is notable that for him, the two simply fuse together in one grand vision. There is no sense of dialogue between the two distinct disciplines of theology and evolutionary science.

Teilhard de Chardin saw the development of human consciousness as a key breakthrough in evolution. In that I think he was essentially correct, as I indicated in Chapter 2. I also very much welcome his emphasis on the evolution of *consciousness* in approaching evolutionary Christology. Perhaps what was most distinctive in de Chardin was the way he handled the question of where the evolution of human consciousness might lead. His answer, in brief, was that it would lead on to the spiritualization of humanity. Though the way in which he worked out this vision was original, there is a long history of this kind of theology. Some of the roots of it can be found in St Paul's vision, at the end of 1 Corinthians 15, of a spiritual or incorruptible body. Among the Fathers, it was Origen who best embodied the kind of approach that came to a late flowering in Teilhard de Chardin.

The key question in this context is the place of Christ in this evolutionary process. Here he seems to me to be ambiguous. On the one hand, he seems to see an inevitability in the evolutionary process. Evolution seemed to him to cry out for the spiritualization that he foresaw. However, he also wanted to say that it was only because Christ had united himself with the creation and humanity that we could be confident that this spiritualization would be carried through. It is another example of the problem that all onwards-and-upwards evolutionary Christologies have. How can you give a convincing account of how Christ makes a crucial difference to something that is predictable anyway, and really just a continuation of discernible evolutionary trends? Teilhard de Chardin undoubtedly had a strong view of Christ as both the goal and the crucial facilitator of the evolutionary process, but he found it easier to make the case for Christ being the goal of the process, than for his making a decisive difference to it.

I want now to step outside the mainline orthodoxy of evolutionary Christology and to consider other approaches. In particular, I want to go even further than Teilhard de Chardin in linking Christ specifically to the evolution of consciousness. In doing so, it will be helpful to follow up what has already been said about the Fall from the perspectives of C.G. Jung and Rudolf Steiner, and to how they approach the significance of Christ.

Jung on Christ

Jung's approach to Christ needs to be placed in the context of his distinction between the ego and the Self. Jung saw Christ as a symbol of the Self, and so Christ represents the goal of individuation. Individuation is, in that sense, a journey towards Christ. A powerful symbol of the Self, such as Christ, is not only the goal of individuation, but can also facilitate the process of individuation. Edward Edinger in *Ego and Archetype* (1972) has a slightly different perspective from Jung himself on how Christ relates to individuation. He sees Christ more as a paradigm of the individuating ego, an example to ego-based humanity of how to move forwards towards individuation. Edinger's approach is compatible with Jung's own view, but enriches it and extends it.

Both the story of Jesus' life, and much of his teaching recorded in the Gospels, can be interpreted from this perspective, as Edinger shows. For example, Jesus' teaching about the priority that needs to be given to seeking the kingdom as the 'pearl of great price' (Matthew 13:46), parallels the overarching priority that needs to be given to seeking individuation. Sayings as 'blessed are the poor in spirit for theirs is the kingdom of heaven' (Matthew 5:3) echo the humility that the ego needs to adopt towards the Self if individuation is to be successfully accomplished. Individuation requires that limited ego-based life be given up if the new life of individuation is to be found, and there is a parallel in Jesus' teaching about how his followers need to lose their life in order to find it.

The life of Jesus can also be seen in terms of individuation (Edinger, 1987). His life shows a continuation of the sometimes painful acquisition of the differentiated consciousness that is a central focus of the story of the Fall. This is especially true of the temptations in the wilderness, with its distinction between the path that Jesus actually took in his ministry and the path that he rejected in the temptations. In Jesus, 'knowledge of good and evil' is thus taken to new depths. Also, the relationship of Jesus to the Father that is revealed so clearly in his baptism can be seen as parallel to the relationship of the ego to the Self. Furthermore, Jesus' remarks, especially in the fourth Gospel, about his relationship to the Father can be seen as a paradigm of the relationship of the ego to the Self.

However, this Jungian perspective on Christ can be taken further. As we saw in connection with the Fall, an analogy can be drawn between the individuation of the individual and a parallel process that humanity as a whole is undergoing. In this way, Christ can be seen as marking a stage in humanity's 'individuation'. As Jung's thought developed, he seemed to take an increasingly realist view of archetypes, such as that of the Self. In his late book, *Answer to Job* (1954), he is talking about the development of God as an archetype, and this process of development seems to be the same kind of individuation process that people undergo. For example, at the time of the encounter between God and Job, Jung considers that God was not very far along this road of individuation, and that God's incarnation as Christ marked a further decisive step in his individuation. In this vein, Jung *mis*interprets the Trinity sequentially, seeing Father, Son and Spirit as a series of stages in the individuation process: primitive unity, differentiation, and then reintegration.

As is so often the case with Jung, it is not quite clear what he is doing here. Some of what he says in *Answer to Job* seems to presuppose a very realist view of God, and could be construed as being about the evolution of God's own consciousness. However, it is equally possible that he was talking about changes in how the symbol of God has been experienced in the human psyche, which would be an aspect of the evolution of human consciousness.

Steiner on Christ

As with the Fall, there are parallels between the approaches of Jung and Rudolf Steiner, though Steiner is closer to theological orthodoxy. The interesting and distinctive thing about Steiner's approach to the place of Christ in the evolution of consciousness is his claim that Christ marks a turning point in that evolution. I have already said that the conventional view that sees Christ as a staging point in the linear development of human consciousness makes it hard to give an adequate account of what difference Christ makes. Steiner overcomes that problem by postulating a change in the direction of human consciousness. Christ is seen, not just a marker of that change, but responsible for it. Even if Steiner's own view is not accepted, it is helpful in showing that linking Christ with the evolution of consciousness is not necessarily tied to a progressivist view of evolution.

The change that Steiner postulates is from a relatively passive mode of religious consciousness before Christ to a more active mode subsequently. This is reflected, for example, in a change in how the relationship between humanity, nature, and the spiritual world is experienced. In the animistic consciousness that existed before Christ, the spiritual world was experienced as speaking to humanity through nature, and humanity was relatively passive in that process. Since Christ, the gift of the spirit to humanity has made possible a new kind of spiritually active perception of the natural world, in which the spirit guides and enhances humanity's perception of nature. The spirit is no longer experienced as beyond nature, but within humanity.

Owen Barfield is one of the most helpful exponents of this Steinerite view of the relationship of Christ to the evolution of consciousness. He links it, for example, to his own technical interest in etymology, using the rise and fall of different categories of words as a guide to the evolution of consciousness. His proposal is that there has been a change from

> a period in which, with the help of language, man is drawing his self-consciousness, as it were, out of the world around him, to a period in which he is, again, with the help of language, in a position to give back to nature something of the treasure he once took from her (Barfield, 1977, p. 234).

Moreover, Barfield suggests that this change in the direction of consciousness can be roughly located historically, falling somewhere 'between the death of Alexander the Great and the birth of St Augustine'.

Why link this change specifically to Christ? Barfield suggests that the change can be seen as one in which the man's 'spiritual selfhood entered into the body of man', a process that invites the term 'incarnation', and is strikingly similar to what is claimed in the Christian gospels. Thus, around the middle of the period during which Barfield, on etymological grounds, suggests that a change in the direction of consciousness occurred:

a man was born who claimed to be the son of God, and to have come down from Heaven, he spoke to his followers of 'The Father in me and I in you', that he told all those who stood around him that 'the kingdom of God is within you', and then startled them, and strove to reverse the direction of their thought – for the word 'metanioa', which is translated 'repentance', also means a reversal of the direction of the mind – he startled them and strove to reverse the direction of their thought by assuring them that 'it is not that which cometh into a man which defileth him, but that which goeth out of him' (p. 235).

There is much else in the Judeo-Christian story that lends itself to being interpreted in this way. Elsewhere, Barfield (1957) has drawn attention to the importance that is attached in the Old Testament to overcoming the tendency to treat external objects as idols, and suggested that was a necessary precondition for the change in consciousness that was launched among the Jewish people by Christ. As he sees it, the eradication of idolatry made possible the new era in which, in the terms of the parable of the sower, the Word of God was sown within.

There is also much in the teaching of St Paul that lends itself to interpretation in a similar way (see Hiebel, 1980) such as the emergence in the thought of St Paul of a new concept of conscience. Indeed, much of the thought of St Paul about how, through Christ, 'the love of God has been shed abroad in our hearts by the Holy Spirit which has been given us' (Romans 5.5) can be interpreted in this way. In this view, the work of Christ is mediated crucially though this gift of the Word, and the Spirit within. Despite this strong emphasis on the Spirit, Steiner did not neglect the work of Christ on the cross, and came to see what he called the 'mystery of Golgotha' as the turning point of time, and especially of the evolution of consciousness.

Barfield (1957), developing Steiner's insights, sees human consciousness as evolving from an undifferentiated state of 'original participation' towards what he calls 'final participation'. That final state of consciousness will build on the freedom and individuality that are among the chief benefits of the Fall, but overcome the sense of alienation and disconnectedness, which have been among its chief problems. Barfield sees Christ as pivotal to this transition from original to final participation. Indeed final participation will be a 'Christ consciousness'.

A somewhat related proposal has been developed in a more explicitly psychological way; though with no reference to the work of Christ, by the Dutch psychologist of religion, Han M.M. Fortmann (1964) in his massive *Alsziende de Onzienlijke* (As Seeing the Invisible). This has not yet been translated, but it has been summarized by Faber (1976). Fortmann describes the consciousness of our time as being a 'shrunken' perception in which religion has become problematic, and he looks forward to it being replaced by a 'second primitiveness' that would be a new kind of 'unshrunken' perception.

The evolution of consciousness is a central theme in Steiner's work, and what I have said here abstracts certain key themes from a much broader and very detailed theory. Though there are aspects of his methodology that are difficult to evaluate, and though his claims about the distant past and future of the evolution of consciousness are hard to relate to other knowledge, there is a central core to his theory which is very plausible. He has a rich theory of how consciousness has continued to evolve through the Christian era. It is definitely not a theory of linear progress, partly because new developments are often seen as recapitulations of old ones in a new context, but also because each change in the evolution of consciousness is seen as bringing both new dangers and new opportunities.

Certainly, there would be widespread agreement that animistic consciousness has receded, though that has happened unevenly in different parts of the world. Particularly interesting is Steiner's interpretation of the period since around 1450 as one in which the 'consciousness soul' has developed (see Barfield, 1959/1966; Davy, 1961). It enables him to weave a coherent story that makes sense of many developments of the modern period, making use of key themes such as the growing sense of inwardness and subjectivity, a new sense of objectivity, but also a new capacity for imagination. His approach leads to a vivid sense of the spiritual possibilities presented by continuing developments in human consciousness, and he has the resources to offer an interpretation of them within the context of a broad, Christocentric approach to the evolution of consciousness.

It is not just that Steiner uses New Testament themes to elucidate changes in human consciousness, though there is much of interest there. To the best of my knowledge, he is alone in evolutionary Christology in offering a coherent theory of how Christ has actually changed the course of human evolution. It is also a strikingly objective theory. That point is worth emphasizing because it is often feared that relating theology to psychology will inevitably lead to a rather subjective approach. However, for Steiner, it is simply an objective fact that Christ has changed the course of the evolution of consciousness, and that would be true even if no one realized that it had happened. While not endorsing every aspect of Steiner's far reaching proposals, it seems to me that his work could set evolutionary salvation history off in a more fruitful direction than it has generally followed so far.

Nature, Salvation and Consciousness

In the final section of this chapter, I want to consider the implications of the approach to salvation history that I have set out here for the redemption of nature. It is not a fashionable theme in current theology, though St Paul is very explicit about it in Romans 8. The Fall is, for St Paul, not something that has only affected human beings; the creation also was 'subjected to futility', but it will be 'set free from its bondage to decay'. For this it 'waits with eager longing', 'groaning in travail', just as we ourselves wait for the 'redemption of our bodies'. This linking of the future of creation to the future of the human body evokes what St Paul says elsewhere about how a physical body is sown, but a spiritual body will be raised up (1 Corinthians 15: 42–4).

Prompted in part by remarks of Owen Barfield mentioned earlier, I want now to take up the relation of the Fall to nature, and to natural biological processes. Notice that the Jungian reading of the Fall is an account of the origin of human (or moral) evil only. It has nothing to say about natural evil, and indeed belongs to the contemporary worldview in which moral and natural evil are seen as completely unconnected issues. Such an account of the origin of evil in terms of the evolution of consciousness seems to assume that there was no evil before human consciousness evolved to the point at which there could be deliberate moral evil. There may have been tragic aspects of the process of evolution, but nothing that could properly be called evil. Polkinghorne (1991) takes a similar view when he argues that the world has always contained natural evil but with the development of human consciousness, there was a 'further fall into moral evil' (p. 100).

Clearly there is a distinction to be made between natural and moral evil, but an oversharp division between them can be uncomfortably dualistic. I am reminded here of Lash's point that focusing on the human predicament in our reading of the doctrine of original sin 'in no way licenses the confining of the interest to the human'. He warns that we are led by dualistic habits of thought to relegate the natural or material 'to the status of the stage or floorboards on which is played out the "drama" of man's redemption' (1985, p. 279). At very least I think it can be argued that fallen human beings see nature in a new way, with themselves less as part of it than hitherto. There is thus a valid sense in which fallen humanity sees nature itself as being fallen too. Whether there was a fall of nature itself, in a strong realist sense, is perhaps another matter. Clearly, there have been consequences for nature of the way in which fallen humanity has seen it as separate and distinct, something that 'green' theology has begun to explore.

Steiner saw the Fall as being associated with a new sense of distance from nature. People developed a new sense of being set apart from nature, even over against it. It is entirely likely, on general grounds, that as human consciousness evolved there was indeed such a growing sense of distinctness from nature. This is something that Owen Barfield (1966) focused on in 'The Fall in Man and Nature'. He puts his central point succinctly when he says that 'Man did not fall *from* nature, or from a state of nature, but Nature fell *with* him (1966, p. 207), and quotes Milton's comment on Eve's eating of the Apple in Paradise Lost, that:

Earth felt the wound, and Nature from her seat
Sighing through all her works gave signs of woe
That all was lost.

There seem to have been long-term historical changes in the extent to which the outside world has been felt to be distinct from the inner one. Most, perhaps all, of our current vocabulary seems to have crystalized out from what were originally 'double aspect' terms, referring both to inner and outer aspects of experience. As I indicated at the end of Chapter 7, these double-aspect concepts seem to have lost their immediacy. The indication from linguistic research (Barfield, 1928) is that our present sense of separateness from our environment has developed gradually.

It is hard for us to keep sufficiently in mind that our way of seeing human consciousness and nature as being separate and distinct is not the only way of looking at things. There is a kind of dualism that arises here between the inner and the outer that parallels that between mind and body. It leads us to see evolution as a purely physical process that eventually led to the emergence of subjective consciousness. To refer back to issues considered in Chapter 2, I would want to see consciousness as arising more within a total system constituted by emerging human beings *and* their environment, rather than as being the result of selection pressures exerted *by* the external environment *on* human beings. The problem of the biological basis of human consciousness needs to be tackled in a broadly biological way, rather than in a narrowly neurological one. We need to learn, as Varela *et al.* (1991) in the put it in *The Embodied Mind*, 'to see organisms and environments as mutually enfolded structures' (p. 199). This line of thought may lead in a direction in which it is more credible once again to link moral and natural evil.

Steiner's theory of how the direction of consciousness has changed is relevant to the salvation of nature. He suggests that there is no longer a sense of the spiritual speaking to humanity through nature, but of the spirit within humanity guiding the perception of nature. On this view, the only way to avoid seeing nature as increasingly dead, and therefore ripe for exploitation, will be to have the spirit endowed imagination to re-enchant it through how we perceive it. Nature can no longer be imbued with spirit in the old animistic way. In that sense the redemption of nature may need to be mediated through human consciousness, even if ultimately the capacity to do so is one of the fruits of the spirit.

Chapter 10

Eschatology:
Subjective and Objective Aspects

In this chapter I will examine Christian eschatology, the theology of God's purposes for the future, in the context of the interdisciplinary dialogue with the sciences. My particular purpose will be to shed light on the dialogue between psychology and theology over Christian doctrine, and to place that in the context of the wider dialogue between science and theology. To that end, I will examine eschatology in the light of *both* cosmology *and* psychology. It will become apparent that which other discipline is chosen for dialogue with theology affects how theology itself is understood. In particular, dialogue with cosmology emphasizes its propositional aspects, whereas dialogue with psychology emphasizes its attitudinal aspects. I will argue that the these different aspects need to be held together in authentic eschatological thinking, and that it is important to conduct the dialogue between theology and the sciences in a way that is not destabilizing.

This will also allow me to consider another theme, the pathologies of eschatological hope. Here I will argue that authentic hope depends on holding together these objective (propositional) and subjective (attitudinal) strands. Hope can disintegrate into *either* a mere propositional expectation that the future will be good (which is optimism rather than hope) *or* a mere wishfulness or fantasy about the future, which equally fails to inspire hope. Pathologies of hope can be discerned in which, in different ways, there is a breakdown of the proper relationship between the here and now and the hoped for.

Having considered hope, I will consider fears about the future in a similar way. Again, there is an interesting relationship between objectively based fears about the future and the more subjective mood of apprehension about it. It is an interesting feature of the current scene that, while hell is being relatively neglected in theology, there is a widespread, secular preoccupation with scenarios that can be seen as a kind of hell on earth. Again the dialogue between theology and psychology over the fear of hell raises issues about how to hold together objective and subjective aspects.

Eschatology and Natural Science

First, let us consider how dialogue with the natural sciences affects eschatological thinking. The natural sciences make predictions about the future of the universe. One basis for such predictions is the Second Law of Thermodynamics, which appears to predict that the universe is running down into disorder. Indeed it was the Second Law which first initiated a dialogue between eschatology and natural science. People became concerned that the disordered future predicted by science was incompatible with the Christian hope. Actually, it is not entirely clear what the Second Law does predict about the universe, because it is not clear that the universe is the kind of closed system to which the Second Law applies; also the second Law does not necessarily predict inexorable progress towards disorder (see Peacocke, 1986). However, leaving aside such complications, it is historically correct that the Second Law focused the question of whether the Christian hope was compatible with bleak cosmological predictions.

These days the Second Law is less central to such cosmic anxieties than the issue arising from big bang cosmology of the long term future of the universe. There are two possible scenarios, one in which the universe will implode on itself in a 'big crunch', and another in which it will expand infinitely, with gradual heat loss. Both scenarios are bleak, and again raise issues about compatibility with the Christian hope. For a fuller discussion of the theological significance of these cosmological predictions, see Polkinghorne and Welker (2000).

However, Christian eschatology belongs to a completely different world from the impersonal predictions of cosmology. For one thing, eschatology is essentially moral; it is about a *good* future; the Christian future is one promised by a loving and faithful God. When theologians speak of the hoped for future they are not generally speaking of a particular point in temporal chronology that will one day be the present, and then the past. Rather, they are speaking of a different kind of future, intended by God and hoped for by mankind. Indeed, eschatology is more a matter of promise than of prediction, and relates to eternity more than to the chronological future.

It is thus clear that Christian eschatology operates in a very different world from scientific predictions about the future of the universe. But yet Christians feel a residual unease about how the cosmology of the future impinges on their eschatological thinking. Granted that Christian eschatology is not *primarily* a set of propositions about the future of the universe, can it be completely independent of the future predicted by cosmology? To press the point, supposing that there was a confident scientific prediction that the whole universe was going to implode next year, would that really make no difference at all to the proclamation of the Christian hope? Bringing scientific predictions about the future of the universe into dialogue with eschatology can lead to a misrepresentation of eschatology as being more concerned with the scientific future than it really is. However, to say that eschatology has nothing whatsoever to say about the scientific future may misrepresent it in a different direction.

It may be helpful here to refer to Lindbeck's (1984) well-known identification of three ways of understanding Christian doctrine, in which the first is propositional. The dialogue between doctrine and science can easily result in taking doctrine more propositionally than it should be. As Lindbeck points out, there are other ways of taking doctrine, the expressive and the linguistic. Dialogue with the natural sciences can lead to neglect of these latter aspects of the function of doctrine. Many theologians would probably feel concern about the nature of Christian doctrine becoming misrepresented in this way. But how far should that unease be pressed? Does eschatology involve propositions about the future of the universe at all?

There is a parallel point about the relationship of the doctrine of creation to natural science. Here again it is easy for those operating in the interface between natural science and theology to misunderstand the doctrine of creation being about the origin of the universe. Surely it is not primarily about that, but about a different kind of dependence of everything in creation on God. Yes, but does it have any implications at all for what we think about the origin of the universe? And if not, how can it altogether avoid having such implications without becoming empirically vacuous? There are different instincts here. Many would be inclined to say flatly that the doctrine of creation is just not about the origin of the universe at all. Others would say that it must have some implications for the origin of the universe, even if that is not its primary focus.

Theologians have often been concerned about doctrine becoming over psychologized. The widespread reaction against Tillich's theology in recent decades arose in part from sensing a danger that, along the road on which Tillich was travelling, Christian doctrine would be psychologized away. Against that danger, if that is what it is, theologians have often wanted to claim some kind of propositional content or objectivity for Christian doctrine. Yet it is not easy to see how the objective aspects of Christian eschatology can be explicated without saying something propositional about the future of the universe and the human race.

Popular scientific writing about the future of the universe, whether it will end in a big crunch or in heat death, appears to be propositional. However, it may not in fact be as narrowly propositional as it seems. There is currently what Larry Bouchard (2000) has called a 'moodiness' about cosmology. It is reasonable to ask why people are so intrigued by bleak predictions about the future of the universe. In fact, cosmology is not the only source of bleak predictions; concerns about a nuclear holocaust or a major environmental disaster have gripped the imagination in similar or even more vivid ways. It can be argued that what seem to be mere impersonal predictions about the future might in part be projections of spiritual realties and concerns onto the scientific or political arenas.

Jungian psychology has taken a particular interest in how ideas that are important in our culture, such as scientific theories, can be projections of the human mind (von Franz, 1985). Reflecting in a similar way, John Davy (1985) has argued that we need to 'begin to read what we call the external world as the 'outer face of our own inner realities'. The way in which we are preoccupied with the end of the universe says something about us, not just about the universe. The boundary between the objective and the subjective is not always to be drawn where we first think.

The nature of eschatology arises in a particularly acute form in popular integrations of science and eschatology developed by scientists. Over the last hundred years or so, many areas of apparently secular thought have taken over religious themes and given them new life. Eschatology is no longer a theological preserve, and contemporary practitioners of quasi-eschatology in popular science are now more widely read than any recent theological eschatology. As we saw in Chapter 4, AI is one area of modern science where ideas of a recognizably eschatological character are strongly entrenched. However, it is not clear that such secular eschatology is really a message of hope in the way that traditional eschatology has always been. For example, it is not clear why anyone should care whether their personal ways of processing information will be preserved indefinitely in computer form, in the way that Tipler (1995) foresees.

It is also not clear how that eschatology makes much sense without God. Christian eschatology maintains a careful balance, saying neither that we are helpless victims of fate, nor that we are masters of our future. That sense of balance is missing in scientific eschatology. The assumption is often that we will have the power to bring about the future that we wish, an optimistic assumption that on the face of things seems exaggerated, even irrational. A key part of the appeal of scientific eschatology seems to lie precisely in this proclaimed ability to control our destiny. To put it crudely, God-like powers are implicitly being claimed for human beings. Since theology ascribes omnipotence to God, an atheist eschatology seems to need to claim it for humanity.

Eschatology and Psychology

Let us now to turn to the very different dialogue between eschatology and psychology, which brings out the subjective aspects of eschatology more explicitly.

In eschatological hope, there is a distinctive relationship between the here and now and the hoped for. There has probably never been a settled tradition of Christian eschatology that is wholly consistent internally. From the earliest years, there have been contrasting strands of thought, albeit sometimes held concurrently. Some, such as Bultmann, have adopted a wholly 'realized' eschatology, that the Kingdom is now; eternal life is nothing more than a quality of life in the present. At the other extreme, eschatology can be located wholly in the future, though there have been further divisions about where this future was to be located. Some have seen it as beyond the grave, or have allowed it to recede into a wholly indeterminate future. Yet others, though mostly on the unorthodox fringes of Christianity, have adopted a specific and detailed futurist eschatology, in the sense of believing that there is a specific date in the future when Christ will come again, establish his Kingdom and the dead will be raised. During Christian history there have been repeated outbreaks of eschatological extremism along these lines. The sensible and predominant view is that eschatological extremes will not do. The Kingdom is 'inaugurated'; it is both 'now already' *and* ' not yet'.

I want to emphasize why this matters psychologically. Hope requires a sense of continuing inauguration. In a completely realized eschatology, there is nothing left to hope for. In a wholly futurist eschatology of a confident and specific kind, the future can seem too inevitable and predictable for *us* to be part of the hope. Hope thrives on a sense of what is inaugurated and possible, but always still coming into being.

It is important to make clear what kind of future we are concerned with in eschatology. We can think about the future in various ways. There is, for example, an ideal future to which we might aspire. In contrast, there is the foreseeable future that we expect or predict will actually come to pass. Moltmann (1970) has made a distinction between the 'futurum', the anticipated future, and the 'adventus', the radically new future. One danger is simply to confuse these two very different concepts. The other danger is to allow the link between the foreseeable future and the ideal future to become too tenuous. The transforming power of the hoped for future depends on it being adequately linked to the present and to the expected future. In eschatology, the hoped for future needs to remain inseparably linked to the predicted future without being confused with it. Proper eschatological thinking does not confuse the present and the future; and also does not confuse the predicted future with the hoped for future in the way that millenarianism does. Equally, proper eschatology does not so rupture the link between the present and the hoped for future that there is no transaction between the two.

In a similar vein, Meissner (1995) has recently offered a Freudian account of the pathology of eschatological thinking found in Utopian millenarianism. He sees millenarian eschatology as involving an undifferentiated fusion of the ego and ego-ideal; the two are simply not distinguished in the way that they need to be. He suggests that this failure to differentiate the ego and ego-ideal has its roots in infantile narcissism. Often the millenarian vision is wedded to violent and destructive fantasies about the events by which the final union of the 'hoped for' with the 'here and now' will be realized, indicating an abdication of the super-ego. However, not all eschatological hope has the features which Meissner diagnoses in extreme millenarianism. We need, as he says:

> to draw a distinction between the hopeful illusions that sustain life and increase the measure of tolerance for human existence and those fanatical visions that exceed the bounds of meaningful hope and sow the seeds of ultimate despair and discord, between an authentic faith that confirms life and identity and the fanaticism that leads away from reality and dooms its adherents to autistic solutions that solve nothing but substitute pure fantasy for the harshness of reality (p. 349).

Hope needs to maintain a clear link between the foreseeable future and the ideal future. It is only if this connection is maintained in human consciousness that the actual future is likely to take on some of the characteristics of the hoped-for future. Otherwise, the hoped for degenerates into something that is merely wished for, or fantasised about, with no actual hope for it, and consequently no commitment to bring it to pass.

Meissner's Freudian analysis of millenarian eschatology could be given a parallel in Jungian thought in terms of the axis between the ego and the 'Self' (that is, the complete and true self). In a healthy personality, the axis between the ego and Self remains open. The ego does not become so diminished or alienated that it has no contact with the Self. Equally, the ego does not become so inflated that it masquerades as the Self, failing to recognize its 'otherness'.

Dysfunctions of eschatological hope can, in this sense, be seen as parallel to a dysfunctioning of the ego-Self axis. The 'hoped for' in eschatological thought can function, for a whole religious movement, in a way that parallels how the symbol of the Self functions for the individual. Equally, the relationship of the present to the eschatological future can become dysfunctional, rather as the relationship of the ego to the Self can become dysfunctional within the individual.

In millenarian eschatology, there seems to be an 'inflation' of the imminent chronological future that fails to distinguish it adequately from the hoped for future. In completely realized eschatology, there is a different kind of inflation in which the present is wholly identified with the hoped-for future. There are other pathologies of eschatological thinking in which the eschatological future has no discernible link with the present, and so is not able to inspire hope. That represents a rupturing of the axis between the present and the hoped for that is equivalent to a rupturing of the ego–Self axis.

The Grammar of Hope

Authentic Christian hope depends on avoiding the extremes of over propositional and over attitudinal interpretations. Hope is not just a matter of holding optimistic propositional beliefs about the future. Neither is it simply a matter of a wish or desire about the future that fails to engage with what is actually likely to happen. Grasping the nature of hope makes it clear that it necessarily stands in a transitional world between the objective and the subjective. A good starting point for a conceptual analysis of hope is the excellent monograph, *Rules of Hope*, by James Averill *et al.* (1990). The view of hope taken there is broadly consistent with that taken, within a different intellectual tradition, by Gabriel Marcel in *Homo Viator* (1982) but Averill's formulation is more systematic. In elucidating the nature of hope, there are two related concepts from which it needs to be distinguished. Hope is different from optimism; it is also different from wishing, wanting or desiring.

Though a clear *conceptual* distinction can be made between optimism and hope, the situation is muddied by the fact that the word 'hope' can be used in a way that is virtually synonymous with optimism. The clearest difference between hope and optimism lies in the confidence with which a future event is predicted. The more likely something is to happen then, by definition, the more optimistic you are that it will happen. This is not true of hope. Indeed, hope characteristically occurs in situations of darkness or uncertainty in which optimism would be impossible or out of place. For example, when you are seriously ill, you may hope to recover, even though the medical prognosis does not allow you to be optimistic. Or if you are being held in a concentration camp, you may hope to live and eventually to be released, though the circumstances hardly justify optimism.

Hope thus differs from optimism in its relation to the rational probability of an occurrence. Because of this, it commands less confidence about the future to talk about hope than about optimism. Politicians who said only that they 'hoped' the economy would improve would inspire no confidence that it would actually happen. On the other hand, to say that you are 'optimistic' that the economy will improve is at least intended to convey a measure of confident expectation.

Extreme pessimism about the future makes hope as inappropriate as does extreme optimism. There is a prudence about hope. People feel it is imprudent to hope for what is extremely unlikely to happen. Many maxims about hope warn again imprudent hope, for example, 'the houses hope builds are castles in the air'. Indeed, as Lash (1996) has pointed out, hope eschews the certainties of both optimism and pessimism. It is altogether more reticent; it adopts an 'interrogative' mood in relation to the future.

The difference between hope and optimism is one of four 'rules of hope' that Averill *et al.* have formulated in their grammar of hope. The second they call a moralistic rule. Hope is circumscribed by moral values in a way that optimism is not. You can be optimistic about any desired event, but you can only allow yourself to hope for what is good. Again, it is instructive to listen to how politicians talk. They use the language of hope, not for more technical matters of public policy, but when they are trying to reach for the moral high ground. They might talk, for example, of their hopes for a society that is kinder, more tolerant, more just. Hoping is intertwined with morality in a way that optimism is not.

Thirdly, you normally only hope for what is important to you. Hoping is such a serious matter that people rarely hope for trivial things. Optimism is again unconstrained in this way. The fourth rule of hope is an action rule. People are normally prepared to take action to bring about what they hope for. Optimism does not carry any specific commitment to action. If you confidently expect something to happen, you can simply wait for it to arrive. Hope, in contrast, demands action. That constrains what you can hope for. Unless you are prepared to work for something, you are in effect constrained from hoping for it.

These rules of hope are also relevant to distinguishing wishing, wanting or desiring from hope. Wishing is unconstrained by probabilities. In particular, it is unconstrained by considerations of prudence. Though people generally do not allow themselves to hope for what is very unlikely, there are no constraints on *wishing* for something that is pure fantasy. Again, wishing is not constrained by morality. You can wish for purely selfish gratifications. What you wish for may be not only *a*moral, it may actually be *im*moral. Thirdly, what you wish for may be quite trivial. You can wish for a delicious dessert, but it would be stretching the grammar of hope, as Averill formulates it, to say that you hoped for one. Finally, wishing carries no commitment to action. It can be simply be a matter of 'wouldn't it be nice if ... '; with no obligation to try to ensure that it comes to pass.

The commitment to action is a key factor in translating wishes into hopes, as Meissner has also pointed out (1987). You may have wishes that have the potential to become hopes in that they are important and moral, but it is the engagement with reality involved in accepting a commitment to bring them about that marks the dividing line between wishing and hoping. Wishing may sometimes be the source from which hoping arises. However, even if wishing is a necessary pre-condition for hoping, it is certainly not a sufficient one.

Optimism and wishing are equally unconstrained by the rules of hope, but in other aspects they are very different, even opposite. Optimism is objective, in the sense that it reflects probabilities that can be determined in a purely rational, even mathematical way. Wishing, in contrast, can be highly subjective, and represents a retreat into a personal, primitive, even autistic world. It *can* be, though it perhaps need not always be, a retreat into the infantile world in which wanting something is all-important; whether it is actually available in the real world is an irrelevant distraction from the subjective power of the wish.

The nature of hope can be elucidated further by looking at its antithesis, that is, hopelessness, or despair. Is hopelessness a lack of optimism, or a lack of hope (as defined above)? The current psychological research literature on hopelessness defines it in terms of expectations, either the expectation that highly desired outcomes will not occur (which would be a lack of optimism) or the expectation that highly aversive outcomes will occur (which would be pessimism) (for example,

Alloy, 1988). Such definitions of hopelessness thus link it conceptually to optimism, pessimism, and expectations for the future, rather than to a lack of hope in the strict sense.

However, I suspect that a lack of optimism is, psychologically, a less significant phenomenon than a lack of hope. The hypothesis under consideration in current psychological research is that hopelessness is a sufficient cause of depression. However, I doubt whether lack of optimism about the future always leads to depression. We live in a bleak world, in which negative expectations about the future are often justified by the reality of our situation. It is implausible that such negative expectations always lead to personal depression. Also, negative expectations about the future are by no means incompatible with hope. Indeed, if we follow Gabriel Marcel, it is precisely in situations in which the future looks bleak that hope comes into its own. My suggestion is that negative expectations about the future only lead to depression where there is a failure of hope, as defined here with the aid of Averill's grammar of hope.

James Hillman (1964) writes movingly about the value and importance of the abandonment of hope, though I think he is thinking more of the abandonment of optimism. When he says, for example that the 'religious meaning of hope implies the sacrifice of all hoping', I think he means that it is optimism that has to be sacrificed. In the loss of optimism that accompanies the suicidal moment, he sees a time of opportunity. He also suggests that the abandonment of what he calls hope (I think he means optimism) is a valuable precondition for psychoanalysis:

> To be weak and without hope ... is often a highly positive condition at the beginning of analysis. It does not feel positive.... But death is going on and a transformation is probable. An analyst may encourage his patient to experience these events, to welcome them, even to treasure them – for some get better by getting worse. If he starts to hope with the patient to 'get rid of' them he has begun to repress in a medical way (p. 159).

The task of the therapist, as Hillman sees it, is to be 'with' patients in their moments of hopelessness, and that is surely also sometimes the task of the Christian pastor. Hopelessness cannot always be cured, and perhaps should not be. Out of the collapse of optimism, a new hope can be rebuilt that does not depend on optimism.

So, is hope objective or subjective? I suggest that it stands at the intersection of the two. It arises at a point of intersection at which creativity, imagination, emotion and religion also stand. Indeed, in this sense, there may be no more religious emotion than hope. In the terms I have used in this chapter, hope integrates the propositional and the attitudinal.

The concept of hope, as I have defined it, and distinguished it from optimism and wishing, was relatively rare in Greek literature before the New Testament. Certainly the word 'elpis' and related forms occurred, and these are often translated as hope. However, as Myers (1949) has pointed out, it is clear that the concept involved was really 'rationally based optimism'. Hoping for something that could not be rationally expected, that is, hope as defined here, was a usage first found in Thucydides, but one that came into its own in the New Testament.

The Old Testament had a rather different concept of hope, focusing mainly on trust, especially in the context of hoping in God, and often lacking any specific concern with future events. There are passages in the New Testament, especially those quoting the Old Testament directly, that use hope in exactly this sense. In Paul, both concepts of hope are found, sometimes one sense being predominant, sometimes the other. However, the significant thing is that Paul brings together strands of the Greek concept of hope as optimism and the Jewish concept of hope as trust (Romans 8:25). In talking about hope for what is unseen, he makes it clear that he is not talking about mere optimism. It would be going too far to say that this broader concept of hope was coined within Christianity. However, I think it would be reasonable to say that the blending of elements of trust and optimism in the concept of hope was one that Christianity found very congenial, and which was given impetus by Christianity.

Resurrection

It may be helpful in focusing on these issues about eschatology further to look briefly at the nature of the resurrection. The resurrection of Christ can be discussed in dialogue with either the natural or the human sciences, and which dialogue partner is chosen again nudges the understanding of the doctrine in one direction or the other.

It is, of course, the idea of the resurrection of a *body* in which the natural sciences would take most interest. One question would be about the possibility of physical resurrection, and many would be inclined to say that it was a scientific impossibility. Certainly, in ordinary experience, bodies simply do not resurrect. However, it seems to me that science always has to be careful about saying that events *could* not happen. What we call the 'laws of nature' operate under a certain range of conditions. Outside their boundary conditions, it is unpredictable what might happen. Jesus may have been such an unusual person that the normal boundary conditions, under which resurrection is impossible, were transgressed in a way that made it possible.

Another question the natural sciences would want to raise about the resurrection is the nature of the resurrection body of Christ. The indication from the New Testament is that it was not an ordinary mortal body. That is clear both from the Gospel resurrection narratives, and also from St Paul's interesting discussion in 1 Corinthians 15 about different kinds of flesh. If there was indeed a physical resurrection of some kind, it seems clear that the resurrection body was not an ordinary mortal one; it was not simply a resuscitation. That leads to the interesting question about what kind of body the resurrection body was, something that could be discussed in dialogue with the natural sciences.

Yet another area of dialogue with natural sciences about the resurrection is its relation to time and space, something that has already been fully discussed by Torrance (1976). One could suggest that the resurrection body has the same kind of relationship to ordinary space as the eternity of the risen Christ bears to time. The latter has been much discussed, the former much less. However, the understanding of the relationship between space and time in our post-Einsteinian world might nudge us towards developing parallel accounts of the relationship of the resurrection to space and time. There is also the question that Torrance addresses of the 'Lordship of Christ' over space and time, and the way in which space and time in general may have begun to be transformed by the resurrection.

These are matters that could be pursued at length, but my concern here is more with whether these are appropriate questions to be pursuing at all. It is clear that they are questions that most contemporary theologians do not choose to pursue. That might be either because they do not feel competent to do so, or because they feel that such questions involve a misunderstanding of the nature of the resurrection. They might seem to imply too literal and propositional an understanding of the resurrection.

Certainly, the resurrection is not just about what happened to a body; the New Testament certainly sees it as having a much broader significance. Some would say that it is not primarily a physical event but a spiritual event. Yes, but is it exclusively a spiritual event? We are back to an issue that is rather like the relationship of the doctrine of creation to the origin of the universe. The doctrine is not primarily about origins, but does it have any implications for origins at all?

Of course, the worldview of the New Testament (and indeed most pre-modern theology) does not make a sharp division between the physical and the spiritual, and it would not be faithful to that worldview to interpret the resurrection as a purely physical event. However, it does not do any better justice to that New Testament worldview to see the resurrection as a purely spiritual or social event, and not a physical one at all. The wariness of many theologians about getting into dialogue with the natural sciences about resurrection seems to come from the fear that this will make the concept of resurrection appear indefensible. The implicit assumption seems to be that many key tenets of Christian doctrine would be indefensible in the contemporary world if they were interpreted in a way that left them open to scientific challenge. It is a matter for concern that contemporary science seems to exercise such a tyranny over theological discussion, but that this is not often admitted openly.

Shall we then choose a different dialogue partner and consider resurrection in connection with psychology? Here again, there is much of interest to be discussed. One obvious line of interest is the way in which belief in the resurrection arose out of the grief processes of the disciples. In fact, it is very common for bereaved people to see and hear their loved ones after they have died. That is surely part of the background for the disciples seeing and hearing the risen Jesus. For example, the way in which the Johannine farewell discourses deal with the departure of Jesus maps very closely on to our modern psychological understanding of grief processes (Spiegel, 1978). There is also much to be explored in the sociology of collective grief, for example about how memory is transformed in the grief process, and the role of cultural memory in resurrection belief (Welker, 2000).

However, the key question is again about the relationship of such interdisciplinary dialogue to how the doctrine of resurrection should be understood. One possibility is to take the resurrection in a sharply reductionist way, that the belief in the risen Jesus was 'nothing but' the manifestation of a standard grief process. A focus on the role of grief processes in resurrection experience need not be reductionist. It would also be compatible with a more 'realist' understanding of the role of God in the resurrection, along the lines that

God fostered a belief in the risen Jesus through the kind of processes by which people normally respond to a bereavement.

Looking at resurrection in dialogue with psychology or sociology thus presses the interpretation of resurrection in a different and opposite direction from looking at it in dialogue with the natural sciences. It can take us towards seeing resurrection as essentially a matter of faith, in which the disciples came to believe in the risen Jesus, experience his spiritual presence with them beyond the cross, were transformed by it, and embarked on the dissemination of what has become a major world faith tradition.

But, if taken too far, this also seems not quite right either. Just as looking at resurrection in dialogue with the natural sciences seems to overemphasize the objectivity of the event, so looking at it in connection with the human sciences seems to overemphasize its subjectivity in a way that very easily leads to the conclusion that the resurrection was a merely subjective or cultural event. My conclusion is that the natural and human sciences can illuminate different aspects of the nature of resurrection, but that it is elucidated most adequately, and in the most balanced fashion, when they are both taken into account.

The Concept of Hell

Let us now turn from the hope of heaven, and the nature of resurrection, to the fear of hell. We will find that a parallel set of issues arises.

It will be helpful to begin with some general remarks about the concept of hell. There is an important asymmetry between belief in heaven and in hell, with heaven being more central to Christian belief than hell (for example, Kung, 1984). Hell perhaps needs to be retained as a possibility, if there is to be freedom of choice, but it is not essential, theologically, that anyone should actually choose it. Universal salvation would not contradict the fundamental tenets of Christian belief, but it would be a bizarre theology that foresaw universal consignment to hell. Similarly, though most people have seen heaven as eternal, at least some theologians have seen a permanent hell as inconsistent with the loving purposes of God (Hick, 1976). Yet again, there are particular individuals, the saints, who the Church has been confident have been received into heaven, but there has not generally been the same confidence about any particular individual going to hell.

Traditionally, concepts of physical punishment and pain, especially fire and burning, have been an important part of the concept of hell. However, this has not been the only way of conceiving it. In British theology, F.D. Maurice was a key figure in arguing for an understanding of hell in present experience as a separation from God (Rowell, 1974). Increasingly, priority has been given to hell as separation from God, or as total and permanent annihilation. John Stott (Stott and Edwards, 1988) has argued that much Biblical language about hell is concerned with destruction rather than suffering.

The position that particular theologians take up on this matter is often a reflection of where they stand generally on the liberal-conservative dimension, but the correlation is by no means a perfect one. For example, some liberal theologians (for example, Dearmer, 1929) have painted a fairly full-blooded portrait of hell to strengthen the case for discarding the whole idea. Also, within Jungian theology, hardly a conservative tradition, there have been those who have resisted what they would see as an over-sanitized idea of hell. Particularly interesting here is the way Jim Garrison (1982) links the contemporary issues of nuclear warfare with the theological one of the wrath of God.

Despite the growing theological reticence about hell, there is much that seems to make hell, or something like it, a vivid contemporary experience. The Nazi programme of exterminating the Jewish people, and the accompanying horror of the concentration camps, has been the focus of rich theological reflection (see Cohn-Sherbok, 1989), and can easily be seen as representing a kind of 'hell on earth'. The 'ethnic cleansing' that has taken place in former Yugoslavia could be seen in the same way. To treat human life as essentially worthless, and to casually inflict suffering on such a vast scale, brings about something close to what most people imagine hell to be like.

There are also dire possibilities for the future of the human race that can be seen, in some ways, as like a fear of hell on earth. For example, the fear of a nuclear 'Armageddon' seems to represent a fear of a kind of hell, an unprecedented destruction of life on earth from which hardly anything would survive (Race, 1988). It is also possible to foresee a kind of hell in an environmental catastrophe that would leave the planet unable to support human life, even though this has so far attracted less interest of an explicitly apocalyptic kind. The total destruction that is feared in both cases links in an interesting way with the kind of contemporary evangelical thinking, represented by John Stott that sees hell primarily in terms of annihilation.

The idea of hell on earth, as opposed to hell in the future is, of course, not a theological impossibility. The issues are parallel to those concerning heaven on earth. As we have seen, there has been a near-consensus in favour of an 'inaugurated' eschatology that sees the partial manifestation of heaven on earth as a foretaste of the heaven that is to come. Just as there can be an anticipatory experience of heaven on earth, so there can perhaps be an anticipatory experience of hell on earth. There is no reason why, on this point, there should be an asymmetry between heaven and hell.

However, is it any more than loose talk to speak about the Nazi holocaust or a nuclear Armageddon as being in some sense 'hell on earth'? Despite the appalling evil and suffering in Nazi concentration camps, and the equally appalling possibility of global nuclear warfare, it is not clear that these really help us to believe in hell in the strict sense of the concept. There is more to hell than extreme suffering; there also needs to be separation from God. Of course, life in a concentration camp would put anyone's belief in God under strain. However, there are many moving examples of people whose faith in God held firm in those appalling conditions, and notable examples of people who managed to see the crucified God as being present with them in their own experience of suffering.

There is also no reason why being in a concentration camp should strengthen anyone's belief in a future, more complete hell. Contemporary experiences of 'hell on earth' may give us a model of what hell might be like, but they do nothing to help us to believe in an ultimate hell. Concentration camps were an appalling present reality, and they carried fear of either natural death of extermination, but they did not obviously represent a threat of anything beyond themselves. Also, there was no sense in which being in a concentration camp represented God's punishment for the moral failings or faithlessness of those concerned; those consigned to them were generally innocent. Hell is, in a strict sense, a just judgment, something that people bring on themselves by how they lead their lives. There was nothing of that in the 'hell' of concentration camps.

It is not clear that global nuclear warfare would come any closer to representing hell on earth. Despite the widespread physical death it would bring, it would not necessarily bring separation from God. Also, because it would necessarily involve the death of many innocent people, it is hard to see it as representing the just judgment of God on the lives of those caught up in it. Those who have been attracted by the idea of nuclear warfare as Armageddon have seen the judgment involved as being a collective one, served on the human race as a whole. However, this causes the destruction of the innocent. Despite the presence in the Old Testament of a line of thinking about destruction of whole peoples because of the sin of some individuals, Christians have generally been uneasy about the idea of the judgment of God being visited on the innocent.

Hell and Psychology

Though there are problems in seeing twentieth century experiences of 'hell on earth' as representing hell in the full theological sense, there may be a case for seeing them as the outcome of deep-seated spiritual forces of destruction. This approach redirects the focus of interest towards the psychological and spiritual roots of hell on earth. C.G. Jung (1954) made an important contribution to this way of thinking in *Answer to Job* and elsewhere. It is a specific example of the general trend in Jungian psychology to see social and cultural phenomena as the outcropping of psychological forces. Jung's theoretical apparatus makes him better equipped than most psychologists to make this kind of connection. The key concept is that of the collective unconscious, a world of archetypes that belong to the collective world rather than to the individual psyche. Of more specific relevance to the concept of hell is Jung's emphasis on the reality of evil and the dark side of God. Jung took fierce exception to the traditional Thomist notion of evil as the mere absence of good (*privatio boni*) because he thought it denied the reality and power of evil. However, it is not clear that this is a necessary implication of the *privatio boni*, and it has been argued (Philp, 1958), that Jung did not fully understand the doctrine he was criticizing.

Jung's emphasis on the reality of evil led him to a concept of God which was broad enough to encompass evil; though Jung's use of the term 'God' here is not the traditional one. In Jungian thought, such as that of Garrison (1982), the paradox that God is ultimately good, but also the source of evil, is one that leads us to an important insight about God. He is experienced as 'antinomial', encompassing good and evil with Godself. Within more orthodox systematic theology, John Robinson (1979) has gone some way towards articulating a related position in his *Truth is Two-Eyed*.

Particularly interesting in the present context are Jung's reflections, in his article on Wotan, on the collective psychological disorder represented by Nazi Germany, because it was Nazi Germany that produced the Jewish holocaust and the concentration camps that are one of the most vivid examples of 'hell on earth' in the twentieth century. Part of the precondition for what happened in Nazi Germany, on Jung's analysis, was the absence of the Christian God. This is highly relevant to the idea of the concentration camps as a kind of hell, in view of traditional thinking about hell as the absence of God:

> Christianity was accepted as a means to escape from the brutality and unconsciousness of the ancient world. As soon as we discard it the old brutality returns in force, as has been made overwhelmingly clear by contemporary events. This is not a step forward but a long step backwards into the past ... Who throws Christianity overboard and with it the whole basis of morality, is bound to be confronted with the age-old problem of brutality. We have had bitter experience of what happens when a whole nation finds the moral mask too stupid to keep up. The beast breaks loose, and a frenzy of demoralization sweeps over the civilized world.' (*Collected Works*, Vol. X, pp. 179–93.)

What is this beast? Jung suggests that it was Wotan, 'the ancient God of storm and frenzy', the principal God of the pre-Christian Teutons. With the conversion of the people to Christianity, Wotan had lived on in local traditions as a devil. However, Jung says, an archetype is 'like an old watercourse along which the water of life has flowed for centuries'. When the opportunity presented itself, the power of Wotan reasserted itself over the German people.

One of the interesting things in Jung's analysis is that, despite his hostility to the *privatio boni* doctrine, he sees the absence of the power of moral goodness inherent in Christianity as being the key factor that made the return of evil possible. Jung picked up another aspect of this theme in his 1945 paper, 'After the Catastrophe' (*Collected Works*, Vol. X, pp.194–217). Here he suggests that the absence of the Christian God allowed archetypal supernatural qualities to be transferred to human beings, filling them with arrogance and arousing evil. 'It produces a diabolical caricature of man, and this inhuman mask is so unendurable, such a torture to wear, that he tortures others.'

It is difficult to find satisfactory criteria by which to evaluate this analysis. Given the basic presuppositions of Jungian psychology, it is a plausible theory of its kind. However, it is advanced with little of the supporting evidence and arguments that might convince the sceptic. What it does do, nevertheless, is to offer a theoretical analysis of the Nazi holocaust that helps to put flesh on the intuitive idea that, in some sense, it represented a manifestation of hell on earth.

In a similar way, questions can be raised about the psychological and spiritual significance of a possible nuclear holocaust. The key starting point for such an analysis would be to grasp that a nuclear holocaust is not so far an actuality, but a threatened possibility. If the theology of hell is 'threat discourse', discourse about a possible nuclear holocaust can also be threat discourse. The fear of nuclear catastrophe functions in some ways like the fear of hell. The threat of a global environmental catastrophe can also function in a similar way, and may have superseded the nuclear threat as the dominant global anxiety.

For many people, an awareness of these dangers leads to strenuous efforts to avert them. It can raise people to new levels of responsible conduct. However, this is not the only possible response. It is equally possible to respond to the possibility of global catastrophe, whether nuclear or environmental, with a mood of fatalism. The nuclear threat seems to present people with a clear choice about whether to acquiesce in fatalism or to strive against it (Corner, 1988).

For Christians, this is linked to a dilemma about how to see global catastrophe in relation to the sovereignty of God. As Kaufman (1985) has pointed out, the prospect of nuclear destruction raises the question of whether or not God is sovereign. In stark terms, it might be felt that either God is willing the catastrophe, or that he is not sovereign. There are, of course, within the twists and turns of Christian theodicy, ways of finessing this apparent dilemma. Perhaps the most important point to note in the present context is that the dilemma is not so very different from the parallel one about the relation of God to hell, where it takes the form of the question of whether hell is the will of God, or whether hell is outside his sovereignty.

One rather unsubtle way of dealing with these dilemmas in relation to nuclear catastrophe is to see it as the direct expression of God's punishment. This approach is central to those who see a nuclear holocaust as God's Armageddon. This, at least has the attraction of seeing continuity of God's purpose going through and beyond nuclear destruction. However, despite this initial appeal, it is in many ways a theologically unsatisfactory resolution of the problem. The Armageddon theory sees God as acting in time, to end history as we know it, ushering in God's eternity. However, like almost all popular apocalyptic theology, this represents an unsatisfactory confusion of God's eternity with a specific temporal act. Also, from a moral point of view, it introduces a degree of helplessness into the human situation. If God is bringing in Armageddon, what does it matter whether or not people try to act responsibly to avert the catastrophe?

The threat of both nuclear and environmental catastrophe is, of course, a very real one. The possibility of nuclear war between the superpowers may have receded, but the possibility of a nuclear war being launched by a small, maverick state is still all too real. Also, though the risk of serious climatic change and environmental crisis is difficult to quantify, it is hard to avoid the conclusion that it is really quite likely to occur.

Despite the reality of these threats, and the urgent need for action to avert them, there is something strange about the way in which these anticipated crises have gripped the imagination. This applies both to those who fear the catastrophe, and to those who, in the Armageddon tradition, almost welcome it as a manifestation of the power of God's judgment. As with the current preoccupation in cosmology over the eventual end of the universe, the possibility needs to be considered that the threat of global annihilation that haunts the modern imagination is, in part, the projection of a psychological or spiritual reality onto the material and historical domain.

Apocalyptic discourse has always been, in part, a way of talking about present realities under the guise of apparently talking about the future. It thus seems that apocalyptic discourse about impending nuclear or environmental catastrophe may be discourse about present psychological or spiritual realities as much as about future material realities.

We are talking here about a strange kind of future. Just as with the future that Christians hope for, it is not clear that the future events that are feared represent a point in chronological time that will ever become a time in the past. They seem to exist, in part, in some different kind of future. This should not be taken as arguing against the need for action to ensure that future catastrophes do not come to pass. However, it is helpful to be aware that the kind of apocalyptic future that we fear may be as much spiritual or psychological as chronological. The two should not be muddled up.

Perhaps, as John Davy (1985) has pointed out, it was something of this sort that Christopher Fry (1951) was referring to in that vivid phrase, spoken by Tim Meadowes in *A Sleep of Prisoners*, that 'affairs are now soul-size'. Maybe the response that is needed is a response of the soul as well as a practical one. Later in the play, Meadowes says:

> Thank God our time is now
> When wrong comes up to meet us everywhere
> Never to leave us till we take
> The greatest stride of soul
> Men ever took.

This discussion of hell has entered territory in which it is difficult to walk in a sure-footed way. We do not adequately understand the hellish aspects of modern life that I have considered here. Also, theological thinking about hell has become too impoverished to provide a well honed theoretical resource with which to seek to understand them. It is remarkable that the main pressures to rethink the idea of hell seem to come from contemporary experience rather than from within theology. As belief in hell has declined it has become, for many people, a concept that refers only to the separation of the individual from God. In contrast, the twentieth-century experiences that can be seen as representing a kind of hell on earth are collective ones. They have the potential to lead Christian thinking back to a more collective understanding of hell. In the process, it will become necessary to grapple more deeply with the psychological and spiritual roots of darkness and annihilation in modern life.

Conclusion

Both in the first part of this chapter concerned with the hope of heaven, and this latter part concerned with the fear of hell, we have found a complex relationship between subjective and objective aspects of eschatology. It is hard the keep the right balance between the two. Part of the problem is the way in which our general thought world fragments into the objective (propositional) and the subjective (attitudinal). We seem to be dealing here with a fault line in modern consciousness. Neither pure objectivism nor pure subjectivism are a good choice. There are increasing voices suggesting that we need to hold the two together (for example, Bernstein, 1983).

Specifically, we should resist choosing between an over objective and an over subjective way of interpreting Christian doctrine. As we have seen, problems arise both from the over-propositional understanding of eschatology that results when it comes into dialogue with the natural sciences, and from the over-attitudinal understanding of it that results when it comes into dialogue with psychology. Theology is best located in the in-between land that is neither wholly objective nor wholly subjective. This place, where the objective and the subjective meet, is the place where good theology is done.

For those of us committed to the interdisciplinary study of Christian doctrine, the question is how to benefit from interdisciplinary partners without allowing them to dislodge us from this important intermediate space. To hold the balance between the objectifying tendencies that come from dialogue with the natural sciences, and the subjectifying tendencies that come from dialogue with human sciences such as psychology, we may need both dialogue partners.

Chapter 11

Dichotomous Thinking in Theology

Theology is continually beset by pressures towards sharp antitheses and over-strong dichotomies: something is said to be this *or* that. Further, it is often assumed that 'this' and 'that' are mutually incompatible and that there can be no relationship between them. In this chapter, I hope to show that the consequences of giving way to such pressures to dichotomous thinking in theology are pernicious, both theoretically and practically.

Dichotomous thinking is not merely a matter of making conceptual distinctions. Distinctions are usually helpful and aid clarity of thought. They only become dichotomous if it is assumed that the things distinguished are unrelated to each other, sharply contrasting and incompatible. Coleridge was clear about the difference between distinguishing and dividing, welcoming the former but castigating the latter. Above all, he emphasized that what is distinguished need not be – and usually should not be – divided: 'It is a dull and obtuse mind that must divide in order to distinguish, but it is a still worse, that distinguishes in order to divide' (cited in Barfield, 1971, p. 19).

I will consider three contexts in which such dichotomous thinking arises in theology. The first is epistemological, the over-sharp distinction between self and world, between the knower and what is known, and between the subjective and the objective. Second, I will consider dichotomies in Christian doctrine. In eschatology, as we have seen, there can be a dichotomy about whether eternal life is already now, or still to come. But there are many such either/or dichotomies in doctrinal thinking: concerning the relationship between God and humanity, between the immanent and the transcendent, and so on. Thirdly, there is the dichotomy between, on the one hand, obedience to authority and tradition and, on the other, personal freedom and autonomy in religion. Each one tends to be seen in either/or terms, but I want to suggest that such dichotomies should be resisted.

These issues could be approached from the standpoint of various different disciplines but I will approach them here from the standpoint of psychology. Epistemological dichotomies raise issues that can be tackled from the standpoint of cognitive psychology. Doctrinal dichotomies have parallels in psychological polarities that shed light on their human significance. Finally, the dichotomy between authority and autonomy can be approached from the standpoint of the psychology of human relationships.

Epistemological Dichotomies

In the last chapter, we confronted the problem of how far eschatology should be interpreted objectively, and how far it should be seen subjectively. There are

Theology and Psychology

dangers either way. If all contact with objective prediction is lost, it becomes vacuous. However, unless there is emphasis on human significance and personal implications, Christian doctrine becomes detached from faith and serves no function. With eschatology, as with all doctrines, the tendency to reduce them to the merely objective, or the merely subjective, needs to be resisted.

To gain some historical perspective, let us note that the present connotations of the terms 'objective' and 'subjective' are a development of the Enlightenment. A *volte-face* took place in the meaning of the word 'subjective' in the seventeenth and eighteenth centuries, from the Aristotelian sense of 'existing in itself' to the modern one of 'existing in human consciousness' (Barfield, 1953). 'Objective' also changed meaning, albeit less decisively, and in a roughly opposite direction. These changes in meaning are an indication of the radical rethinking of the nature of objectivity and subjectivity that occurred in the early modern period, with the dawn of the 'onlooker' or 'spectorial' consciousness. It culminated in the sharp division in the latter part of the nineteenth century between science on the one hand and art, poetry, religion on the other (Bowker, 1998).

The Enlightenment period saw an overemphasis on the rationality of Christian doctrine. The 'natural theology' project of the Enlightenment too easily fell into the trap of imagining that God was a being whose existence could be fully proved, and whose nature could be studied by rational human beings. At worst, that fostered a detached attitude to matters of faith, as though assessing Christian belief was like weighing up a new scientific hypothesis. It neglected the power of belief to move the heart, to shape behaviour, and to build community.

Fideism (the overemphasis on the basis of religious belief in pure faith, rather than in any kind of rationality) was a reaction against such an over-objective approach. Once it was assumed that faith could not simply be a matter of objective knowledge, it was tempting to safeguard faith by placing it on foundations altogether different from those of knowledge. Then it became 'pure faith', or even 'blind faith'. Of course, fideism has been right about some things, particularly about the way in which faith is a matter of personal commitment, not just the detached acceptance of a certain intellectual position. However, once faith is located in a domain altogether separate from knowledge, there is no possibility of integrating religious faith and secular knowledge in a broad worldview. Fideism shared with the over rational approach to religion of the Enlightenment too strong a dichotomy between the objective and the subjective. It is central to the present task of healing the inheritance from modernity that this unnecessary dichotomy should be overcome.

I will approach these issues from the standpoint of cognitive psychology rather than philosophy. Theology has made much use of epistemology, the branch of philosophy concerned with human knowledge. However, it is surprising, given the strength of theological interest in the grounds of religious beliefs, that theology has not shown a comparable interest in the psychological study of cognition. Cognitive psychology is the counterpart of philosophical epistemology.

Epistemology is usually evaluative, concerned with whether we are justified in holding our beliefs. The study of cognition is more attentive to how people actually arrive at their beliefs. It is not concerned with the ideal of certainty in knowledge, that has been the cause of so much epistemological trouble. Rather, it recognizes, in its more pragmatic way, that it would be inefficient for human beings to wait until they were certain before they adopted particular beliefs. There are some highly obsessional people who do actually aspire to certainty (Watts, 1995). Anyone who knows such a person will have seen a vivid demonstration of what an impossible target it is to operate in practice.

In *The Psychology of Religious Knowing* (Watts and Williams, 1988), I approached religious cognition by looking for parallels between religious knowing and other related forms of knowing. There are parallels, for example, with artistic perception, empathy with other people, and understanding of oneself. Though not alike in all respects, they all represent a reading of reality that is neither obvious nor arbitrary. They all require sustained effort, imagination, integrity and seriousness of purpose. Insights into the nature of oneself provide a particularly good analogue of religious insight. Of course, many people go through life with a relatively superficial understanding of themselves, and there are sometimes long periods when self understanding does not advance much. However, it is when people are making discernible progress towards more profound levels of self understanding that something like religious insight occurs.

Psychotherapy provides a rich context in which to observe this process. Though there is no single way in which personal insights and religious insights always arise, a common pattern is discernible. To gain insight, people need to set aside stereotyped ruminations and patterns of thought about themselves. That applies in both personal and religious contexts. To gain religious insight, you need to gain a certain distance from doctrinal clichés and religious obsessions. Equally, to gain personal insight in psychotherapy, you need to develop a style of attentiveness to your feelings and thoughts that is broad, sustained and penetrating. It is often necessary to hold many things in mind at once in order to begin to see their pattern and significance. That frequently has to be done at a tacit rather than a fully explicit level of consciousness. Equally, religious insights, which often arise in what Ian Ramsey (1964) called moments of 'disclosure', require a similar style of broadband attentiveness.

There follows a struggle to conceptualize and articulate such insights adequately. Often, at important moments of personal insight in psychotherapy, people have a sense of beginning to understand something important before they can articulate it. The effort to articulate is often a struggle, and the results may seem inadequate and disappointing. The insight, once expressed in words, often seems not to fully capture what the person was beginning to understand. In a not dissimilar way, Christian contemplatives, though they have written volumes, have nearly all emphasized both the difficulty of finding words that capture adequately what they want to express, and the importance on occasions of not articulating things in words. As we saw in Chapter 6, cognitive psychology can provide a plausible theory of why that should be so.

In going deeper into the question of how religion relates to objectivity and subjectivity, it will be helpful to take as a springboard Freud's (1927/1951) question of whether religion is concerned with 'reality' or 'illusion'. This sounds like a sharp dichotomy, though close attention to Freud reveals that it is a little less sharp than it has often been taken to be. For Freud, 'illusion' is a technical term meaning 'wish fulfilment'; it is not the same as delusion. Psychotic delusions are often internally consistent but impervious to the influence of all observations and other beliefs, which are either ignored, or distorted to support the delusional system. Where there is an over-sharp dichotomy between faith and knowledge, religious beliefs risk being held in a way similar to how delusions are held. As Jung (1958) remarks, 'The rupture between faith and knowledge is a symptom of the split consciousness which is so characteristic of the mental disorder of our day' (p. 74).

Illusion, as Freud defines it, is comparable to 'myth', which also has a technical meaning rather different from its popular meaning. When myth is used in the technical sense, the contrast between truth and myth is not as sharp as may at first appear, because mythological truth can be seen as one form of truth. Similarly, for Freud, 'illusion' is not as sharply antithetical to truth as is delusion. This nuance of meaning in Freud has recently been developed in a rich and fruitful way, by Paul Pruyser (1983) and W.W. Meisner (1984), to lay the foundations for a new psychodynamic understanding of religion. They have drawn on Winnicott's (1971) concept of the 'transitional', seeing religion as a transitional activity, along with art and play (see Watts and Williams, 1988).

The key point about the transitional is that it does not belong either to the real external world or to the private world of fantasy. It is a hybrid world, which combines elements of both. Winnicott's concept of the transitional arose from his observations of child development, but he extended it to adult activities, and developed its general theoretical importance. It is a concept that is helpful in releasing us from the over dichotomous question of whether religion belongs to a world of external public reality or to a world of private fantasy.

There are many philosophical questions to be raised about the concept of the transitional. Though it is welcome that at least some things are located within this domain, what is strange is that so many things are implicitly excluded from it. Outside the limited domain of the transitional, the distinction between external reality and private fantasy is apparently allowed to remain intact in psychoanalytic thinking. This is not satisfactory. Those who have concerned themselves with the implications for patterns of human understanding of how language is used will not be happy with such an unreconstructed concept of external reality. Neither will it commend itself to psychologists who have been concerned with the cognitive processes which enter into all human understandings of the world.

The world we 'know' is shaped by our previous experience and background assumptions. The concerns of cognitive psychology here seem to be somewhat broader than those of hermeneutics. Their resulting critique of the notion of external reality is perhaps more comprehensive, because cognitive psychology gives proper weight to the influence of memory and attention, as well as of language, on how we understand reality.

It is thus doubtful whether there is any knowledge of reality that, in one sense, should *not* be located in what Winnicott called the transitional world. However, religion, art and play perhaps have it in common that they are imaginative, and equip people for conduct in the real world, even though they are not content with descriptions of the obvious features of that world. What is needed now is a richer understanding of the *particular* ways in which the private and objective are intertwined in religion, and how this differs from how they combine elsewhere.

There are the beginnings of such an understanding in the work of Pruyser, Meissner and others. However, it remains to be developed and systematized.

There is another dichotomy, related to that between external reality and private fantasy, that has been influential in much religious thinking. This is the question of whether religious beliefs are making material or non-material claims about the world. This issue often surfaces in discussions about metaphor (for example, Barbour, 1974; Soskice, 1985), as there is usually an implicit assumption that the literal use of a word is the material one, and the metaphorical use a non-material one. As we saw in the last chapter, it is a debate that often occurs in connection with the resurrection. Those of conservative leanings want to interpret these claims about resurrection literally, that is, in a material, spatio-temporal sense. Those of more liberal outlook are inclined to take them metaphorically. As with many debates that do not move towards a resolution, one wonders whether the real problem might not be with the tacit assumptions that both sides share. I am suspicious of the underlying dichotomy between the material and the non-material worlds on which the dichotomy between the literal and the metaphorical is built.

The concept of metaphor is not a straightforward one. Janet Soskice in *Metaphor and Religious Language* defines metaphor as 'that figure of speech whereby we speak about one thing in terms which seem to be suggestive of another'. She rejects the idea that *words* are metaphorical in any general sense. Rather, it is speakers and hearers who *use* words metaphorically. She also rejects the notion that metaphorical words have two meanings. Rather, metaphorical uses of words have about them a 'tension' that reflects the fact that the metaphorical use has not yet become sufficiently lexicalized to justify, for example, a dictionary entry.

This is a good account of metaphor in a strict sense. However, I am doubtful whether much religious thinking is 'metaphorical' in this sense. Clearly, linkages between material and non-material meanings abound in religious thought, but they are so well established that there is little of the tension about their use that this strict concept of metaphor would require. Rather, the use of images in religious thinking is, as Soskice aptly calls it, 'emblematic'; it represents a constant reworking and enrichment of an established network of associations. The problem with emphasizing the role of the *usage* of words in metaphor is that it tends to steer things in a non-realist direction. It is easy to assume that the usage of words is essentially an arbitrary matter, and that alternative metaphors could perfectly well have been developed. This leaves us with too sharp a dichotomy between the world that is being described, and the language used to describe it.

It is helpful here to refer to what the social psychologist, Solomon Asch (1958), has called, 'double-aspect' terms. These are terms which have two established meanings, one material and one non-material, such as 'bitter', a bitter taste and a bitter experience (see Watts and Williams, 1988, Chapter 9). The same linkages between material and immaterial meanings appear in a variety of different, historically independent languages. That suggests that the linkages are not an arbitrary choice of language users, but that they reflect linkages between material and non-material aspects of reality. That, in turn, challenges the dichotomy between the material and the non-material.

Many of the images that are central to theological thinking are more like double-aspect concepts than they are like metaphors, in the strict sense in which Soskice and others define them. Consider a religious double-aspect term such as light which has both a material, or at least spatio-temporal, sense of daylight, and also a series of related non-material meanings such as the intellectual light that facilitaties knowledge, the moral light in which good and evil is revealed, and finally the nature of God himself as light. The idea of God as light seems to be a double-aspect (or multiple-aspect) concept rather than a metaphor in the strict sense.

To see the idea of God as light as a mere metaphor, originating in the contrived application of a word with a material meaning to convey a non-material idea, contains too sharp a sense of division between the material and non-material senses of light. It also locates this development in usage entirely in the speaker's use of language, and not sufficiently in the nature of the reality which is being described. Bultmann's (1961) programme of 'demythologising' religious language seems to reflect a lack of appreciation of the 'double-aspect' nature of religious thinking.

At a deep level, the psyche does not seem to respect the dichotomy between the material and the non-material, or between the literal and the metaphorical. This is seen most clearly in dreams. Dream language, like double-aspect terminology, straddles material and non-material domains as though they were two facets of the same reality. I suggest that religious thinking will similarly need to eschew sharp dichotomies between the material and the non-material, between the literal and the metaphorical. Thinking that is over dichotomous on these matters will risk being either merely intellectual, or as encapsulated as a psychotic delusion.

That does not mean that we should fail to make the relevant distinctions. Remember Coleridge's point that we can distinguish without dividing. If you look at how children attempt to comprehend metaphors, it seems that they often fail to make distinctions between the different ideas held together in a metaphor (see Watts and Williams, 1988, pp. 141–3). Maybe this was how it was for primitive humanity. Dreams suggest it is still like this for what might be called the 'deeper' levels of the mind or psyche. I cannot see that it is feasible or desirable for modern humanity to attempt to recapture such a non-analytical, undifferentiated style of thinking. But neither, I suggest, are we justified in retaining sharp dichotomies between the material and the non-material, or between the literal and the metaphorical.

Currently, we have two broad views about epistemology, one that believes in a rather naive way in the possibility of complete objectivity ('subjectless objectivity'), and another that assumes that no objectivity is possible ('non-objectifying subjectivity'). Sadly, all too many people seem totally entrenched on one side or other of this divide. Scientific discovery is often accompanied by a failure to recognize that all discoveries are in an important sense discoveries about language and point of view. Equally, those who have grasped the importance of language and point of view often have no interest in any kind of objective discoveries; too often postmodernism seems to want to win the battle against any kind of objectivity. I do not intend to imply here that reality and language can be separated, nor that one is primary to the other. However, I would reject the view that language is primary, just as strongly as I would reject the view that some non-linguistic or unencoded reality is primary.

There is nothing to be gained from trying to win this battle for one side or the other; what is needed is co-operation. As Owen Barfield (1977) puts it:

Perhaps each needs the clasp and support of the other in his half-blinded staggering towards the light. Perhaps there is not one prison cell but two: the non-objectifying subjectivity in which the humanities are immured, and the adjoining cell of subjectless objectivity, where science is locked and bolted; and maybe the first escape for the two prisoners ... is to establish communication with one another (p. 140).

Doctrinal Dichotomies

I will now consider doctrinal dichotomies in a parallel way. There are many such dichotomies. The eschatological dichotomies have already been considered in the last chapter. In 'realized' eschatology, the kingdom is now, and eternal life is a quality of life in the present. Others, though mostly on the unorthodox fringes of Christianity, have adopted a wholly futurist eschatology, that there is a specific date in the future when Christ will come again, establish his Kingdom and the dead will be raised. Fortunately, these strong dichotomies have been widely resisted, and an inaugurated eschatology has been adopted which holds the balance between extreme positions.

In Christology, there also tend to be dichotomies. There is a tendency either to see Jesus as just an outstandingly good and wise man, or as God wearing human flesh. The christological controversies of the early centuries strove to find a path between these extremes about the person of Jesus, and the eventual Chalcedonian formulation which insisted on his being both God and man set that out clearly. Indeed, there is no dichotomy that has been more strenuously resisted in classical theology than the idea that Jesus was either God *or* man, but not both. I wish that other theological dichotomies had been resisted as resolutely.

The Athanasian Creed also has a neat formulation of a similar point when it talks about neither confounding nor dividing the persons of the Trinity. It thus calls for an approach which makes the necessary distinctions (that is, not confounding) without completely separating (dividing). The specific example with which the Creed is concerned is, of course, 'neither confounding the persons nor dividing the substance' of the persons of the Trinity. However, the way in which the persons of the Trinity need to be distinguished without being divided is a model for how Christian thinkers should approach the danger of over dichotomous thinking in other contexts.

There are also important dichotomies concerning the Church and sacraments which became sharply polarized at the time of the Reformation. Indeed, it is only in the twentieth century that good progress has been made in overcoming them. Among the many ways in which the Church has been seen (Dulles, 1974), there are the extremes of it being either a mystical body or just a human assembly. Equally what is received in the Eucharist has been seen either as mere bread, albeit rich in symbolism, or literally as the body of Christ. Such dichotomies have often been maintained by a means of an unhelpful, low theory of the nature of symbolism, which has assumed that if something is 'merely symbolic' it has little real value or status. In the last section, I argued that such a theory is an inadequate view of metaphor; the same is true of symbolism.

There are also dichotomies concerning the relationship between God and humanity. For example, the emphasis tends to be either on God as immanent or God as transcendent. In some strands of modern theology, process theology for example, God is seen as the ground of the world. In other strands, such as Barthian theology, there has been a strong emphasis on the radical otherness of God, and on the sharp disjunction between God and humanity. Similarly, God can be characterized either by his judgment or his forgiveness, with some people emphasizing God's acceptance and forgiveness of humanity, and others emphasizing his radical call and the sternness of his judgment.

In the twentieth century, these are probably the theological dichotomies that have been hardest to resist. There do not seem to be the same classical resources to help in keeping a balance here as there are, for example, in Christology. The danger in conservative theology lies not so much in a strong sense of the 'otherness' of God, but in holding it in a way that does not sufficiently allow for the complementary sense of the relatedness of God to humanity and creation. Such theology cannot do justice to the unity of God with his creation and tends to lead to the marginalisation of God in relation to his creation. Equally, there are dangers in liberal theology, not with the wholly proper emphasis on God's relation to the world, but with surrendering too much of the power and mystery of God that some feel cannot easily be assimilated into modern thought.

There are parallels to these doctrinal dichotomies in psychological thought, which I will now explore. In the first chapter I pointed out how parallels to the idea of original sin can be seen in both sociobiology and in Freudian psychology. Psychology is replete with concepts that are parallel to theological ones. I propose now to approach this question of the relationship between God and humanity from the standpoint of Jungian psychology.

The axis between the ego and Self in Jungian thought presents a helpful analogue of these doctrinal dichotomies. Similar points could be made, though perhaps not quite so easily, in Freudian thought in relation to the ego and ego-ideal or, in more general personality psychology, in connection with the real self and ideal self. As we have noted already, the ego, in Jung as in Freud, is the centre of consciousness. The 'Self', in contrast, is the centre of the whole personality, conscious and unconscious, the wholeness to which each person can potentially move. What is required for movement towards individuation is to maintain a healthy relationship between ego and Self.

The axis between them can go wrong in one of two ways. The ego can 'inflate', become grandiose and, in a shallow and inadequate way, usurp and imitate the deeper functions of the Self. Alternatively, the ego can be alienated from the Self, or crushed by it, so that it cannot develop properly in relation to the Self (as a child may not develop properly if alienated from its parents). The relationship between the ego and the Self in Jungian thought is in some ways analogous to that between God and humanity. Humanity can become 'inflated' and usurp the functions of God, or can become 'alienated' and disconnected from God. In both cases the axis between them malfunctions.

Just as there needs to be a healthy axis between the ego and the Self, so, I suggest, there needs to be a healthy balance between the sense of imminence and transcendence of God. If there is too exclusive an emphasis on the transcendent otherness of God, the human person is left feeling disconnected from God, and in a position of helpless dependence or abasement before him. Alternatively, if people over-identify themselves with God, there is no sense of the 'beyond', of grace, or of possibilities beyond the obvious.

Different theological traditions about the immanence or the transcendence of God have been paralleled by different traditions of spirituality. The dominant Western tradition is stronger on separateness from God than on unity with him. The Eastern tradition, with its concept of the divinization of man has had a stronger sense of union with God, as have many Western mystics, and the currently fashionable 'creation spirituality' (Fox, 1983). Again, there needs to be a balance between a sense of the otherness of God and of the possibility of union.

Another psychological analogy that may be helpful is the process of socialization. Spiritual development can be seen as a socialization process, albeit one that continues in adulthood and is not only found in children. The socialization of children depends on parents both making demands on children that represent the intrusive reality of the social world, and being on the child's side, providing a dependable, supportive presence to help them cope with social demands. With only one or the other, children become either spoiled or frightened. The same combination arises in many other contexts. Industrial supervisors need to be demanding as far as work tasks are concerned, but also encouraging. So do psychotherapists need to be both challenging and supportive.

In a similar way, spiritual growth seems to depend on a sense of a God who is 'other', righteous and holy, before whom we will inevitably feel naked and inadequate. However, it also needs a sense of God who is one with us, who identifies himself with us and we with him, whose support is unfailing. Without a sense of the otherness of God, there will be little growth and change, just as there is little change in psychotherapy which is not challenging. Equally, without a complementary sense of oneness with God, there will be no feeling for what it is possible to become, and no confidence to embark on the journey.

In theology, it is necessary to maintain a 'both/and' formula about people both being made in the image of God, and also being sinful and fallen. There is an analogy between theological ideas about the sinfulness or fallenness of humanity and psychological ideas about human disability or a damaged personality. There are severe limits to what can be achieved in psychological therapy, even though progress occasionally exceeds what can reasonably be hoped for. Therapists need to develop a realistic sense of the constraints on change, just as they need a sense of the surprising opportunities for change that might actually be present. Psychiatry recognizes the disability of many of its patients, including those disabilities that antedate any specific episodes of distress or illness. There is a kind of parallel there with theological ideas about fallenness, about how humanity will always fall short of the ideal.

There are also analogues in psychotherapy of the sense of grace. Many therapists would recognize that there are limits to the extent that change can be planned in advance and worked for strategically. Many things are initially unpredictable: the course that personal development will take, the nature of the adjustment that will eventually be reached, the context in which change will take place, and its speed and time scale. Therapists often recognize that progress depends on working with a constellation of opportunities and constraints that are initially outside the knowledge and control of both client and therapist. Sensitivity to the givenness of these opportunities and constraints, and a spirit of cooperation with them, is analogous in some ways to the religious sense of working with the grace of God.

Theology should always maintain the possibility of redemption alongside a sense of the fallenness of man. The dark side of humanity should not be neglected or denied, but neither should it be regarded as the last word. There is an interesting analogy here with the role of the Jungian 'shadow' in individuation. Jung makes a distinction between the 'persona', (the presentable, public face of personality), and the shadow, (its unpresentable flipside that people conceal from others, perhaps even from themselves). An important feature of Jung's concept of the shadow is its relationship to the whole personality. It needs to be reintegrated with the rest of the personality on the path towards individuation.

Similar points can be made, theologically, about evil. It is tempting to think that there are some aspects of us which reflect our relatedness to God, but other aspects which are evil and show no relationship to God whatsoever. Theologically, this does violence to the understanding of God as the creator of all, and to the redemptive purpose of God. The doctrine of creation stands as a bulwark against a fundamental dualism between good and evil. To view evil as something which must simply be jettisoned on the religious path also does violence to the understanding of God as redeemer. The doctrine of the redemptive purpose of God teaches us not to attempt to discard what we may regard as the evil parts of our personalities. Even the lost sheep is sought out and brought back.

Theodicy has grappled with these issues. The Jungian view that the shadow is necessary for individuation seems close to the kind of theodicy espoused, for example by John Hick (1976) which recognizes the value of evil in 'soul-making'. This idea of the constructive 'soul-making' role of evil is perhaps at its weakest when presented as a justification for why there is evil in the world. However, taken as a matter of fact statement about the psychological and spiritual blessings that can come through overcoming evil, it is close to Jungian ideas about the value and indispensability of the shadow in individuation. Trying to separate out what people think are their good and bad aspects ignores the human reality that good and evil are intertwined. The Jungian concept of the shadow is helpful in capturing the interrelatedness of the light and dark sides of human nature.

In this section, I have tried to draw parallels between theological dichotomies and related patterns of thought in psychology. In doing such parallels, I am not trying to argue that psychology is really implicitly theological, nor conversely that it has appropriated theological ideas for its own secular enterprise and turned them into something anti-theological. My interest in these parallels is rather for the light they shed on the human significance of patterns of theological thought. There is more at stake in theology than simply whether it is intellectually correct, but also the practical matter of the effect it has on people. An over dichotomous style of theology can be unhelpful, personally and spiritually. The parallels between theology and psychology that I have drawn here provide the resources for showing why that is so.

Authority and Autonomy

Finally, I will consider the over sharp dichotomies that are often drawn in the Christian life between the acceptance of authority, and personal autonomy in religious matters. There are parallel issues about continuity and change in Christian thinking and living. Again, I will suggest that there are unnecessary dichotomies that need to be overcome. Robert Runcie (1988) called for 'an escape from the either/or of radical permissiveness and reactionary authoritarianism'. It would be neither practicable, nor attractive, to attempt to reverse recent liberal trends. However, a complete absence of authority seems equally unattractive, and can have damaging consequences. We therefore need to find a constructive middle-way between permissiveness and authoritarianism.

Authority has been exercised in different ways at different periods of history (see Meissner, 1971). In the last two centuries there has seen a dramatic erosion of traditional forms of authority, political, moral and religious. In recent times authority has become increasingly a matter of relationship, in which two inter-dependent people participate, one to offer authority and one to accept it. Both are free people, and choose to engage in a role relationship voluntarily, out of an explicit awareness of its functional purpose and creative potential. The occupancy of a position of authority is the occasion for a relationship which, in its functional characteristics, is voluntary.

Most discussion of religious authority has focused on where authority should be located. There has been relatively little discussion of *how* authority should be presented and what response to it is appropriate. This is the issue to which psychology, and the social sciences, can make a particular contribution. It is an approach that has often been neglected though there are some discussions of religious authority which have made use of the social sciences; for example Rowan Williams (1982) made use of Simon's (1980) general theory of authority, and Stephen Sykes (1984) made use of Wrong's (1979) social analysis of power. There has been surprising little psychological contribution to discussions of religious authority, though an important exception is William Meissner's (1971) book on authority.

In developing a psychological approach to this problem, it may be useful to begin with authority in pastoral care. There is a place in pastoral care for structure and guidance that parallels the place of authority in the Church, and the use of authority in pastoral counselling can provide an example of the middle path between permissiveness and authoritarianism that Runcie suggested that we need to find. Authority need not be coercive; it can also be enabling and empowering. As we saw in the last section, socialization relationships are most effective and helpful when they combine demands with support.

There is often a general need for the provision of structure and guidance in counselling, especially with certain kinds of client such as those who are not particularly 'psychologically minded'. Good counselling needs to adapt its approach to the personality of the client, and some clients need the provision of external structure. The predominant ethos in counselling is simply to facilitate clients' exploration of their own problems, but that is not always the most helpful approach.

For example, students may come to a student counselling service because they are having difficulty in disciplining themselves to do their work, despite the fact that they understand the need to do it. This can produce a desire for the sympathetic external authority that would enable them to do the work they basically want to do. The need for authority is not confined to such students. There are many people with behaviour problems, such as compulsive gambling, who have similar needs. Faced with this, it seems right, at least sometimes, to provide the structure that is sought. Of course, the long-term objective would be to help the person concerned to develop capacities for self-regulation that would render external authority unnecessary. However, the nature of the crisis is often such that more immediate help is needed.

There are rules of practice concerning the provision of authority in counselling. First, it should be made explicit that the authority is only being offered, and that the client can make a free decision about whether or not to accept it. The counsellor who uses authority should always make it clear that any authority he or she may have is only what is bestowed on him by the client. Secondly, when authority is used in counselling, it should not be to achieve objectives that counsellors have for their clients, but only to help clients achieve objectives that they themselves explicitly and consciously desire, but have been unable to achieve by themselves. Thirdly, the offering of structure and authority must be combined with a caring attitude, and should not be attempted unless it can be done in that spirit.

Similar issues arise in the use of authority in the Church. One criterion by which the proper use of authority in the church should be evaluated is how far it is experienced as enabling by those to whom it is offered. Authority in the church is most likely to be constructive and enabling in its effects when it is explicitly offered and accepted, rather than when it is imposed.

It is common in discussions of religious authority to make a distinction between authority and power, and the claim is often made that religious authority is not a matter of power. However, there is a danger of this point being made too easily. There is a marked reluctance in theological discussion to have anything to do with the concept of power. This leads, in turn, to the danger that the church will *claim* not to be involved in the exercise of power, but will continue to exercise it nonetheless. There are perhaps few things more distasteful than power struggles in the Church being waged under the camouflage of theological disagreements.

One of the practical consequences of exercising authority well is that the charisma of the person in authority will be enhanced. However, there is more to institutional authority than charisma. Social psychologists make a distinction here between a social position and a social role (for example, Kelvin, 1970). Institutional authority begins with the occupancy of a relevant social position. Occupancy of a social position creates the opportunity for the functional exercise of a particular social role. However, it remains a contingent matter how effectively this social role is exercised in practice. Occupying a position of authority in the Church merely creates the opportunity for the provision of enabling authority within the role relationships that the position creates.

Lash (1978) makes a similar distinction between external, formal authority (the authority associated with the holder of a particular position), and internal, 'material' authority (the authority a statement or command acquires when it is self-authenticating). External authority needs to be accompanied by material authority. Authority should strive to inspire allegiance because it is felt to be merited; it will also understand that it is not right to require obedience when such allegiance is not forthcoming. That leads towards the proffering of enabling authority.

Let us now see how this approach applies to finding a middle way between authoritarianism and permissiveness in matters of doctrine and morality. It is difficult to discuss this at the present time without falling into the polarization between liberals and traditionalists within the Church. In seeking to move beyond that increasingly sterile debate, it is useful to make a clear distinction between *what* beliefs and principles are upheld, and *how* they are upheld. Liberalism has often involved a retreat from traditional positions. Religious beliefs such as the virgin birth, or moral principles such as those concerning sexual behaviour, that used to be firmly upheld are now called into question. That is a quite separate issue from the one that is being raised here about *how* authority can be exercised without sliding into authoritarianism or permissiveness. This latter issue arises in exactly the same way regardless of whether it is the full range of traditional beliefs that are being maintained, or some slimmed-down subset of them.

The way in which a path can be steered between permissiveness and authoritarianism is to offer authority rather than impose it. It is important, if doctrinal positions and moral principles are to operate creatively within a believer, that they should be personally tested and freely adopted. This avoids the snares of authoritarianism. However, it is also important, if mere permissiveness is to be avoided, that matters of doctrine and morality should be presented sufficiently clearly and firmly that they cannot be simply fudged or evaded.

If religious belief is to play a constructive role in someone's Christian life, it is necessary that it should be fully assimilated, and not just intellectually accepted. A helpful analogy can again be drawn between the assimilation of religious beliefs and of personal insights of the kind that arise in psychotherapy. Patients very often achieve 'intellectual insight' into the nature of their problems at an early stage of therapy; indeed the main outlines may be apparent within the first session. The real challenge comes in developing this into 'effective insight' that changes their lives and experience. Mere repetition of correct interpretations is of no more help here than it is with religious belief. The full meaning and significance of the insights need to be probed, their emotional implications need to be felt, their significance for other personal beliefs needs to be worked through, and their behavioural implications have to be lived out.

Perhaps the central, pragmatic objection to attempting to maintain correct belief solely by authority is that it distracts from, and undermines, this process of the assimilation of religious insights. It is thus pastorally damaging and stunts spiritual growth. If people are to assimilate religious beliefs, they have to be left to perform for themselves at least part of the task of arriving at those beliefs. There is a parallel here with the well established principle that people are much more likely to implement decisions when they have participated in taking them. If people reach beliefs at least partly on their own, those beliefs will have far wider implications for their lives. Authority, in matters of doctrine, thus needs to be complemented by a personal path of seeking belief on the basis of experience. What is being advocated here is not an exclusive reliance on personal religious experience, but rather a process of sustained and imaginative reflection that draws on experience, and interprets it in the light of traditional belief, reworking and assimilating it.

Philosophy of science suggests a parallel, drawing on the analogy of how theory relates to observation and experiment. Recent thinking has emphasized that theory and observation are not as separate as used to be supposed, but that all data is itself 'theory-laden' (Hanson, 1958), selected and interpreted with reference to a theoretical perspective. This is a pointer towards the way in which doctrine and experience interact in the life of a believer, in a single act of contemplation in which there is a doctrine laden assimilation of experience. To realize the potential of this fully, theology needs to move beyond the categorical barrier between doctrine and experience, just as philosophy of science has gone beyond a sharp dichotomy between theory and experiment.

A similar approach is needed regarding moral principles. Once again, it needs to be emphasized that the question being raised is not *what* religious morality should consist of; whether or not particular controversial items of conduct should be regarded as morally acceptable. That is a proper subject for debate, but not the focus of concern here. The concern here is rather with *how* moral principles are presented and maintained. The argument is an exactly parallel one, that if the adoption of moral principles is to have a creative effect in people's lives, they must be left room to arrive at those principles for themselves. It is the proper role of moral authority to set out principles and to encourage people to reflect on them and to assimilate them. That is very different from saying that moral principles simply carry authority, and that there are no questions to be asked about them. Moral principles, like doctrine, need to be offered rather than imposed if they are to operate creatively. Again, they are more likely to be heeded if presented in this way.

This has implications for the form in which moral principles are communicated. There is a strand of thinking in moral philosophy, represented in postwar thinking by R.M. Hare (1952), that the essential and necessary feature of morality is its prescriptiveness. Morality, it is suggested, is by definition a matter of 'do this'. Such an emphasis on the prescriptiveness of morality has often been accompanied by a parallel emphasis on the disjunction between moral statements and descriptive statements. The idea that morality can be derived from fact has been dubbed the 'naturalistic fallacy'. This view of the nature of morality is, in its strongest form, both philosophically unnecessary and pastorally unhelpful. There has been a growing consensus that, though there is a distinction between 'fact' and 'value', there need not be a complete dichotomy between the two. Facts are relevant to moral judgments, even if they do not fully determine them.

Ethical principles are sometimes best communicated, not as set of imperatives, but as factual statements about the consequences of particular kinds of conduct. There is an eloquent statement of this approach in a brief discussion of marriage and divorce in Werner Pelz's (1963) *God is No More*, once deservedly a best seller:

> When the church, through the doctrine of the indissolubility of marriage wants to say to bridegroom and bride: 'This is your partner, through him or her you may discover the whole of mankind. If you want to bypass him or her because you want more, you will discover that you get less', points towards a real insight. When it turns this insight into a law, it obliterates it and becomes responsible for distorting our understanding of marriage

more gravely than any number of divorces. To separate responsibility from joy, and duty from love, corrupts man's personality at its roots ... When we destroy the unity of desire and obligation we turn man into a schizophrenic 'moral' animal (p. 42).

There is a similar point to be made about forgiveness. Religious teachings have often emphasized the close linkage between feeling forgiven oneself and forgiving others. It is often portrayed as a matter of moral duty to forgive others in order that we might be forgiven ourselves. However, it can also be advocated on pragmatic grounds. Not harbouring grievances helps people to be free themselves. Seen in this way, the linkage between being forgiven oneself and forgiving others is not just a moral imperative, but an emergent property of the way human psychology operates.

The function of proper authority is thus to liberate, nurture and enable. The validity of authority can be assessed by whether it does this. In order to liberate, authority needs to be offered rather than imposed. Authority needs to be available, but the response to it must be a free one. This is not mere liberalism. Authority can and should provide a rock of truth to which they can return or (better) a secure dwelling that they can inhabit. However, where it seeks to coerce it loses its capacity to enable.

For Christians, the key point to remember is that authority ultimately belongs to God, not to any human person. This leads on to the distinction between legitimate authority and coercive power. Authority is properly 'that kind of structured reality, whether social or personal, which through nurture and cultivation enables individuals to become truly centred selves or persons, and thus, relatively free beings' (Skinner, 1987). Such authority clearly resides in a relationship, not in the source of authority alone. In contrast, coercive power alienates people and destroys the possibility of openness to transcendence. Ideology can be used as an ally of coercive power, and can also destroy trust. As John Skinner says, it is the 'idolatrous substitution of what is proximate and finite for what is ultimate and transcendent'. Because such authority and ideology have no sense of transcendence beyond themselves, they cannot encourage such a sense in others.

In a similar vein, Rowan Williams (1982) points out that Christian obedience is obedience to the Paschal symbol, not obedience to a command. The authority of the symbol, unlike that of the command, always points beyond itself and so fosters growth. Obedience to it is not blind, but rather leads to enlightenment. The leaders of the church owe their authority to this symbol, and the validity of religious authority depends on faithfulness to it, a validity which is lost if the authority of command is substituted for that of symbol. Human authority, if it is to maintain validity, must always remember its transcendent basis, and point towards that basis in the way it is exercised. Only then can it lead people, not to itself, but to the transcendent source from which the authority comes.

Conclusion

The theme of this chapter has been the importance of overcoming dichotomies in theology. First we considered the epistemological dichotomies that arise between the private and subjective on the one hand, and the external and objective on the other. Then, similar points were made about doctrinal dichotomies concerned with God and man, about immanence and transcendence, and concerning the present time and the ultimate eschaton. Finally, we considered the dichotomies between authority and autonomy, and between tradition and development.

At each point, I have tried to suggest the psychological and spiritual importance of avoiding such dichotomies. Faith can only develop in a healthy way when people are operating in a transitional world between the subjective and objective. Equally, a healthy sense of relationship to God requires that the sense of separateness from him, and union with him, are both given an adequate place. Finally, to develop their faith, people need to be offered a secure body of tradition and authority, but they need to be left the freedom to rework that tradition for themselves.

Bibliography

Addinall, P. (2000), 'The Fall: history or myth?', *Science and Christian Belief*, **12** (1), 47–52.

Alexander, R.D. (1987), *The Biology of Moral Systems*, New York: Aldine DeGruyter.

Alloy, L.B. (ed.) (1988), *Cognitive Processes in Depression*, New York: Guilford Press.

Anderson, R.S. (1982), *On Being Human: Essays in Theological Anthropology*, Grand Rapids, Michigan: Eerdmans.

Andresen, J. (ed.) (in press), *Religion in Mind: Cognitive Perspectives on Religious Belief, Ritual and Experience*, Cambridge: Cambridge University Press.

Arbib, M.A. and Hesse, M.B. (1986), *The Construction of Reality*, Cambridge: Cambridge University Press.

Asch, S.E. (1958), 'The Metaphor: A Psychological Inquiry', in Tagiuri, R. and Petrullo, L. (eds), *Person Perception and Interpersonal Behaviour*, Stanford: Stanford University Press.

Averill, J.R., Catlin, G. and Chon, K.K. (1990), *Rules of Hope*, New York: Springer-Verlag.

Ayala, F.J. (1987), 'The biological roots of morality', *Biology and Philosophy*, **2**, 235–52.

Ayala, F.J. (1988), 'Can "Progress" Be Defined as a Biological Concept?', in Nitecki, M.H. (ed.), *Evolutionary Progress*, Chicago: University of Chicago Press, pp. 75–96.

Baars, B.J. (1998), *A Cognitive Theory of Consciousness*, Cambridge: Cambridge University Press.

Barbour, I.G. (1974), *Myths, Models and Paradigms*, New York: Harper and Row.

Barbour, I.G. (1998), *Religion and Science: Historical and Contemporary Issues*, London: SCM.

Barfield, O. (1928), *Poetic Diction: A Study in Meaning*, London: Faber and Faber.

Barfield, O. (1953), *History in English Words*, London: Faber and Faber.

Barfield, O. (1957), *Saving the Appearances: A Study in Idolatry*, London: Faber and Faber.

Barfield, O. (1959/1966), 'The Fall in Man and Nature', in Barfield, O. (ed.), *Romanticism Comes of Age*, London: Rudolf Steiner Press.

Barfield, O. (1971), *What Coleridge Thought*, Middletown, Connecticut: Wesleyan University Press.

Barfield, O. (1977), *The Rediscovery of Meaning, and Other Essays*, Middletown, Connecticut: Wesleyan University Press.

Barkow, J., Cosmides, L. and Tooby, J. (eds) (1992), *The Adapted Mind: Evolutionary Psychology and the Generation of Culture*, New York: Oxford University Press.

Barlow, C. (1994), *Evolution Extended: Biological Debates on the Meaning of Life*, Cambridge, Mass.: MIT Press.

Barr, J. (1992), *The Garden of Eden and the Hope of Immortality*, London: SCM.

Batholomew, D.J. (1984), *God of Chance*, London: SCM.

Bechtel, W. and Abrahamsen, A. (1991), *Connectionism and the Mind*, Oxford: Blackwell.

Behe, M.J. (1996), *Darwin's Black Box: The Biochemical Challenge to Evolution*, New York: Free Press.

Bennan, B. (1988), *Psychotherapy and the Spiritual Quest*, London: Hodder and Stoughton.

Bergin, A.E. (1980), 'Psychotherapy and religious values', *Journal of Consulting and Clinical Psychology*, **48**, 95–105.

Bergson, H. (1907/1983), *Creative Evolution*, trans. A. Mitchell, Lanham, MD.: University Press of America.

Bernstein, R.J. (1983), *Beyond Objectivism and Subjectivism*, Oxford: Blackwell.

Berry, R.J. (1999), 'This cursed earth: Is "The Fall" credible?', *Science and Christian Belief*, **11** (1), 29–49.

Berry, R.J. (2000), 'The Fall is history', *Science and Christian Belief*, **12** (1), 53–63.

Blackmore, S.J. (1999), *The Meme Machine*, Oxford: Oxford University Press.

Bouchard, L.D. (2000), 'Contingent Futures: Imagining the Ethics of Cosmology', in Polkinghorne, J. and Welker, M. (eds), *The End of the World and the Ends of God: Science and Theology on Eschatology*, Harrisburg, Pennsylvania: Trinity Press International.

Bowker, J. (1995), *Is God a Virus? Genes, Culture and Religion. The Gresham Lectures, 1992-3*, London: SPCK.

Bowker, J. (1998), 'Science and Religion: Contest or Confirmation', in Watts, F. (ed.), *Science Meets Faith*, London: SPCK.

Boyer, P. (1994), *The Naturalness of Religious Ideas: A Cognitive Theory of Religion*, Berkeley: University of California Press.

Breakwell, G. (ed.) (1992), *Social Psychology of Identity and the Self Concept*, Surrey: Surrey University Press.

Brown, W.S. (1998), 'Cognitive Contributions to Soul', in Brown, W.S., Murphy, N. and Malony, H.N., *Whatever Happened to the Soul? Scientific and Theological Portraits of Human Nature*, Minneapolis: Fortress Press.

Browning, D. (1966), *Atonement and Psychotherapy*, Philadelphia: Westminster Press.

Browning, D. (1980), *Pluralism and Personality*, Lewisburg: Bucknell University Press; London: Associated University Presses.

Browning, D. (1987), *Religious Thought and the Modern Psychologies*, Philadelphia: Fortress Press.

Brummer, V. (1984), *What Are We Doing When We Pray?* London: SCM.

Buckley, M. (1987), *At the Origins of Modern Atheism*, New Haven: Yale University Press.

Bull, T.M. (1998), *Artificial Intelligence and the Doctrine of Sin*, Undergraduate Dissertation, University of Cambridge.

Bultmann, R. (1961), 'New Testament and Mythology', in Bartsch, H. (ed.), *Kerygma and Mythos*, trans. R.H. Fuller, New York: Harper.

Campbell, D.T. (1975), 'On the conflicts between biological and social evolution and between psychology and moral tradition', *American Psychologist*, **30**, 1103–26.

Carter, J. and Narramore, B. (1979), *The Integration of Psychology and Theology*, Grand Rapids, Michigan: Zondervan.

Charles, D. and Lennon, K. (eds) (1992), *Reduction, Explanation and Realism*, Oxford: Clarendon Press.

Clark, S.R.L. (1995), *How to Live For Ever: Science Fiction and Philosophy*, London: Routledge.

Clocksin, W.F. (1988), 'Artificial Intelligence and Human Identity', in Cornwell, J. (ed.), *Consciousness and Human Identity*, Oxford: Oxford University Press.

Coakley, S. (1997), *Religion and the Body*, Cambridge: Cambridge University Press.

Cohn-Sherbok, D. (1989), *Holocaust Theology*, London: Lamp Press.

Combs, A. (1995), *The Radiance of Being: Complexity, Chaos and the Evolution of Consciousness*, Edinburgh: Floris Books.

Compton, J. (1972), 'Science and God's Action in Nature', in Barbour, I. (ed.), *Earth Might Be Fair: Reflections on Ethics, Religion and Ecology*, Englewood Cliffs, New Jersey: Prentice Hall.

Copeland, J. (1993), *Artificial Intelligence: A Philosophical Introduction*, Oxford: Blackwell.

Corey, M.A. (1994), *Back to Darwin: The Scientific Case for Deistic Evolution*, Lanham, Maryland: University Press of America.

Corner, M. (1988), 'The Armageddon scenario', in Race, A. (ed.), *Theology Against the Nuclear Horizon*, London: SCM.

Cotterill, R. (1989), *No Ghost in the Machine: Modern Science and the Brain, the Mind and the Soul*, London: Heinemann.

Crabbe, M.J.C. (ed.) (1999), *From Soul to Self*, London: Routledge.

Craig, E. (1987), *The Mind of God and the Works of Man*, Oxford: Clarendon Press.

Crick, F. (1994), *The Astonishing Hypothesis: The Scientific Search for the Soul*, London: Simon and Schuster.

Crook, J.H. (1980), *The Evolution of Human Consciousness*, Oxford: Clarendon Press.

Cupitt, D. (1998), *Mysticism After Modernity*, Oxford: Blackwell.

d'Aquili, E.G. and Newberg, A.B. (1998), 'The Neuropsychology of Religion', in Watts, F. (ed.), *Science Meets Faith*, London: SPCK, pp. 73–91.

d'Aquili, E.G. and Newberg, A.B. (1999), *The Mystical Mind: Probing the Biology of Religious Experience*, Minneapolis: Fortress Press.

Daly, G. (1988), *Creation and Redemption*, Dublin: Gill and Macmillan.

Davies, M. and Humphreys, G.W. (1993), *Consciousness: Psychological and Philosophical Essays*, Oxford: Blackwell.

Davy, C. (1961), *Towards a Third Culture*, London: Faber and Faber.

Davy, J. (1985), 'Discovering Hope', in Davy, J. (ed.), *Hope, Evolution and Change*, Stroud: Hawthorn Press.

Dawkins, R. (1976), *The Selfish Gene*, New York and Oxford: Oxford University Press.

Dawkins, R. (1982), *The Extended Phenotype: The Gene as the Unit of Selection*, Oxford, W.H. Freeman.

Dawkins, R. (1986), *The Blind Watchmaker*, London: Penguin.

Dearmer, P.D. (1929), *The Legend of Hell*, London: Cassell.

Deikman, A. (1966), 'Implication of experimentally produced contemplative meditation', *Journal of Nervous and Mental Disease*, **142**, 101–16.

Dennet, D. (1995), *Darwin's Dangerous Idea: Evolution and the Meanings of Life*, New York: Simon and Schuster.

Dennett, D.C. (1991), *Consciousness Explained*, London: Allen Lane.

Dixon, T. (1999), 'Theology, anti-theology and atheology: From Christian passions to secular emotions', *Modern Theology*, **15**, 297–330.

Dobzhanzsy, T. (1969), *The Biology of Ultimate Concern*, London: Rapp and Whiting.

Doctrine Commission of the Church of England (1988), *We Believe in God: Report of the Doctrine Commission of the Church of England*.

Dreyfus, H.L. and Dreyfus, S.E. (1986), *Mind Over Machine*, New York: Free Press.

Dulles, A. (1988), *Models of the Church (second edn)*, Dublin: Gill and Macmillan.

Eaves, L.J., D'Onofrio, B. and Russell, R. (1999), 'Transmission of religion and attitudes', *Twin Research*, **2**, 59–61.

Edelman, G.M. (1992), *Bright Air, Brilliant Fire: On the Matter of Mind*, London: Allen Lane.

Edinger, E.F. (1972), *Ego and Archetype*, Harmondsworth: Penguin.

Edinger, E.F. (1987), *The Christian Archetype: A Jungian Commentary on the Life of Christ*, Toronto: Inner City Books.

Eiser, J.R. (1994), *Attitudes, Chaos and the Connectionist Mind*, Oxford: Blackwell.

Elliott, C. (1995), *Memory and Salvation*, London: Darton, Longman and Todd.

Emmet, D. (1979), *The Moral Prism*, London: Macmillan.

Faber, H. (1976), *Psychology of Religion*, London: SCM.

Farley, E. (1990), *Good and Evil: Interpreting a Human Condition*, Minneapolis: Fortress Press.

Farrer, A. (1967/88), *Faith and Speculation: An Essay in Philosophical Theology: Containing the Deems Lectures 1964*, Edinburgh: T. & T. Clark.

Fenton, G.W. (1981), 'Psychiatric Disorders of Epilepsy: Classification and Phenomenology', in Reynolds, E. and Trimble, M. (eds), *Epilepsy and Psychiatry*, New York: Churchill Livingstone.

Fenwick, P. (1996), 'The Neuropsychology of Religious Experience', in Bhugra, D. (ed.), *Psychiatry and Religion*, London: Routledge, pp. 167–77.

Flanagan, O. (1992), *Consciousness Reconsidered*, Cambridge, Mass.: MIT Press.

Fleck, J.R. and Carter, J.D. (eds) (1981), *Psychology and Christianity: Integrative Readings*, Nashville: Abingdon.

Foerst, A. (1996), 'Artificial Intelligence: walking the boundary', *Zygon*, **31**, pp. 681–93.

Foerst, A. (1998a), 'Cog, a humanoid robot, and the question of the image of God', *Zygon*, **33**, 91–111.

Foerst, A. (1998b), 'Embodied AI, creation and Cog', *Zygon*, **33**, 455–61.

Forman, R.K.C. (1990), *The Problem of Consciousness: Mysticism and Philosophy*, Oxford: Oxford University Press.

Fortmann, H.M.M. (1964), *Als Zeinde de Onzienlijke*, Hilversum.

Fox, M. (1983), *Original Blessing: A Primer in Creation Spirituality*, Santa Fe: Bear and Company.

Franz, M-L. von (1980), *Projection and Re-Collection in Jungian Psychology: Reflections of the Soul*, trans. W.H. Kennedy, la Salle (Ill.)/London: Open Court.

Freud, S. (1927/1951), *The Future of an Illusion*, London: Hogarth.

Fry, C. (1951), *A Sleep of Prisoners*, London: Oxford University Press.

Furse, E. (1993), November: Letters, *The Tablet*.

Garrison, J. (1982), *The Darkness of God: Theology after Hiroshima*, London: SCM.

Gebser, J. (1985), *The Ever-Present Origin*, trans. N. Barstad with A. Mickunas, Athens, Ohio: Ohio University Press.

Gellner, E. (1985), *The psychoanalytic Movement or the Cunning of Unreason*, London: Paladin.

Gerhart, M. and Russell, A.M. (1998), 'Cog is to us as we are to God: a response to Anne Foerst', *Zygon*, **33**, 263–9.

Gimello, R.M. (1978), 'Mysticism and Meditation', in Katz, S.T. (ed.), *Mysticism and Philosophical Analysis*, London: Sheldon Press, pp. 170–99.

Good, D.A. and Watts, F.N. (1996), 'Qualitative research', in Parry, G. and Watts, F.N. (eds), *Behavioural and Mental Health Research: A Handbook of Skills and Methods, 2nd edn*, Erlbaum UK: Taylor and Francis.

Goodwin, B. (1994), *How the Leopard Changed Its Spots: The Evolution of Complexity*, London: Weidenfield and Nicholson.

Gore, C. (ed) (1889), *Lux Mundi: A Series of Studies in the Religion of the Incarnation*, London: John Murray.

Gould, S.J. (1996), *Life's Grandeur*, London: Jonathan Cape.

Green, J.B. (1998), 'Bodies-That is, Human Lives: A Re-examination of Human Nature in the Bible', in Brown, W.S., Murphy, N. and Malony, N.H. (eds), *Whatever Happened to the Soul? Scientific and Theological Portraits of Human Nature*, Minneapolis: Fortress Press.

Greenwood, J.D. (1994), *Realism, Identity and Emotion*, London: Sage.

Gregersen, N.H., Drees, W.B. and Gorman, U. (eds) (2000), *The Human Person in Science and Theology*, Edinburgh: T. & T. Clark.

Habgood, J. (1998), *Being a Person: Where Faith and Science Meet*, London: Hodder and Stoughton.

Hampson, S.E. (1988), *The Construction of Personality: An Introduction, 2nd edn*, London: Routledge.

Hanson, N.R. (1958), *Patterns of Discovery*, Cambridge: Cambridge University Press.

Hare, R.M. (1952), *The Language of Morals*, Oxford: Oxford University Press.

Harré, R. (1970), *The Principles of Scientific Thinking*, London: Macmillan.

Harré, R. (1979), *Social Being, second edn*, Oxford: Blackwell.

Harré, R. (1983), *Personal Being: A Theory for Individual Psychology*, Oxford: Blackwell.

Harré, R. (1986), *The Social Construction of Emotions*, Oxford: Blackwell.

Harré, R. (1991), *Physical Being: A Theory for Corporeal Psychology*, Oxford: Blackwell.

Harré, R. (1998), *The Singular Self: An Introduction to the Psychology of Personhood*, London: Sage.

Haught, J.F. (2000), *God After Darwin: A Theology of Evolution*, Boulder: Westview Press.

Hay, D. (1987), *Exploring Inner Space: Scientists and Religious Experience (2nd edn)*, London: Mowbray.

Hefner, P. (1993), *The Human Factor: Evolution, Culture and Religion*, Minneapolis: Fortress Press.

Hegel, G.W.H. (1807/1977), *The Phenomenology of Spirit*, trans. Miller, Oxford.

Hick, J. (1976), *Death and Eternal Life*, London: Collins.

Hiebel, F. (1980), *The Epistles of Paul and Rudolf Steiner's Philosophy of Freedom*, trans. A. and M. Howard, Spring Valley, New York: St George Publications.

Hillman, J. (1964), *Suicide and the Soul*, London: Hodder and Stoughton.

Hillman, J. (1975), *Re-visioning Psychology*, New York: Harper and Row.

Hillman, J. (1979), 'Peaks and vales: The soul/spirit distinction as basis for the differences between psychotherapy and spiritual discipline', in *Puer Papers*, 54–74, Dallas: Spring Publications.

Hinde, R.A. (1999), *Why Gods Persist: A Scientific Approach to Religion*, London: Routledge.

Hood, R.W. (Jr.), Spilka, B., Hunsberger, B. and Gorsuch, R. (1996), *The Psychology of Religion: An Empirical Approach (2nd edn)*, New York: Guilford Press.

Hull, D.L. and Ruse, M. (1998), *The Philosophy of Biology*, Oxford: Oxford University Press.

Hunsinger, D. van Deusen (1995), *Theology and Pastoral Counseling: A New Interdisciplinary Approach*, Grand Rapids, Michigan: William B. Eerdmans Publishing Company.

Huxley, A. (1946), *The Perennial Philosophy*, London: Harper and Brothers.

James, W. (1960) (First published 1902), *The Varieties of Religious Experience: A Study in Human Nature*, London: Collins.

Jaynes, J. (1976), *The Origins of Consciousness in the Breakdown of the Bicameral Mind*, London: Allen Lane.

Jeeves, M. (1976), *Psychology and Christianity: The View Both Ways*, Leicester: Inter-Varsity Press.

Jeeves, M. (1984), *Behavioural Science: A Christian Perspective*, Leicester: Inter-Varsity Press.

Jeeves, M. (1994), *Mind Fields: Reflections on the Science of Mind and Brain*, Leicester: Inter-Varsity Press.

Jeeves, M. (1997), *Human Nature at the Millennium: Reflections on the Integration of Psychology and Christianity*, Leicester: Inter-Varsity Press.

Johnson, E.L. and Jones, S.L. (eds) (2000), *Psychology and Christianity*, Illinois: Inter-Varsity Press.

Johnson-Laird, P.N. (1988), *The Computer and the Mind*, London: Fontana.

Jones, S.L. (1994), 'A constructive relationship for religion with the science and profession of psychology: perhaps the boldest model yet', *American Psychologist*, **49**, 184–99.

Jung, C.G. (1954), *Answer to Job*, London: Routledge and Kegan Paul.

Jung, C.G. (1958), *The Undiscovered Self*, London: Routledge and Kegan Paul.

Jung, C.G. (1970), *The Archetypes and the Collective Unconscious, Collected Works IX (I) second edn*, London: Routledge and Kegan Paul.

Jung, C.G. (1970) 'After the Catastrophe', *Collected Works, Vol. X second edn*, London: Routledge and Kegan Paul, pp. 194–217.

Jung, C.G. (1970) 'Wotan', *Collected Works, Vol. X second edn*, London: Routledge and Kegan Paul, pp. 179–93.

Kasper, W. (1976), *Jesus the Christ*, trans. V. Green, London: Burns and Oates.

Katz, S.T. (1978), 'Language, Epistemology and Mysticism', in Katz, S.T. (ed.), *Mysticism and Philosophical Analysis*, London: Sheldon Press, pp. 22–74.

Kauffman, S. (1995), *At Home in the Universe: The Search for Laws of Self-Organization and Complexity*, Oxford: Oxford University Press.

Kaufman, G. (1985), *Theology for a Nuclear Age*, Manchester: Manchester University Press.

Kelvin, P. (1970), *The Bases of Social Behaviour*, London: Holt, Rinehart and Winston.

Kim, J. (1979), 'Causality, identity and supervenience in the mind-body problem', *Midwest Studies in Philosophy*, **4**.

Kirk, K. (1927), *Conscience and Its Problems*, London: Longmans Green.

Kitcher, P. (1985), *Vaulting Ambition: Sociobiology and the Quest for Human Nature*, Cambridge, Mass.: MIT Press.

Knox, C.(1993), *Changing Christian Paradigms*, Leiden: E.J. Brill.

Kung, H. (1984), *Eternal Life?*, Garden City, New York: Doubleday.

Lake, F. (1966), *Clinical Theology: A Theological and Psychiatric Basis to Clinical Pastoral Care*, London: Darton, Longman and Todd.

Langford, M.J. (1981), *Providence*, London: SCM.

Lash, N. (1976), *Voices of Authority*, London: Sheed and Ward.

Lash, N. (1984), 'Materialism', in Richardson, A. and Bowden, J. (eds), *A New Dictionary of Christian Theology*, London: SCM, pp. 353–4.

Lash, N. (1985), 'Production and Prospect: Reflections on Christian Hope and Original Sin', in McMullin, E. (ed.), *Evolution and Creation*, Notre Dame: University of Notre Dame Press.

Lash, N. (1988), *Easter in Ordinary: Reflections on Human Experience and the Knowledge of God*, London: SCM.

Lash, N. (1996), 'Chapter 4: Observation, Revelation and the Posterity of Noah', *The Beginning and the End of Religion*, Cambridge: Cambridge University Press.

Lazarus, R.S. (1982), 'Thoughts on the relations between emotion and cognition', *American Psychologist*, **37**, 1019–24.

Lazarus, R.S. (1999), 'The Cognition-Emotion Debate: A Bit of History', in Dalgleish, T. and Power, M.J. (eds), *Handbook of Cognition and Emotion*, Chichester: John Wiley.

LeDoux, J. (1996), *The Emotional Brain: The Mysterious Underpinnings of Emotional Life*, New York: Simon and Schuster.

Leventhal, H. (1984), 'A Perceptual-Motor Theory of Emotion', in Berkowitz, L. (ed.), *Advances in Experimental Social Psychology*, **17**, New York: Academic Press.

Lindbeck, G.A. (1984), *The Nature of Doctrine*, London: SPCK.

Locke, J. (1960), *An Essay Concerning Human Understanding*, London: Collins. (Originally published 1690.)

Logan, R.D. (1987), 'Historical Change in Prevailing Sense of Self', in Yardley, K. and Honess, T., *Self and Identity: Psychosocial Perspectives*, Chichester: John Wiley.

Lumsden, C.J. and Wilson, E.O. (1981), *Genes, Mind and Culture*, Cambridge, Mass.: Harvard University Press.

Lumsden, C.J. and Wilson, E.O. (1983), *Promethean Fire: Reflections on the Origin of Mind*, Cambridge, Mass.: Harvard University Press.

MacIntyre, A.C. (1989), *After Virtue: A Study in Moral Theory*, London: Duckworth.

MacKay, D.M. (1991), *Behind the Eye*, Oxford: Blackwell.

Marcel, A.J. (1992), 'The Personal Level in Cognitive Rehabilitation', in von Steinbuchel, N., von Cramon, D. and Poppel, E. (eds), *Neurological Rehabilitation*, Berlin: Springer-Verlag, pp. 155-168.

Marcel, A.J. and Bisiach, E. (eds) (1988), *Consciousness in Contemporary Science*, Oxford: Clarendon Press.

Marcel, G. (1982), *Homo Viator: Introduction to a Metaphysics of Hope*, New York: Harper and Row.

Mark, B. (2000), *Mysticism and Cognition: The Cognitive Development of John of the Cross as Revealed in his Works*, Aarhus: Aarhus University Press.

Markus, H. and Nurius, P. (1986), 'Possible selves', *American Psychologist*, **41**, 954–69.

McClelland, D.C. (1964), *The Roots of Consciousness*, Princeton: D. Van Nostrand Co.

McFadyen, P. (1990), *The Call to Personhood*, Cambridge: Cambridge University Press.

McGrath, J. and McGrath, A. (1992), *The Dilemma of Self-Esteem: The Cross and Christian Confidence*, Wheaton, Illinois and Cambridge, England: Crossway Books.

McMullin, E. (ed.) (1985), *Evolution and Creation*, Notre Dame: University of Notre Dame Press.

McNamara, P. (in press), 'Religion and the Frontal Lobes', in Andresen, J. (ed.), *Religion in Mind: Cognitive Perspectives on Religious Belief, Ritual and Experience*, Cambridge: Cambridge University Press.

Meissner, W.W. (1971), *The Assault on Authority*, Maryknoll, New York: Orbis Books.

Meissner, W.W. (1984), *Psychoanalysis and Religious Experience*, New Haven: Yale University Press.

Meissner, W.W. (1987), *Life and Faith*, Washington D.C.: Georgetown University Press.

Meissner, W.W. (1992), *Ignatius of Loyola: The Psychology of a Saint*, New Haven: Yale University Press.

Meissner, W.W. (1995), *Thy Kingdom Come: Psychoanalytic Perspectives on the Messiah and the Millennium*, Kansas City: Sheed and Ward.

Midgley, M. (1985), *Evolution as Religion*, London: Methuen.

Midgley, M. (1992), *Science as Salvation: A Modern Myth and its Meaning*, London: Routledge.

Midgley, M. (2000), 'Consciousness, Fatalism and Science' in Gregersen, N.H., Drees, W.B. and Goerman, U. (eds), *The Human Person in Science and Theology*, Edinburgh: T. & T. Clark.

Milbank, J. (1990), *Theology and Social Theory*, Oxford: Blackwell.

Mithen, S. (1996), *The Prehistory of the Mind: A Search for the Origins of Art, Religion and Science*, London: Thomas and Hudson.

Moltmann, J. (1970), 'Theology as Eschatology', in Herzog, F. (ed.), *The Future of Hope*, New York: Herder and Herder.

Monod, J. (1972), *Chance and Necessity*, New York: Random House.

Moore, J. (1979), *The Post-Darwinian Controversies*, Cambridge: Cambridge University Press.

Moravec, H. (1988), *Mind Children: The Future of Robot and Human Intelligence*, Cambridge, Mass.: Harvard University Press.

Morea, P. (1997), *In Search of Personality: Christianity and Modern Psychology*, London: SCM.

Murphy, N. (1994), 'What has Theology to Learn from Scientific Methodology?', in Rae, M., Regan, H., and Stenhouse, J. (eds), *Science and Theology: Questions at the Interface*, Edinburgh: T. & T. Clark.

Murphy, N. (1998), 'Human Nature: Historical, Scientific, and Religious Issues', in Brown, W.S., Murphy, N. and Malony, H.N. (eds), *Whatever Happened to the Soul? Scientific and Theological Portraits of Human Nature*, Minneapolis: Fortress Press.

Myers, D. and Jeeves, M. (1987), *Psychology Through the Eyes of Faith*, London: Harper and Row.

Myers, J.L. (1949), 'Ελπις, ελπω, ελπομαι, ελπιζειν', *The Classical Review*, **63**, p. 46.

Nagel, T. (1974), 'What is it like to be a bat?', *Philosophical Review*, **83**, 435–50. (Reprinted in Nagel, T. (1979), *Mortal Questions*, Cambridge: Cambridge University Press.)

Nelson, J.B. (1979), *Embodiment*, New York: Pilgrim Press.

Neumann, E. (1954/1973), *The Origins and History of Consciousness*, Princeton: Princeton University Press.

Oatley, K. and Jenkins, J. M. (1996), *Understanding Emotions*, Oxford: Blackwell.

Oyama, S. (1985), *The Ontogeny of Information: Developmental Systems and Evolution*, Cambridge: Cambridge University Press.

Pailin, D.A. (1989), *God and the Processes of Reality: Foundations of a Credible Theism*, London: Routledge.

Pattison, S. (1993), *A Critique of Pastoral Care, second edn*, London: SCM.

Peacocke, A. (1985), 'Biological Evolution and Christian Theology – Yesterday and Today', in Durant, J. (ed.), *Darwinism and Divinity: Essays on Evolution and Religious Belief*, Oxford: Blackwell.

Peacocke, A. (1993), *Theology for a Scientific Age: Being and Becoming – Natural, Divine and Human*, London: SCM.

Peacocke, A. (1999), 'The Sound of Sheer Silence: How Does God Communicate with Humanity', in Russell, R.J., Murphy, N., Meyering, T.C. and Arbib, M. (eds), *Neuroscience and the Person: Scientific Perspectives on Divine Action*, Vatican City State:Vatican Observatory Publications.

Peacocke, A.R. (1986), *God and the New Biology*, London: Dent.

Pelz, W. and Pelz, L. (1963), *God is No More*, London: Gollancz.

Penrose, R. (1989), *The Emperor's New Mind*, Oxford: Oxford University Press.

Penrose, R. (1994), *Shadows of the Mind*, Oxford: Oxford University Press.

Persinger, M.A. (1987), *Neuropsychological Bases of God Beliefs*, New York: Prager.

Peters, T. (1999), 'Resurrection of the very embodied soul?', in Russell, R.J., Murphy, N., Meyering, T. and Arbib, M.A. (eds), *Neuroscience and the Person: Scientific Perspectives on Divine Action*, Vatican City State: Vatican Observatory Publications.

Philp, H. (1958), *Jung and the Problem of Evil*, London: Rockliff.

Pinker, S. (1994), *The Language Instinct: How the Mind Creates Language*, New York: William Morrow.

Pinker, S. (1997), *How the Mind Works*, New York: Norton, and London: Allen Lane.

Plotkin, H. (1997), *Evolution in Mind: An Introduction to Evolutionary Psychology*, London: Allen Lane.

Polkinghorne, J.C. (1989), *Science and Providence*, London: SPCK.

Polkinghorne, J.C. (1991), *Reason and Reality*, London: SPCK.

Polkinghorne, J.C. (1994), *Science and Christian Belief: Theological Reflections of a Bottom-Up Thinker: The Gifford Lectures for 1993-4*, London: SPCK.

Polkinghorne, J.C. (1996), *Scientists as Theologians: A Comparison of the Writings of Ian Barbour, Arthur Peacocke and John Polkinghorne*, London: SPCK.

Polkinghorne, J.C. (2000), *Faith, Science and Understanding*, London: SPCK.

Polkinghorne, J.C. and Welker, M. (eds) (2000), *The End of the World and the Ends of God*, Harrisburg, Pennsylvania: Trinity Press International.

Proudfoot, W. (1985), *Religious Experience*, Berkeley: University of California Press.

Pruyser, P. (1991), *Religion in Psychodynamic Perspective*, Oxford: Oxford University Press.

Pruyser, P.W. (1983), *The Play of Imagination: Towards a Psychoanalysis of Culture*, New York: International Universities Press.

Puddefoot, J. (1996), *Artificial Intelligence and the Mind Machine*, London: SPCK.

Putnam, H. (1975), *Mind, Language and Reality*, Cambridge: Cambridge University Press.

Putnam, H. (1998), *Representation and Reality*, Cambridge, Mass.: MIT Press.

Race, A. (ed.) (1988), *Theology Against the Nuclear Horizon*, London: SCM.

Rahner, K. (1978), *Foundations of Christian Faith: An Introduction to the Idea of Christianity*, trans. W.V. Dych, New York: Crossroad.

Ramachandran, V.S. and Blakeslee, S. (1998), *Phantoms in the Brain: Human Nature and the Architecture of Mind*, London: Fourth Estate.

Ramsey, I.T. (1964), *Models and Mystery*, Oxford: Oxford University Press.

Reich, K.H. (1988), 'Cog and God: a response to Anne Foerst', *Zygon*, **33**, 255–62.

Ricoeur, P. (1967), *The Symbolism of Evil*, Boston: Beacon Press.

Ridley, M. (1999), *Genome: The Autobiography of a Species in 23 Chapters*, London: Fourth Estate.

Rizzuto, A.M. (1979), *The Birth of the Living God*, Chicago: University of Chicago Press.

Robinson, J.A.T. (1979), *Truth is Two-Eyed*, London: SCM.

Rogers, C. (1961), *On Becoming a Person*, Boston: Houghton Mifflin.

Rose, H. and Rose, S. (eds) (2000), *Alas, Poor Darwin: Arguments Against Evolutionary Psychology*, London: Jonathan Cape.

Rottschaeffer, W.A. (1998), *The Biology and Psychology of Moral Agency*, Cambridge: Cambridge University Press.

Rottschaeffer, W.A. and Martinsen, D. (1990), 'Really taking Darwin seriously: an alternative to Michael Ruse's Darwinian metaethics', *Biology and Philosophy*, **5**, 149–73.

Rowell, G. (1974), *Hell and the Victorians*, Oxford: Oxford University Press.

Runcie, R. (1988), *Authority in Crisis: An Anglican Response*, London: SCM.

Ruse, M. (1995), *Evolutionary Naturalism: Selected Essays*, London: Routledge.

Ruse, M. (2001), *Can a Darwinian Be a Christian? The Relationship between Science and Religion*, Cambridge: Cambridge University Press.

Russell, R.J., Murphy, N., and Isham, C.J. (eds) (1993), *Quantum Cosmology and the Laws of Nature: Scientific Perspectives on Divine Action*, Vatican City State: Vatican Observatory; Berkeley Calif.: Center for Theology and Natural Sciences.

Russell, R.J., Murphy, N. and Peacocke, A. (eds) (1995), *Chaos and Complexity: Scientific Perspectives on Divine Action*, Vatican City State: Vatican Observatory; Berkeley, Calif.: Center for Theology and the Natural Sciences.

Russell, R.J., Stoeger, W.R., Ayala, F.J. (eds) (1998), *Evolutionary and Molecular Biology: Scientific Perspectives on Divine Action*, Vatican City State: Vatican Observatory; Berkeley, Calif.: Center for Theology and the Natural Sciences.

Russell, R.J., Murphy, N., Meyering, T.C. and Arbib, M.A. (eds) (1999), *Neuroscience and the Person: Scientific Perspectives on Divine Action*, Vatican City State: Vatican Observatory; Berkeley, Calif.: Center for Theology and the Natural Sciences.

Ryle, G. (1949), *The Concept of Mind*, London: Hutchinson.

Saunders, N. (in press), *Divine Action and Modern Science*, Cambridge: Cambridge University Press.

Schachter, S. (1964), 'The Interaction of Cognitive and Physiological Determinants of Emotional States', in Berkowitz, L. (ed.), *Advances in Experimental Social Psychology*, **1**, New York: Academic Press, 49–80.

Searle, J. (1997), *The Mystery of Consciousness*, London: Granta.

Sheldrake, R. (1988), *The Presence of the Past, Morphic Resonance and the Habits of Nature*, London: Harper Collins.

Sheldrake, R. (1995), *Seven Experiments That Could Change the World*, New York: Riverhead Books.

Sheldrake, R. (1999), *Dogs That Know When Their Owners are Coming Home*, London: Hutchinson.

Sheldrake, R. (2000), 'The "sense of being stared at" does not depend on known sensory clues', *Biology Forum*, **93**, 237–52.

Short, L. (1995), 'Mysticism, mediation, and the non-linguistic', *Journal of the American Academy of Religion*, **63**, 659–75.

Simon, Y. (1980), *A General Theory of Authority, 2nd edn*, Notre Dame: University of Notre Dame Press.

Skinner, J.E. (1987), 'Ideology, Authority and Faith', in Sykes, S.W. (ed.), *Authority in the Anglican Communion*, Toronto: Anglican Book Centre.

Soskice, J.M. (1985), *Metaphor and Religious Thought*, Oxford: Clarendon Press.

Sperber, D. (1996), *Explaining Culture: A Naturalistic Approach*, Oxford: Blackwell.

Spiegel, Y. (1978), *The Grief Process*, London: SCM.

Stace, W.T. (1960), *Mysticism and Philosophy*, Philadelphia: J.B. Lippicott.

Stannard, R. (1996), *Science and Wonders; Conversation about Science and Belief*, London: Faber and Faber.

Starbuck, E.D. (1899), *The Psychology of Religion*, New York: Scribner.

Sternberg, R.J. (1990), *Metaphors of Mind: Conceptions of the Nature of Intelligence*, Cambridge: Cambridge University Press.

Stott, J. and Edwards, D.L. (1988), *Essentials: A Liberal-Evangelical Dialogue*, London: Hodder and Stoughton.

Swinburne, R. (1979), *The Existence of God*, Oxford: Clarendon Press.

Sykes, S.W. (1984), *The Identity of Christianity*, London: SPCK.

Taliaferro, C. (1994), *Consciousness and the Mind of God*, Cambridge: Cambridge University Press.

Taylor, C. (1989), *Sources of the Self: The Making of the Modern Identity*, Cambridge: Cambridge University Press.

Teasdale, J.D. and Barnard, P.J. (1993), *Affect, Cognition and Change*, Hillsdale, New Jersey: Lawrence Erlbaum.

Teilhard de Chardin, P. (1959), *The Phenomenon of Man*, London: Collins.

Theissen, G. (1984), *Biblical Faith: An Evolutionary Approach*, London: SCM.

Tillich, P. (1952), *The Courage to Be*, London: Nisbett.

Tipler, F.J. (1994), *The Physics of Immortality*, Basingstoke: Macmillan.

Torrance, T. (1976), *Resurrection, Time and Space*, Edinburgh: Handsel Press.

Tucker, D.M., Novelly, R.A. and Walker, P.J. (1987), 'Hyperreligiosity in temporal lobe epilepsy: redefining the relationship', *Journal of Nervous and Mental Diseases*, **175**, 181–4.

Turner, D. (1995), *The Darkness of God: Negativity in Christian Mysticism*, Cambridge: Cambridge University Press.

Varela, F.J., Thompson, E. and Rosch, E. (1991), *The Embodied Mind*, Cambridge, Mass.: MIT Press.

Ward, K. (1992), *Defending the Soul*, Oxford: Oneworld.

Watts, F. (1983), 'Affective cognition: a sequel to Zajonc and Rachman', *Behaviour Resolution Therapy*, **21**, 89–90.

Watts, F. (1992), 'Is psychology falling apart?', *The Psychologist*, 5, 489–94.

Watts, F. (1995), 'An information processing approach to compulsive checking', *Clinical Psychology and Psychotherapy*, **2**, 69–77.

Watts, F. (1996), 'Psychological and religious perspectives on emotion', *International Journal for the Psychology of Religion*, **6**, 71–87. (Reprinted in *Zygon*, **32**, 243–60.)

Watts, F. (1997), 'Revelation in the Mind', in Burridge, R., Watts, F. and Brown, D. (eds), *Where Shall We Find God? Lincoln Lectures in Theology, 1997*, Lincoln Cathedral Publications.

Watts, F. (ed.) (1998a), *Science Meets Faith*, London: SPCK.

Watts, F. (1998b), 'Science and Religion as Complementary Perspectives', in Gregersen, N.H. and van Huyssteen, W. (eds), *Rethinking Theology and Science: Six Models for the Current Dialogue*, Grand Rapids, Michigan: Fortress Press.

Watts, F. (2000), *Christians and Bioethics*, London: SPCK.

Watts, F. (2001a), 'Prayer and Psychology', in Watts, F. (ed.), *Perspectives on Prayer*, London: SPCK.

Watts, F. (2001b), 'Shame, Sin and Guilt', McFadyen, A. and Sorot, M. (eds), *Forgiveness and Truth*, Edinburgh: T. & T. Clark.

Watts, F. and Williams, M. (1988), *The Psychology of Religious Knowing*, Cambridge: Cambridge University Press. (Republished by Cassell: 1994.)

Watts, F., Nye, R. and Savage, S. (2001), *Psychology for Christian Ministry*, London: Routledge.

Webb, C.C.J. (1919), *God and Personality*, Aberdeen: Aberdeen University Press.

Webster, R. (1996), *Why Freud Was Wrong: Sin, Science and Psychoanalysis*, London: Harper Collins.

Weimer, W.B. (1977), 'A Conceptual Framework for Cognitive Psychology; Motor Theories of Mind', in Shaw, R. and Bransford, J. (eds), *Perceiving, Acting and Knowing: Towards an Ecological Psychology*, New Jersey: Hillsdale.

Weiskrantz, L. (1997), *Consciousness Lost and Found: A Neuropsychological Exploration*, Oxford, New York, Toronto: Oxford University Press.

Welker, M. (2000), 'Resurrection and Eternal Life: The Canonic Memory of the Resurrected Christ, His reality, and His Glory', in Polkinghorne, J. and Welker, M. (eds), *The End of the World and the Ends of God*, Harrisburg, Pennsylvania: Trinity Press International.

Westen, D. (1985), *Self and Society: Narcissism, Collectivism, and the Development of Morals*, Cambridge: Cambridge University Press.

Wilber, K. (1983), *Up From Eden: A Transpersonal View of Human Evolution*, London: Routledge and Kegan Paul.

Wildman, W.J. and Brothers, L.A. (1999), 'A Neuropsychological-Semiotic Model of Religious Experiences', in Russell, R.J., Murphy, N., Meyering, T.C. and Arbib, M.A. (eds), *Neuroscience and the Person: Scientific Perspectives on Divine Action*, Vatican City State: Vatican Observatory Publications.

Wiles, M.F. (1986), *God's Action in the World*, London: SCM.

Williams, G.C. (1989), 'A Sociobiological Expansion of Evolution and Ethics', in Paradis, J. and Williams, C. (eds), *Evolution and Ethics: T.H. Huxley's Evolution and Ethics with New Essays on its Victorian and Sociobiological Context*, Princeton, New Jersey: Princeton University Press, pp. 179–214.

Williams, H.C.N. (1967), *Nothing to Fear*, London: Hodder and Stoughton.

Williams, J.M.G., Watts, F.N., Macleod, C. and Mathews, A. (1997), *Cognitive Psychology and Emotional Disorders, second edn*, Chichester: John Wiley.

Williams, R. (1982), 'Authority and the Bishop in the Church', in Santer, M. (ed.), *Their Lord and Ours*, London: SPCK.

Wilson, E.O. (1975), *Sociobiology: The New Synthesis*, Cambridge, Mass.: Harvard University Press.

Wilson, E.O. (1998), *Consilience: The Unity of Knowledge*, London: Little, Brown and Company.

Winch, P. (1958), *The Idea of a Social Science*, London: Kegan Paul.

Winkler, F. (1960), *Man: The Bridge Between Two Worlds*, New York: Harper.

Winnicott, D.W. (1971), *Playing and Reality*, New York: Basic Books.

Wright, D. (1971), *The Psychology of Moral Behaviour*, Harmondsworth: Penguin.

Wright, R. (1994), *The Moral Animal: Why We Are the Way We Are: The New Science of Evolutionary Psychology*, New York: Pantheon.

Wright, R. (2001), *Non Zero: The Logic of Human Destiny*, London: Abacus.

Wrong, D.H. (1979), *Power: Its Forms, Bases and Uses*, Oxford: Blackwell.

Yardley, K. and Honess, T. (eds) (1987), *Self and Identity: Psychosocial Perspectives*, Chichester: John Wiley and Sons.

Zajonc, R.B. (1980), 'Feeling and thinking: preferences need no inferences', *American Psychologist*, **35**, 151–75.

Thematic Index

AI 44, 49–51, 53–61, 72, 135
altruism 17, 24
archetypes 120, 126, 145
Armageddon 144–5, 147
assimilation 7
atheism 9–10, 46
atonement 15
authority 7, 15, 23–5, 41, 78, 151, 161–6
autonomy 107, 151, 161, 166

behaviourist 11, 35
bicameral mind 119–120
biological psychology 10
blindsight 34–5
body 3, 11, 20, 35, 38, 42, 46–7, 56–8,
        63, 69–71, 106, 119, 125, 127,
        129–130, 141–2, 157, 166
brain 8–10, 13, 23, 25, 33, 35–44, 46–7,
        54–8, 64, 66–7, 69–71, 78–84, 86,
        97, 103, 105, 110, 119

causal operator 83–4
central nervous system 21, 39
Chalcedonian 8, 157
chance 28, 29
chaos theory 101
Christian pastoral psychology 2
clinical theology 2, 8
Cog 56–7
cognition 6, 11, 13–14, 25, 35, 49, 53,
        55–6, 74, 78, 82, 84, 86, 96, 97,
        152–3
cognitive operators 83–4
cognitive psychology 35, 97, 99, 151–4
collective unconscious 120, 145
complementary perspectives 8
connectionism 56
conscience 105, 109–11, 128
consciousness 11, 13–14, 25–7, 33–46,
        51–3, 57, 64, 70, 72, 79, 82–3,
        85–8, 93–4, 98–100, 114–131, 137,
        148, 152–4, 158
consolation 80

consonance 7
cosmology 4, 58, 133–5, 147
counselling psychology 2, 5
creation 4, 27–30, 59, 69, 79, 97,
        102–104, 114, 124–5, 129, 134,
        142, 158–9, 160

Darwinism 20–21, 23, 37, 113
depression 66, 80, 140
despair 137, 139
determinism 19, 66
dichotomous thinking 151
divine action 14, 22, 79, 101–109
double aspect terms 99, 130, 155
dreams 156
dualism 37–9, 41–3, 56, 71, 79, 103, 130,
        160

ego 120–123, 126, 137–8, 158
ego-ideal 137, 158
embodied AI 56
embodiment 69
emotion(s) 8, 13, 23, 34, 53, 66–7, 74–5,
        85–7, 95–6, 109, 140
Enlightenment 45, 65, 74, 104, 106–7, 152
epigenetic rules 23
eschatology 14, 50–51, 58, 61, 116,
        133–7, 141, 144, 148, 151–2, 157
    futurist 136, 157
    realized 136
ethics 23–5
evolution 4, 14, 20–30, 42, 59, 66, 81, 98,
        102–104, 113–16, 118–120, 122–5,
        127–130
evolutionary Christology 123
evolutionary psychology 13, 17–22, 115

Fall (The) 2–3, 11, 113, 115–130
fideism 152
fluid intelligence 52
forgiveness 3, 158, 165
free will 11, 30, 39, 60, 107
frontal lobes 81–3

Author Index

185